# FRESH SPICE

# FRESH SPICE

### ARUN KAPIL

PAVILION

# CONTENTS

INTRODUCTION                    006
BUYING FRESH SPICES             008
COOKING WITH SPICES             010
BUILDING A BLEND                010
A–Z OF SPICES                   012
THE SCIENCE OF FLAVOUR          020

PORK & BACON                    024
BEEF & VENISON                  042
LAMB & MUTTON                   058

BIRDS 076

FISH 098

SHELLfish & SQUID 118

EGGS & CHEESE 130

GRAINS & PULSES 146

WINTER VEGETABLES 166

SUMMER VEGETABLES 186

WINTER FRUIT 200

SUMMER FRUIT 212

SWEET THINGS 230

RELISHES, CHUTNEYS,
    JAMS & JELLIES 252


BASICS 264

INDEX 268

ACKNOWLEDGEMENTS 272

# INTRODUCTION

I've been around spices all my life. I love them. I love their vibrancy, their huge array of aromas and flavour notes, their provenance, history, cultivation, science; the lot. And I love to cook. Cooking is my dearest passion. I believe any dish can benefit from a touch of spice – just enough to bring out an accent, a nuance, not to cloud or smother. Spices add clarity encouraging tastes to sparkle on your palate. This is food alchemy; the best kind of science there is!

I'd like to show you how I blend and work with spices by introducing you to a new way of cooking with them from a purely flavour and taste perspective. This book's all about how to make the best use of spices in everyday cooking with a whole bunch of well laid-out recipes from snacks and main courses to sides, sauces and sweet things. It sets out the basic building blocks of spice knowledge using fresh spices, freshly ground to most brilliant effect; a celebration of their natural colours, aromas and flavours.

As a child I was in and out of the kitchen, making rock buns with my Yorkshire Mum, Pam, and spicy dishes with my Dad, Gyan. Where most children had model planes, I had spices! When I moved to London I worked in restaurants to supplement my income in the music business before finally and more recently arriving in Ireland. I came to attend the Ballymaloe Cookery School, fell in love with the country and my beautiful wife, Olive. Nurtured by this generous nation I set up my spice company, Green Saffron and began trading in whole spices direct with Indian farms, blending fresh flavours at my Irish base. I'm a spice specialist, and very much a home cook.

I create recipes based on my favourite foods, never limited by genre, region or country, simply focused on making delicious food. I've arranged the recipe chapters into food groups and at the beginning of each chapter I introduce the spices that work best with these foods. Some of the recipes may appear lengthy and a little daunting at first, but the instructions are set out in a step-by-step format. They explain exactly what to do, ensure the spotlight is on the spice and the focus clearly on flavour. So, get stuck in, have a go, enjoy your cooking and relish your food!

# BUYING FRESH SPICES

Spices should be fresh, vibrant and zinging with natural flavour. Capturing their essence in the food we eat has to start at the beginning, with the raw spice itself. So how do you know what to look for? We're bombarded with campaigns for organic this, free-range that, local, sustainable, fresh – but they're seldom applied to spices. They should be. Just as with wines, cheeses, coffee, teas, meat, fish and vegetables, I like to know the provenance of the spices I use, how they're cultivated, and stored, because these things matter to the end product. Spices are parts of plants: like fruit, vegetables and grains they are harvested at certain times of year: black pepper in winter, coriander in spring, nutmeg and mace in summer. After harvesting, each spice then needs to be dried, and in some cases cured or matured, before it is ready for sale; this can take from two hours to six months, depending on the spice. In the past, spices took much longer to make their journey from the farm to our tables. Today, there's no reason why we shouldn't be able to buy 'farm-fresh' spices – and at greensaffron.com, you can – there's certainly no excuse for dull, sad-looking spices that have been stored too long.

Demand the freshest, best-looking spices from the shops and suppliers you use. The easiest thing to do is simply to use your senses, checking for scent and vibrant colour. Asian shops are likely to have a good choice of fresh spices because they have a high turnover. When buying online you may be able to ask more questions about the provenance of your spices; after that it's a matter of finding a supplier that you trust.

Once you're happy you've hunted down the best, stick to buying spices 'little and often': as you need them, rather than a bulk buy that ends up unused at the back of the cupboard. Store spices in airtight containers in a cool, dark place; don't put them in the fridge – there's no need.

Most spices are best bought whole, and ground just before you use them. Freshly ground spices are more intense than the whole ones; as the surface area increases, so does volatility and flavour – but the volatile oils, the compounds that give spices their aromas and flavours, are easily lost, which is why I recommend grinding your own spices 'to order' for each recipe. Think of the difference between fresh and dried herbs, or between dusty, ready-ground black pepper and pungent freshly ground black peppercorns. Now imagine how much more vibrant the flavours of cumin, cinnamon and coriander will be if you grind them only when you need them. You can use a mortar and pestle, an electric spice mill, a small coffee grinder (preferably not the one you use for coffee) – or just put the whole spices in a strong plastic bag, cover it with a tea towel and bash with a heavy pan or rolling pin until they're ground as coarsely or finely as you want. I know this may seem like 'a bit of a grind' at first, but you will notice the flavour difference, your spices will keep better and you will soon get in the habit and enjoy the sensations of the freshly unlocked fragrance.

# COOKING WITH SPICES

The food I love revolves around pure flavour, texture and, particularly, spices. I see spices as flecks of bright, glorious colour in a world of monochrome seasoning. To me, fresh, fragrant, raw spices are everyday ingredients. I believe that everyone can cook, and everyone can cook with spices.

Spices add a wealth of beautiful, vibrant flavours; fragrant, subtle aromas. They can create smoky notes, citrus notes, menthol notes, warmth, depth and a finish that leaves the palate clean yet wanting more. Spices evolved naturally, producing volatile oils as an organic self-defence mechanism. I like to celebrate this 'wild' element when I'm blending and cooking with spices. Not opting for regulated, exactly consistent flavours, but creating a flavour for the moment. Spices are the bold ingredients of the food world: left of centre, unconventional but a positive influence, with their heart in the right place. Solo or blended, they can be used in any dish. When I'm coming up with spice combinations, I see a cast of characters with different moods and emotions, I see colours, and flood my mind with flavour memories, mixing my Eastern and Western sides. So when it comes to spices, forget conventional wisdom; go with your instincts and think flavour!

*To toast or not to toast?*
I shudder every time I hear people say, 'You should always toast your spices.' It really is a bugbear of mine, this willy-nilly toasting, roasting and frying of spice. WHY? The usual answer is that heat brings out the flavour of the spice. But let's think about that for a minute. A vibrant, volatile 'fresh' spice has flavour by its very nature. By heating a spice, you're changing its chemical composition and therefore its flavour profile, compressing it all into the toasty mid-range but losing any high notes. Now that's brilliant for many dishes, but be aware of how such processes affect the ingredients we use. I may decide to toast some spices at the beginning of a recipe so they are not too dominant, but then add a little more of the same spice near the end of cooking to highlight the flavour. The perfect blend of spices is all about getting the right mix of notes while maintaining individual flavour integrity.

# BUILDING A BLEND

When you host a party, you want to invite guests who are going to mix well. You need to know their individual characters so you can create a good group. Now this may not necessarily mean they all get on perfectly. Where would be the fun in that? It makes for a more stimulating event when people have different views and want to get them across. Indeed, isn't the phrase 'to add a little spice to the mix' meant for just such occasions?

It's a similar situation when using spices. Get to know the characteristics of each spice, then you can use them confidently in every dish, either to add balance or to take the dish's overall flavour in an unexpected direction. Flavour characteristics should mix well together, but they should all be able to hold their own in a dish and bring something wonderful to the party. Happy food mixes with happy spices such as fennel, coriander, green cardamom; dark, moody food with sultry, exotic spices such as cloves, star anise, black pepper, black cardamom. Heady, perfumed but astringent rose gets on well with floral, creamy, sweet vanilla. Introduce them to black pepper for its pungent, warming, woody heat, or the perfumed heat of long pepper. Or you might begin with pungent, heavy-hitting asafoetida, adding support from characters like earthy-sweet turmeric, earthy-citrus cumin and a zingy, uplifting touch of ginger.

## Spice characteristics

The essential character of a spice relates to its volatile oil content, the compounds that give it its fragrance and flavour. Freshness is key, as by definition 'volatile' oils are easily lost. Without going into chemistry, there are two key groups of compounds: terpenes and benzenes. Terpenes are responsible for the aromatic freshness of a spice, which we describe as floral, piney or 'spicy' – the pinenes in pepper, the linalool in coriander, for example. Benzenes provide 'sweet', creamy aromas – vanillin in vanilla, eugenol in cloves, cinnamon, cassia, bay leaves and basil. From these examples, you can begin to see how and why we can all relate to spices in similar ways.

## Spice notes

You can tell if a spice blend is right when you simply want to dive into it, when you want the entire fragrance to engulf you and no single spice is too dominant. Without being overly prescriptive, I tend to approach this by thinking in terms of bass, middle and high notes and achieving a balance. Bass notes, low and lasting, provide depth, and come from turmeric, cumin, as well as black cardamom, ginger, vanilla, tamarind and star anise. Middle notes means spices like cassia, coriander, fennel, cloves, pepper and saffron that hold their own flavours. High-note spices are those like green cardamom, mace, nutmeg and cinnamon: top-end, perfumed, cherry-on-the-top types. You can identify these high-note spices by their initial burst of scent and ethereal, volatile nature; they're spices that need to be used sparingly and treated with care – the spice divas, if you will.

## Colours

I don't want to sound like a crazy warehouse party casualty, but I do relate colours to food types, and from there I make a connection to a spice. Colours reflect moods – think about blue and green and you think calm, serenity; yellow suggests happiness and positivity; reds are full of warmth and energy; black and brown are moody, exotic. I use these natural indicators to steer me in the right flavour direction. For example, the deep golden sphere of an egg yolk suggests the all-pervasive warmth of the sun, and that takes me to the warm golden colour of turmeric and the heat of cayenne pepper, which go so well with eggs. When thinking about lamb I might imagine a green and sunny pasture, and a sweet, serene mood; in terms of spices I might turn to the uplifting perfume of green cardamom, the bright citrus hit of coriander, or a touch of floral sweetness from cloves.

# A–Z of Spices

The following pages describe the spices used in this book; I hope they will encourage you to widen your repertoire. Spices, like herbs, are parts of plants that are rich in flavour compounds. Some leaves are usually considered as spices rather than herbs: curry leaves, for example, or cassia leaves, also known as tejpatta or Indian bay leaves. Barks, such as cassia and cinnamon, are also used as spices. Spices can be fruits, such as black pepper and vanilla; seeds, like mustard, fenugreek and nigella (also known as black onion seeds or kalonji); or seed husks or hulls, such as Szechuan pepper. They can be dried gums, or oleoresins, such as asafoetida, which is made by tapping the resin from the roots of ferula plants (related to fennel). Ginger and turmeric are rhizomes – root-like stems – and cloves are dried, unopened flower buds. To me, the most enigmatic spices of all are mace and saffron. Mace, the lacey outer coating to the nutmeg seed, is defined as an aril – an extra seed covering – and saffron is the stigma of a crocus flower.

In this A–Z I use botanical definitions to describe the part of the plant used as a spice. Botanically, a fruit is simply a seed pod; you may be surprised at how many spices commonly referred to as 'seeds' are actually 'fruits', albeit generally dried, unripe fruits, including caraway, cumin and coriander. A fruit is essentially made of two parts: the 'housing' or husk, and the seed. The housing may be hard, like the black skin of peppercorns, or soft and fleshy like mace or the red flesh around a pomegranate seed. The housing is generally called 'pericarp' when hard and 'aril' when soft. White pepper is simply the seed of a peppercorn with the black pericarp removed.

Nature always plays a large part in a spice's flavour. Just as with wine, the soil and climate influence the spice we buy. Even more important are the decisions made by the farmer, such as how and when to harvest and how the spice is processed.

I've included the main volatile oils and other aroma and flavour compounds that contribute to the character of each spice. Each spice also has its 'note': bass, mid or high. These relate to the building blocks I describe on pages 10–11. You will see that certain compounds are common to a number of spices, and this will give you a steer as to which spices work well together in a blend. For example, citrus aromas most likely come from limonene, a compound named because it smells like lemons – a 'happy' spice characteristic. Anethole gives anise-like aromas and is found in caraway, fennel, star anise, as well as in herbs such as tarragon and basil. When combining spices to achieve depth and synergy in a dish I look for characteristics that complement and balance each other.

I have given a little background knowledge about each spice, including where they are mainly cultivated, what to look for when buying fresh spices, and a few ideas on how they are used. Some spices are known by several names, so I've included some of these to help you find them.

## ALLSPICE

(Jamaican pepper, pimento, English pepper)
*Botanical name: Pimenta dioica*
*Part used: fruit ('berries')*
*Main flavour and aroma compounds: eugenol, cineol*
*Character: heady, complex, exotic, sweet*
*Note: mid–high*
*Buy: whole or powdered*

Native to the Caribbean, Mexico and Central America, the evergreen allspice tree grows to about 10–20m tall. The tiny round fruits are picked while still green, just before they are fully ripe, at which point they begin to lose their aroma. They are then dried and change from green to reddish-brown. Allspice 'berries' look like large peppercorns with one pronounced freckle.

Jamaica is the largest producer of the spice; it is also cultivated in Barbados, Cuba and Mexico. I prefer the Jamaican variety to the Mexican as I find it has a sweeter, slightly more complex, flavour.

Christopher Columbus introduced the spice to Europe in the 16th century. An Englishman named it 'allspice' because he thought it smelt like a mixture of clove, nutmeg, cinnamon and pepper. This spice is used whole in pickling and ground in cakes, puddings and pies.

## AMCHOOR (MANGO POWDER)

*Botanical name: Mangifera indica*
*Part used: fruit*
*Main flavour and aroma compounds: ocimene, cubebene, cadinene*
*Character: intense astringency, caramel, sour tang*
*Note: mid*
*Buy: powdered*

Mangoes are native to India and South Asia. Amchoor is a tangy-tart powder made from unripe green mangoes; peeled, sliced, sun-dried and then ground to a light brown powder. It has a fruity, honeyed caramel aroma and sherbet-like flavour, and in northern India it is dusted over all manner of cooked and raw foods as a condiment to make dishes really sparkle and come alive! It's a handy way to add fruity flavour and a savoury tartness without adding extra moisture, and is used with pulses, vegetable dishes, fish, chutneys and pickles. Amchoor also contains certain enzymes that make it work as a meat tenderiser, so it's useful in marinades.

## ANARDANA (DRIED POMEGRANATE SEEDS)

*Botanical name: Punica granatum*
*Part used: seeds*
*Character: tangy sour crunch, fruity sweet end*
*Note: mid*
*Buy: whole or powdered*

Cultivated since ancient times, pomegranates are now grown in many countries around the world. To make anardana, fresh pomegranate seeds are slowly sun-dried, making the flavour deeper and richer, yet they retain some of the fruit's tannic astringency. The fruity sourness works exceptionally well with poultry and game birds such as duck, pheasant, quail, or even poussin, and also with lamb.

Dried pomegranate seeds are great as a snack, rather like crunchy raisins. The best hail from the Himalayan wild 'daru' variety of pomegranate.

The seeds are also sold powdered, usually roasted first to remove excess moisture. This powder is strewn over snacks in northern India to make a zingy condiment. Anardana is a wonderful ingredient: you'll find yourself reaching for it when something's just a little lacklustre and needs to sparkle.

## ASAFOETIDA

(Hing in Hindi)
*Botanical name: Ferula asafoetida*
*Part used: resin gum*
*Main flavour and aroma compounds: propenyl disulfide, pinene*
*Character: pungent, sulphurous, onion and garlic notes*
*Note: bass*
*Buy: small nuggets*

Asafoetida is the dried resin gum tapped from the root of the ferula plant; sometimes known as giant fennel, it is native to Iran and Afghanistan, and cultivated in the north of India. There are two main varieties, the milky white Kabuli Sufaid and the deep brown Lal.

It is usually found in powdered form, mixed with gum arabic, rice flour and turmeric, but I prefer to buy only the pure resin. It is quite difficult to find in shops, but can be bought online. Sometimes called 'devil's dung', this resin is extremely pungent and must be stored in airtight containers to preserve not only its freshness, but also your sanity! However, when used in cooking, it loses its pungency and adds an almost fruity, intense flavour like fried onions and garlic. Reputed to have anti-flatulent properties, it is widely used in lentil-based dishes. I love asafoetida and use it to add depth to meat stews, veg dishes, relishes and chutneys.

## CARAWAY

*Botanical name: Carum carvi*
*Part used: fruit ('seeds')*
*Main flavour and aroma compounds: anethole, limonene, carvone*
*Character: delicate smoky anise*
*Note: mid*
*Buy: whole*

Caraway plants are native to Europe, western Asia and north Africa. The tiny, light brown, ridged, curved fruit (known as 'seeds') are about 3–4mm long and have an anise-citrus flavour. Caraway is popular in northern Europe and Scandinavia, since it grew locally and unlike other spices it didn't need to be imported. The 'seeds' are usually used whole. They are sometimes added to sauerkraut, but are more often used in baking, from rye breads to festive biscuits. In the UK caraway is traditionally used in 'seed cake' and for a Lancashire speciality known as Goosnargh cakes (a type of cookie). In Holland, Germany and Russia it flavours the digestif Kümmel. It doesn't often appear in Indian cuisine, though some translated recipes do mistakenly call for it in biryanis and pilaus.

## CARDAMOM, BLACK

(Elaichi, or Kali elaichi, in Hindi)
*Botanical name: Amomum subulatum*
*Part used: fruit (seed pod)*
*Main flavour and aroma compounds: cineol, terpinene, limonene*
*Character: smoky, sultry, exotic, camphor, complex twisted high notes*
*Note: bass*
*Buy: whole*

A member of the ginger family of flowering plants, black cardamom is native to northern India (I get mine from Darjeeling); its dried seed pods are dark brown, wrinkly and about 2cm long, packed with dark brown seeds. A species with larger pods is grown in China and Vietnam. In India, we say green cardamom for cooling and black for heat; black cardamom is mainly used in savoury dishes, but this is not a rigid rule. Indeed, I use it with mango in my kulfi (ice cream) recipe (see page 244). I love the camphor notes and smokiness, which is created as the pods are dried over smouldering embers. This makes them perfect with game and dark meats, to accentuate depth of flavour.

## CARDAMOM, GREEN

(Elaichi, or Chota elaichi, in Hindi)
*Botanical name: Elettaria cardamomum*
*Part used: fruit (seed pod)*
*Main flavour and aroma compounds: myrcene, limonene and cineol*
*Character: menthol, eucalyptus, heady gingery perfume, uplifting*
*Note: high*
*Buy: whole*

Like black cardamom (above), green cardamom is a member of the ginger family and is one of my favourite spices. It is native to southern India (I get mine from Idduki in Kerala) and Sri Lanka and is extensively cultivated in Guatemala. It is the third most expensive spice after saffron and vanilla, largely because each plant only produces 500g of pods a year. The pods are dried in the sun or, commercially, over electric elements, and each pod, about 1.5cm long, is packed with sticky brown-black seeds. Tease them out with your fingers and grind them, or add the whole pods to more robust and savoury dishes, and in infusions. The whole pods are not meant to be eaten – the flavour is too intense in one hit – if you find one, just leave it on the side of the plate. Green cardamom has a beautiful, uplifting, citrus, gingery, minty, camphor, hoppy, complex perfume, adding high-end 'ping' to both sweet and savoury dishes. Try to search out fat, bright green pods rather than the skinny, wizened, pallid offerings all too often on sale.

## CAROM (AJWAIN, AJOWAN)
*Botanical name: Trachyspermum ammi*
*Part used: fruit ('seeds')*
*Main flavour and aroma compounds: thymol, pinene, cymene, limonene, terpinene*
*Character: peppery, anise, bitter*
*Note: mid*
*Buy: whole*

Like caraway, coriander, cumin and fennel, carom is the dried fruit of a flowering plant, and the spice is usually referred to as seeds. The tiny (about 1.5–2mm), egg-shaped grey fruits smell musty and thyme-like; they are sometimes erroneously called lovage or dill seeds. The spice probably originated in Egypt and was introduced to India at the time of Alexander the Great's conquest, around 300BC. India is the main producer of carom, and it is also grown in Pakistan, Afghanistan, Iran and Egypt.

Carom has quite a kick if eaten raw, but when cooked it mellows to something milder and altogether more complex. It imparts its flavour more readily in fat, and in India the seeds are often fried in ghee, which allows the distinctive flavour to permeate the dish. They are used whole, a fab addition to lentil and root vegetable dishes, adding peppery notes of anise and thyme. The essential oil thymol gives carom medicinal properties, including digestive and anti-flatulent effects.

## CASSIA
*Botanical name: Cinnamomum tamala*
*Part used: bark*
*Main flavour and aroma compounds: eugenol, coumarin (trace)*
*Character: deep clove-like plus high note sweetness, astringent*
*Note: mid*
*Buy: whole*

Cassia is the dried inner bark of an evergreen tree of the laurel family, native to southern China; it now grows throughout South and Southeast Asia. It is often known as Chinese cinnamon. Indeed, the Hindi for cassia, *dal chini*, means 'Chinese wood'. Freshly dried cassia bark has a vibrant, ruddy hue and is highly aromatic, with a slight bitterness. In

some countries cassia and cinnamon are used interchangeably, but cassia has deeper notes than the more delicate, sweeter cinnamon. Cassia's flavour both penetrates and lingers. In India it's considered 'warming' and is usually used in savoury dishes, especially meat. It's also one of the components of Chinese five-spice powder.

Cassia bark is thicker than that of cinnamon (see below) and is very hard to grind. Ideally, blitz it in an electric spice grinder before you start the recipe. Alternatively you could use a mortar – and a lot of elbow grease! Some recipes, especially braises and stews, use whole pieces of cassia: they are not meant to be eaten – you'll soon know if you bite a piece of wood.

## CAYENNE PEPPER
*Botanical name: Capsicum annuum*
*Part used: fruit*
*Main flavour and aroma compounds: capsaicinoids*
*Character: fruity, pungent heat*
*Note: mid*
*Buy: powdered or flakes*

Cayenne peppers are hot chillies, usually harvested when red and fully ripe, then dried and finely ground to make the bright red spice we know as cayenne pepper. The dried chillies can also be crushed and used in the form of chilli flakes. Cayenne peppers are also used fresh, or combined with vinegar to make spicy-hot, pungent sauces, much-loved in the southern USA. They take their name from the city of Cayenne in French Guiana, but are grown in many parts of the Americas and Asia. The chilli heat rating of cayenne pepper usually ranges between 20,000 and 50,000 Scoville units. If you're not a chilli-head, err on the low side, taste your blend and then add a little more cayenne if you feel it needs more of a kick. I particularly enjoy the spicy heat of cayenne in cooked cheese dishes and with shellfish, as part of the dish or sprinkled on as a final colourful flourish.

## CHILLIES
*Botanical name: Capsicum annuum, Capsicum frutescens and other species*
*Part used: fruit*
*Main flavour and aroma compounds: capsaicinoids*
*Buy: fresh or dried, whole or flakes*

Although these are not a spice, I use fresh chillies in a similar way to dried ones (cayenne, Kashmiri, paprika), matching them to the dish and balancing them with other flavours: ají (lemon) chillies for their pronounced fruity notes, fresh bird's eye chillies for perfumed raw heat, and Scotch bonnets for pure devilment!

Chillies are the fruit of a flowering plant

native to Central and South America, and were named 'peppers' by Christopher Columbus because he found their spicy heat similar to the black pepper known in Europe. The Portuguese explorer Vasco da Gama is credited with the introduction of chillies to India in 1498. Over time, the chilli replaced black pepper as India's preferred method of adding deep and pungent heat to a dish and India is now the world's biggest producer (and consumer) of chillies. More than 200 varieties of chillies are grown in many countries around the world.

The 'heat' of chilli peppers is historically measured in Scoville heat units (SHU). It was devised using a panel of tasters and a dilution of the chilli extract, testing when the heat from the capsaicin is no longer detectable; it is therefore a subjective scale. Newer chilli heat scales are more scientific, but Scoville units are still widely used. For example, jalapeño chilies range from about 2500 to 4000 SHU, bird's eye chillies from 50,000 to 100,000, while Scotch bonnets range from 100,000 to 350,000.

## CINNAMON
*Botanical name: Cinnamomum zeylanicum*
*Part used: bark*
*Main flavour and aroma compounds: eugenol, ethyl cinnamate, linalool, coumarin (trace)*
*Character: heady, warm, sweet astringency*
*Note: high*
*Buy: whole*

True cinnamon is the dried inner bark of a tree native to Sri Lanka; is also grown in India, the Seychelles and elsewhere. As a spice it has travelled even more widely. To farm the spice, the tree is coppiced to produce lots of branches; these branches are harvested, the outer bark removed and the inner bark rolled to form cinnamon's easily recognisable 'quills'. Once dried, the tan-coloured quills are cut into 7–10cm 'sticks'. Although it is quite hard to grind, I recommend buying whole cinnamon sticks and grinding them when you need them: blitz them in an electric spice grinder or pound them in a mortar – it's well worth the effort. The flavour of cinnamon quickly deteriorates if it's not sparkling fresh, and the bitterness is more pronounced in the ground spice, especially if overcooked.

In the West, we commonly associate the sweet scent of cinnamon with pastries and desserts, and with mulled wine at Christmas. In South America it's often paired with chocolate in both sweet and savoury dishes. Much more interesting to me is its use in spice blends and savoury dishes, where it adds its heady sweetness to meats such as lamb and chicken.

## CLOVE

*Botanical name: Eugenia caryophyllus*
*Part used: unopened flower bud*
*Main flavour and aroma compounds: eugenol, vanillin*
*Character: assertive, medicinal, deep, fruity*
*Note: mid*
*Buy: whole*

Cloves come from a large evergreen tree (the leaves are also aromatic) native to the Molucca Islands, the original 'Spice Islands' in Indonesia. Each tree produces flower buds for around 80 years – yielding anything from a modest 2kg to a bumper 18kg annually. The unopened flowers are harvested and dried in the sun. The essence of 'aromatic sunshine', they are grown in many countries, including Indonesia, Madagascar, Tanzania, India and Pakistan and are used around the world in both sweet and savoury dishes.

The spice is used both whole and ground. In India it finds special favour in meat dishes. In the West cloves are commonly used with baked ham, stewed fruits and pickles; an onion studded with a clove adds depth to stocks and sauces. Try always to buy fat-looking cloves. The strong flavour of cloves means they need to be used judiciously. They contain large amounts of the oil eugenol, which accounts for their distinctive flavour. Clove oil acts as an anaesthetic.

## CORIANDER

(Dhania in Hindi)
*Botanical name: Coriandrum sativum*
*Part used: fruit ('seeds')*
*Main flavour and aroma compounds: linalool, terpinene, pinene*
*Character: lemony citrus, muted intensity*
*Note: mid*
*Buy: whole*

The flowering plant whose dried fruits are known as coriander seeds is native to a large area around the Mediterranean, but has been established much further afield for thousands of years, and two distinct varieties have developed. In Europe and North Africa the fruits, 3–4mm in diameter, are spherical, brownish, and have a woody-peppery-orange aroma. Far superior, to my mind, are the slightly larger, rugby-ball-shaped greeny-yellow fruits of the Indian coriander; you may think you know coriander, but when you experience it in its freshest form, nothing can prepare you for the intense citrus hit of this lemon bomb!

The aroma fades fast, so – as with most spices – I recommend grinding as and when you need it. The 'seeds' are brittle, so coriander is one of the easiest spices to grind. In Indian cookery, coriander 'seeds' are used in generous quantities and accurate measurements are not so crucial when using this amiable spice. They're used whole or ground, generally in savoury dishes. Around

the Mediterranean and in northern Europe, coriander is used in meat dishes, sausages, and as a pickling spice; it's the traditional spice in Irish corned (preserved) beef.

Fresh coriander leaves are a popular herb in many parts of Asia and Central and South America; their distinctive, strong, grassy-citrus flavour derives from an essential oil that is not present in the dried fruit ('seeds').

## CUMIN

(Zeera or jeera in Hindi)
*Botanical name: Cuminum cyminum*
*Part used: fruit ('seeds')*
*Main flavour and aroma compounds: cuminaldehyde, pinene, cymene*
*Character: earthy citrus, peppery, gentle anise*
*Note: bass*
*Buy: whole*

Cumin is the fruit (usually called 'seeds') of a flowering annual plant that grows well in any country with a long, hot summer. The 'seeds' – about 5mm long and ridged – are harvested when they turn yellow-brown and are then dried. Native to Egypt and the Eastern Mediterranean region, the largest producer and consumer of cumin today is India; Turkey, Iran, Syria, Egypt, Mexico and China are other major producers. The Romans introduced it to much of Europe, and Spanish and Portuguese colonists introduced it to the Americas.

A glorious spice with zingy lemon and anise flavours in equal parts, rounded out with a down-to-earth comforting warmth and almost astringent notes of fresh black pepper. It gives savoury, earthy depth to a dish, a sort of 'bedrock' flavour for lighter aromatics, typically coriander, to dance upon. The seeds can be dry-roasted or fried in ghee to maximise their intensely savoury flavour. Cumin is important in much Indian cooking, and is essential in Garam Masala and Panch Phoran (see pages 266–7). It is highly reputed for its digestive properties – indeed the Hindi for cumin, *jeera*, is derived from a Sanskrit word meaning 'digestive'.

## CUMIN, BLACK

*Botanical name: Bunium bulbocastanum*
*Part used: fruit ('seeds')*
*Main flavour and aroma compounds: cuminaldehyde, terpinene, cymene*
*Character: earthy anise*
*Note: bass*
*Buy: whole*

Black cumin grows wild in Kashmir, Afghanistan and Iran and is sometimes considered superior to 'ordinary' cumin: the flavour is 'darker', sweeter and almost smoky. Each plant yields just 5–8 grams of seed, making it quite a pricy spice. In Hindi it is called *shahi* ('royal') or *kala* ('black') cumin.

The thin black 'seeds' are about 3mm long, and have an earthy, nutty, savoury and somewhat herby, floral flavour. The seeds are usually used whole; not ground, and are often toasted before use, which brings out the nutty qualities. Black cumin is confined mainly to the cuisines of northern India, Iran and Afghanistan, particularly in breads, garlic-onion-ginger pastes and steamed rice dishes.

## FENNEL

*Botanical name: Foeniculum vulgare*
*Part used: fruit ('seeds')*
*Main flavour and aroma compounds: anethole*
*Character: sweet middle, muted anise*
*Note: mid*
*Buy: whole*

Fennel seeds are the fruit of a plant with yellow flowers and feathery leaves, which grows wild in the Mediterranean region, and which has long been established across Asia and in north America. The 'seeds' vary in size and shape; I prefer the slightly smaller, more delicate type, about 3–4mm long, but whichever type you come across they should always be bright, vibrant green.

Fennel is popular in French and Italian kitchens, often used with fish and in pork dishes and salami. The ground spice is an essential constituent of Chinese five-spice powder, while, used whole, the seeds make up one-fifth of the quintessential Bengali spice mixture, Panch Phoran (see page 266). Fennel is equally popular in other parts of India – as a pickling spice, in southern Indian garam masala and paired with ginger in Kashmiri cuisine, where it's also used to flavour baked goods. Toasting mutes the spice's sweetness and it tends to be treated this way when it is used in bread and cheese recipes. Imparting its anise flavour to all it touches, the seeds are often chewed as a breath freshener. The Indian classic Mishri and Soonf, a mixture of crystal sugar and fennel seeds commonly known as *paan*, not only acts as a palate cleanser, but is also a natural digestif.

## FENUGREEK

*Botanical name: Trigonella foenum graecum*
*Part used: seeds*
*Main flavour and aroma compounds: beta-pinene, camphor, beta-caryophyllene*
*Character: bitter, sweet pea flavours*
*Note: mid*
*Buy: whole*

This annual plant, a member of the bean family, flourishes in warm, dry conditions and is cultivated worldwide, especially throughout the Indian subcontinent, the Near East and North Africa. The little sandy yellow-coloured, jagged, cube-shaped seeds aren't used very often in Western cuisine. Some find the spice's bitterness off-putting, although it's possible to temper the bitterness somewhat with toasting. Most recipes advise against letting the seeds darken, but in both Gujarati and Nepalese cuisine they are allowed to almost blacken in oil in order to add a smoky, roasty, almost meaty flavour to both the oil and the entire dish. I use this technique for the potato part of my Bacon Chop recipe (see pages 34–35). Whole fenugreek seeds form one-fifth of the Bengali spice blend Panch Phoran (see page 266). The ground spice is a common component of curry powder, and it is often used in south Indian vegetable and pulse dishes, as well as in the wonderfully hot Ethiopian spice mix, *berbere*. It has recently been discovered to have blood sugar regulating properties, to the extent that is it now a spice suggested to many sufferers of type 2 diabetes.

## GINGER

*Botanical name: Zingiber officinale*
*Part used: rhizome ('root')*
*Main flavour and aroma compounds: pinenes, camphene, cineole, linalool, borneol, turpineol, nerol, geraniol, zingiberene*
*Character: citrus, piney, soft heat*
*Note: bass*
*Buy: fresh or powdered*

Ginger is the root-like fleshy stem of a flowering plant native to southern China and tropical Asia. Its use in Asian cooking dates back some 4000 years; it goes well with both savoury and sweet foods, and was one of the earliest spices to be traded around the Mediterranean; it became one of the most popular spices in Europe. Later traders introduced it to Africa and the Americas.

Ginger is available in a whole host of forms, each with a slightly different expression of ginger's lively, citrusy warmth. When buying the fresh 'root', it should be firm, with smooth, taut, light brown skin (which is usually peeled off before use); if you can see a slice of the flesh it should be light yellow and not too fibrous. Avoid wizened, flabby pieces. Dried ginger is ground to a fine, dark beige powder, preferably with visible tiny fibres. Whole pieces of dried ginger are sometimes used as a flavouring. Chunks of ginger may be preserved in syrup, sometimes known as 'stem ginger', or cooked in syrup and then coated in sugar (crystallised ginger). Mild young ginger can be pickled; paper-thin slices are often served with Japanese food.

'Gingerbread' was first recorded in Europe in AD 992, and in India, ginger increased in popularity from the 13th century, with the rise of Muslim rule. Today, a paste of fresh ginger and garlic is the basis for many savoury dishes in India, Thailand and other Southeast Asian countries.

Sweetly spicy ginger is also well known for its medicinal properties, often brewed up as a tea. The Hindi word for ginger, *adrak*, means 'fire in the belly', and it is known to aid digestion and can help relieve nausea, especially motion sickness and morning sickness in pregnancy.

## INDIAN BAY LEAF

(Tejpatta, Malabar leaf, cassia leaf)
*Botanical name: Cinnamomum tamala*
*Part used: leaf*
*Main flavour and aroma compounds: eugenol and linalool*
*Character: delicate, citrus, top note cinnamon*
*Note: high*
*Buy: whole*

Indian bay are the leaves of the cassia tree, which is also grown for its bark, in India, China and Bhutan. They are quite different from the 'traditional' Mediterranean bay leaves (*Laurus nobilis*), being light green and about three times as long, with a delicate, orangey-citrus, cinnamon-like fragrance that's perfect for Asian stocks. I use them in an ice cream (see page 234) for their gentle perfume and lightly twisted cassia flavour.

## JUNIPER

*Botanical name: Juniperus communis*
*Part used: fruit ('berries')*
*Main flavour and aroma compounds: pinenes, sabinene, limonene*
*Character: pine high note, deep berry perfume*
*Note: high*
*Buy: whole*

This spice is the key flavouring in modern gin and its ancestor, genever – the Dutch word for juniper. It's the unripe green berries that provide the characteristic flavour in your G&T, whereas the ripe purple-black berries are the ones you'll use in the kitchen. When buying, ensure they're plump, round and taut-skinned. To use juniper berries, lightly crush them to release the complex fragrant flavours and aromas.

Juniper 'berries' are the fruit of a prickly evergreen shrub that grows wild throughout Europe and north America. The ancient Greeks and Romans used juniper, and it has been found in Egyptian tombs. These days it is most associated with northern Europe and Scandinavia, often found in fish preparations such as rollmop herrings. Juniper is also perfect paired with cabbage – both braised and pickled – and game, loved for its clean, sharp qualities.

## KASHMIRI CHILLIES

*Botanical name: Capsicum annuum*
*Part used: fruit*
*Main flavour and aroma compounds: capsaicinoids*

*Character: smoky, fruity perfume, gentle heat, glorious red colour*
*Note: mid*
*Buy: whole or flakes*

True Kashmiri chillies are grown in the Kashmir and Jammu region. As the peppers ripen, they turn deep red and the flavours become sweeter and more rounded – and their heat increasingly searing! Kashmiri chillies are usually sold dried; they have a wonderful deep red sheen, and as well as colour and spicy heat from the capsaicin content, they impart a pronounced fruity, slightly smoky flavour. You can buy whole chillies and chop them as required, or as flakes. Always (carefully) taste a few flakes before adding to a recipe – the heat level can vary wildly from batch to batch, but you're looking at around 6000 to 11,000 Scoville heat units.

## MACE

*Botanical name: Myristica fragrans*
*Part used: aril*
*Main flavour and aroma compounds: myristicin, pinene, limonene, borneol, terpineol, geraniol, safrol*
*Character: intense floral perfume, clean-cut astringent warmth*
*Note: high*
*Buy: whole*

Mace is one of my favourite spices. It has a finer aroma than nutmeg, with a slight hint of anise. Mace and nutmeg are both derived from an evergreen tree, native to the Moluccas, the 'Spice Islands' of Indonesia, and now cultivated in Grenada in the West Indies, Malaysia, and southern India. The nutmeg fruit looks like a pale apricot; when ripe it splits to reveal its conker-like seed (nutmeg) in a lacey coat, or aril (mace). The two parts are separated after harvesting; the mace is dried and (usually) flattened. Traditionally and somewhat romantically referred to as a 'blade' of mace, but as the arils are often broken into two or three pieces, a blade may mean different things to different cooks. Fresh mace is a bright pinky-red, highly aromatic, with astringent, almost numbing characteristics; as it dries it fades to an orange colour and loses some of the intensity of the aroma.

You need a light touch: with mace, less is more, as it's a powerful flavour that can easily overwhelm other spices. It's brilliant with potted seafood and meaty dishes of beef and lamb, and it's also a wonderful flavouring for dairy-based desserts and sauces such as béchamel, to which it imparts a warm orange colour. I love the way this spice can add perfume and sweetness yet also cut through richness and add a 'clean finish' to define flavours on the tongue.

Always buy whole mace rather than ready-ground; however, mace can be hard to grind, so I suggest that before adding it to a spice blend you blitz it in an electric spice grinder, or use a mortar and plenty of elbow grease!

## MUSTARD SEEDS, BLACK

*Botanical name: Brassica nigra*
*Part used: seeds*
*Main flavour and aroma compounds: isothiocyanates*
*Character: nutty pungent heat*
*Note: bass*
*Buy: whole*

Mustard plants are part of the Brassica family, like cabbages. Black mustard is native to southern Europe and western Asia, and is one of the oldest spices in the world; it is mentioned in Sumerian texts dating to around 3000BC. I prefer the nutty, more pungent flavour of black mustard to the brown mustard (*Brassica juncea*) that originated in northern India, although the two are more or less interchangeable. Brown mustard is easier to cultivate and is now commonly grown in Europe, while both are now grown in India. The black variety is slightly larger than the brown and has a blueish-black hue.

Mustard's heat is different from chilli heat, travelling up the nose and dissipating quickly. When ground and mixed with cold liquid, the 'heat' is the result of a chemical reaction between two natural compounds found in mustard: sinigrin and the enzyme myrosin. Interestingly, this reaction does not happen when hot liquids are used, because heat (or acidity or alcohol) destroys some of the enzyme. So if you are mixing mustard from scratch, remember to allow the intrinsic heat to build before adding vinegar, which stops the reaction.

The flavour of mustard seeds is quite different when they are cooked whole. They can be dry-roasted, but are more commonly dropped into hot oil, when they make an audible 'pop', become slightly greyish in colour and develop a rounded, nutty flavour that complements savoury dishes, especially fish and pulses. Black mustard seeds are a crucial part of the Bengali spice blend, Panch Phoran (see page 266).

Mustard seeds are also pressed to make a cooking oil that is used in many parts of the Indian subcontinent.

## NIGELLA SEEDS (BLACK ONION SEEDS, KALONJI)

*Botanical name: Nigella sativa*
*Part used: seeds*
*Main flavour and aroma compounds: nigellone, thymoquinone, allyl propyl disulphide*
*Character: floral pepper notes, muted bitterness*
*Note: mid*
*Buy: whole*

Nigella seeds come from a flowering plant native to South and Southwest Asia; it's not related to the onion, although the spice is commonly called black onion seeds. The tiny black seeds are roughly cuboid and have little odour; when ground or chewed they develop a vaguely oregano-like scent. The taste is aromatic and slightly bitter, pungent, smoky, even peppery.

You'll see them sprinkled over Indian naan and breads from Turkey; in fact the Turkish name translates as 'bun's herb'. In north India, Punjabi and Bengali cooks use nigella to flavour cooked vegetables. The spice forms one-fifth of the Bengali spice blend Panch Phoran (see page 266). Dry-toasting or frying in oil makes the complex flavour of nigella more rounded and a little nuttier.

## NUTMEG

*Botanical name: Myristica fragrans*
*Part used: seed kernel*
*Main flavour and aroma compounds: myristicin, pinene, limonene, borneol, terpineol, geraniol, safrol*
*Character: bittersweet heady perfume, astringent*
*Note: high*
*Buy: whole*

Nutmeg is the hard, brown, egg-shaped seed (about 2.5mm long) of the tree that also gives us mace (see above). The tree is native to parts of Indonesia and is cultivated in Malaysia, the Caribbean and southern India. Early traders prized it for its medicinal and aphrodisiac properties, and in large quantities it is a hallucinogen, but not a very good one; it's likely to make you feel queasy and uneasy.

With its uplifting, 'full-on', fragrance, it's a spice that must whisper, not shout, with a tendency to overpower and render a dish unpalatably bitter if overused: 'a grating of nutmeg' means a single rub along a grater. Its slight astringency cuts through richness in both sweet and savoury dishes. Béchamel sauce is lifted by a touch of nutmeg, while the French spice blend Quatre Épices (see page 266) includes nutmeg and is used in sausages and pâtés. The British often use nutmeg in sweet dishes, custards, mulled wine and hot milk drinks. It's widely used in Dutch cooking and in the Caribbean. It also perks up pumpkin – in Italian pasta fillings and in American pumpkin pie. It's often grated over cooked spinach in Italy, and I'd always recommend a generous grating in mashed spud to give it a subtle lift, but to me nutmeg is probably best when used with chocolate to enhance the nuances and notes of cacao.

## PAPRIKA

*Botanical name: Capsicum annuum*
*Part used: fruit*
*Main flavour and aroma compounds: capsaicinoids*
*Character: soft, peppery, fruity*
*Note: mid*
*Buy: powdered*

I tend to associate paprika with Hungary (and goulash) and Spain (and chorizo). But the spice is appreciated elsewhere, too, for example, in the Arabic spice blend *baharat*.

Paprika is a powder made from ground dried red chilli peppers; it is the proportion of fruit, membrane and seeds used that dictates the strength of the final product, rather than the pungency of the pepper variety itself. Paprika can be broadly divided into hot, sweet and smoked. Until the 1920s, when a sweet pepper plant was identified and cultivated, all paprika in Central Europe was the hot type. Today, the product labelled simply 'paprika' is the sweet, mild type.

In Hungary, you'll find salt and paprika, not salt and pepper, as table condiments. Different types of paprika are commonly used within a single dish to create the perfect blend of flavours, much like the use of multiple chilli varieties in Mexican cooking.

Spanish paprika, *pimentón*, comes in mild or 'sweet', medium-spicy and piquant versions. Pimentón de la Vera, from La Vera in western Spain, has a smoky character because the peppers are dried over oak wood. Typically, Spanish paprika is sweeter and milder than its Hungarian counterpart. The sugar content means paprika readily burns and turns bitter, so mind the stove when working with it.

## PEPPERCORNS, BLACK

*Botanical name: Piper nigrum*
*Part used: fruit ('berry')*
*Main flavour and aroma compounds: piperine, chavicine, pinenes, careen, limonene, cubenol, asaricin, 2-ethyl-3,5 dimethylpyrazine (also found in cacao)*
*Character: pungent, fruity, Parma violet, fresh leather*
*Note: mid*
*Buy: whole*

So well-known and distinctive that the term 'peppery' is widely used when describing other aromas, it is pungent with a sharp, yet warming, woody, fresh leather, Parma violet, almost vanilla note. Pungent-hot-pungent.

Peppercorns are the fruits of a perennial climbing vine; picked while unripe, they shrivel and darken as they dry. Green peppercorns are picked even earlier, brined to halt maturation, and may then be dried. Native to southwest India and now widely cultivated in tropical regions – although the best pepper is grown in India. Pepper's popularity largely stems from its ability to transform a dish in an instant, bringing food to life without overpowering it. In India, pepper was the original way to add heat, millenia before the arrival of chilli in the 16th century.

# 17

When freshly ground, black pepper is both pungent and headily aromatic. Add ground black pepper toward the end of the cooking process so that the flavour is not 'cooked out'. Whole peppercorns are often included in marinades and slow-cooked dishes.

Widely acknowledged as the King of spices, pepper has also been called 'black gold', and accounts for more than a quarter of global spice trade. It should be stored in an airtight and opaque container, because light reduces its spiciness.

## PEPPER, CUBEB

(Cubebs, Javanese pepper)
*Botanical name: Piper cubeba*
*Part used: fruit*
*Main flavour and aroma compounds: cubebene*
*Character: intense twist, rounded peppery, rose*
*Note: mid–high*
*Buy: whole*

The dried, unripe fruits of a member of the pepper family, cubebs resemble common black peppercorns, but with a little spiky stalk protruding from each. Native to Java, Indonesia, cubebs were popular in Europe until the 17th century and were used interchangeably with black pepper. Cubeb has a pronounced bitterness, which may well have contributed to its fall from favour, although the flavour mellows with cooking, and in the Middle Ages cubebs were candied and eaten whole. Commonly used to flavour spirits such as gin, this spice reputedly has aphrodisiac and medicinal properties, such as treating respiratory complaints.

I like to use cubebs in place of allspice, except when the more complex sweetness of allspice (Jamaican pepper) is required. In North Africa, particularly Tunisia and Morocco, cubebs appear in some recipes for *ras el hanout* – a blend of around 20 superior spices, often including rose petals, that translates as 'top of the shop'.

## PEPPER, LONG

(Pippali in Tamil)
*Botanical name: Piper longum*
*Part or type: flower spike*
*Main flavour and aroma compounds: piperine*
*Character: intense pepper, clove mid-notes, nutmeg, pine*
*Note: high*
*Buy: whole*

Long pepper is the flower spike of a vine that grows wild throughout India. It is rather hotter and more pungent than the closely related black pepper. Each peppercorn resembles a diminutive greyish-black catkin about 2.5cm long and contains many poppy-seed-sized fruits within, much in the manner of a pine cone and its nuts. Look for it in the Indian grocer's under the name *pippali*.

The Romans valued long pepper more highly than black, and today it is used in Indian pickles, a number of Indonesian and Malaysian dishes, as well as North African spice blends. The incense-like flavour is hard to pinpoint; it tastes rather 'ancient', with a hint of clove, nutmeg and top-note ginger. I like to use it to help define flavours, particularly, and probably not surprisingly, peppery notes. To use, simply rub the spike along a grater.

## PEPPER, SZECHUAN

*Botanical name: Zanthoxylum piperitum*
*Part used: pericarp (seed husk)*
*Main flavour and aroma compounds: linalool, limonene, cineole, pinene, citronellal, turpineol*
*Character: citrus, pepper, high-note perfume, mouth-numbing*
*Note: high*
*Buy: whole*

Szechuan or Sichuan pepper is not related to either black pepper or chilli; it was given this name by Westerners because it produces a perception of 'heat', but it lacks the pungency of other pepper types. The dried seed husk of the shrub-like prickly ash tree, Szechuan pepper can be used either whole or ground. It is usually added at the last stages of cooking in order to preserve the fragrant aromatic quality. Finely ground, it's part of Chinese five-spice powder. The uniquely citrus, hot-and-numbing sensation this spice offers is much prized in Szechuan cuisine and in many a spice blend I create. I love the tingling, numbing, buzzing sensation experienced when biting down on a husk, similar to a cross between licking a battery and drinking a fizzy drink!

The variety called 'Timur' is an important ingredient in Nepal, particularly in pickles and meat dishes, while in India, the *tephal* variety is used predominantly along the Konkan Coast of west India. The Chinese also infuse oil with the spice, or roast it and blend it with salt as a table condiment.

## PEPPER, WHITE

*Botanical name: Piper nigrum*
*Part used: seeds*
*Main flavour and aroma compounds: piperine*
*Character: sweet, pungent, peppery*
*Note: mid*
*Buy: whole*

The same fruits that become black pepper also give us white pepper. White pepper comes from skinned, fully ripe peppercorns. Skinning the corns means that some volatile aromas are lost, but white pepper retains the full pungency of its black counterpart.

The spice is mainly used in the West, often where a 'peppery' flavour is called for but the visibility of black pepper would spoil the appearance of a dish. It will provide pungent heat but not the highly fragrant quality of black pepper. In Japan, it's sometimes used as an alternative to Szechuan pepper.

Once ground, the spice becomes earthier with time, even occasionally described as 'mouldy'. This 'farmyard' taint can actually more commonly be attributed to a fault in outdated processing methods.

## ROSE PETALS

*Botanical name: Rosa centifolia, Rosa damascena and other species*
*Part used: flower petal*
*Main flavour and aroma compounds: citronellol, geraniol, nerol, linalool, farnesol, pinenes, terpinene, limonene, camphene, neral, eugenol*
*Character: heady floral sweetness, deep perfume, soft astringency*
*Note: mid*
*Buy: desiccated petals*

Roses may be a quintessential feature of an English country garden, but the fragrant petals also have a long history of use in a host of culinary applications. Edible species include the cabbage, damask and musk roses largely used in Persian and Middle Eastern cooking and the Indian rose, a very fragrant variety. When buying them dried, look for a deep purple-red colour and strong fragrance. The ancient Egyptians, Persians and Romans used rose petals to decorate food and flavour syrups. In the 11th century the Persian polymath Ibn Sina (Avicenna) is credited with the discovery of the distillation of rose petals to make rose water. In Europe in the Middle Ages, rose water was a key flavouring in sweetmeats such as marzipan, mainly associated with the wealthy nobility. The petals also make wonderful jams and conserves, preserved intact within a soft-set, sweet, fragrant jelly.

The culinary use of rose is largely restricted to sweet preparations (such as the innumerable Indian milk-based sweets and desserts), although the dried petals are found in the North African spice blend *ras el hanout*, and rose water can be sprinkled over biryani and other lavish rice dishes. In the West, the petals are frosted with egg white and sugar and used to decorate cakes, and bitter chocolates filled with a rose fondant cream are an old-fashioned British treat.

## SAFFRON

*Botanical name: Crocus sativus*
*Part used: stigma*
*Main flavour and aroma compounds: picrocrocin and safranal*
*Character: intense, floral, light astringency*
*Note: mid*
*Buy: 'threads' or 'strands'*

Saffron is gathered from certain varieties of the crocus flower. Each flower has three vivid red stigmas. It takes about 150,000 such stigma to make 1kg of saffron, making this spice the most expensive of all. However, a couple of threads of this precious spice will go a very long way, and have the power to totally transform a dish with saffron's inimitable flavour and fragrance. Always buy the fine whole threads: ground saffron is not only vastly inferior and loses fragrance fast, it is very likely to be a fake. Safflower is a thistle-like plant with orange flowers that are often dried and passed off as saffron – but the only thing it has in common is a similar colour. Look for saffron that is purely red, with no lightly coloured wispy filaments. To me, the best saffron comes from Kashmir, but popular growing areas include Iran, Greece, Turkey, Spain and Morocco.

In the UK, the spice was historically cultivated around the Essex town of Saffron Walden, and it was also grown in Ireland. Cornish saffron buns use the spice, but there aren't too many British recipes that include it. Saffron is used in Spain's paella, Italy's risotto Milanese, and France's Provençal fish stew, bouillabaisse. In Asia, saffron is used in both savoury and sweet preparations, notably in dishes with Mughal roots: you'll see it in Persian rice dishes and north Indian biryanis. It also flavours milky Indian sweets, lassis and the sweet, festive Muslim rice dish, fruit-and-nut studded *zarda pilau*.

Unusually among spices, saffron's defining flavour compounds are water-soluble, so it makes sense to soak it in liquid before use in order to get the maximum flavour and aroma from each thread – either water or milk as is most appropriate for the dish. To preserve its delicacy, saffron should always be added toward the end of cooking. It can be stored for longer than other spices – around 2 years in a cool, dark cupboard.

## STAR ANISE
*Botanical name: Illicium verum*
*Part used: fruit (pericarp and seeds)*
*Main flavour and aroma compounds: anethole*
*Character: deep, rich, buttery anise, liquorice, intense perfume*
*Note: bass*
*Buy: whole*

The name denotes the appearance, each pod from the evergreen tree resembling an eight-pointed star. Although it contains the same flavour compound, star anise is not related to the Mediterranean anise (*Pimpinella anisum*). Native to southern China and Vietnam, it is also cultivated in India and many other Asian countries, and in Jamaica.

The ground spice is an important component of Chinese five-spice powder, and the whole spice is used in braised dishes. You will also find star anise in the Vietnamese noodle soup, *pho*, and in some Thai, Persian and Pakistani dishes. In north India it is used in biryani, garam masala and masala chai. In the West, the primary use for the spice is as a flavouring for alcoholic drinks such as pastis.

When using it in a spice blend, restraint is the key. All too often it is given a starring role, beguiling the cook with its dazzling beauty, but this captivating spice can easily smother all flavours it meets.

## TAMARIND
*Botanical name: Tamarindus indica*
*Part used: fruit (pulp)*
*Main flavour, aroma and souring compounds: sugars, tartaric acid*
*Character: sweet–sour, tangy, light astringency*
*Note: bass*
*Buy: paste or dried*

The tamarind tree is indigenous to Africa and grows prolifically on the banks of rivers and lakes of southern India; it is also cultivated in other parts of tropical Asia, Latin America and the West Indies. Its fruit – sometimes called Indian date – is a large bean-like pod, dark brown when ripe, containing a sticky fruity pulp punctuated with large seeds. For ease of use, I generally use the thick, black, concentrated paste of Indian origin available from nearly every Asian shop; I have written the recipes with this product in mind, rather than the more runny brown product normally made in Malaysia or Thailand.

Tamarind is prized for its souring properties, similar to that achieved with lemon, vinegar or tomato. It is widely used throughout South and Southeast Asia, and in Latin America, in both sweet and savoury foods, relishes, sherbets, teas and other drinks. It's not a traditional component of many Western dishes…except, of course, the much-loved Worcestershire sauce!

In India, tamarind chutney and tamarind water are used to dress all manner of snack dishes, collectively called *chaat*. In southern India it's often found in vegetable dishes such as *sambar* and *rasam*, and as the key flavouring in *puliyogare*, spicy-tangy tamarind rice. Intensely sweet-sour tamarind candies are popular in many countries of Asia, Latin America and the Caribbean.

## TURMERIC
*Botanical name: Curcuma longa*
*Part used: rhizome (root)*
*Main flavour and aroma compounds: turmerone, atlantone, zingiberene*
*Character: sweet, earthy, gingery, ethereal astringency*
*Note: bass*
*Buy: powdered*

Fresh turmeric looks very much like fresh ginger – until you slice it and reveal the dazzling orange-gold flesh. To transform the knobbly rhizomes into the more familiar brilliantly coloured powder, fresh turmeric is boiled, dried and ground. Turmeric grows wild in many parts of South and Southeast Asia and is cultivated in India and elsewhere. This wonderful spice has been used medicinally for thousands of years and is now being studied as a treatment for cancer, Alzheimer's and other conditions. The beautiful and auspicious colour is readily transferred to food – and to hands and clothes. In fact it has been used as a dye since at least 600bc. Turmeric is a staple ingredient in Indian cookery. Its musky perfume imparts an earthy background note that rounds out the flavours in many Indian dishes, although its bitter astringency means it needs to be thoroughly 'cooked out', usually in hot oil, and used in small quantities.

## VANILLA
*Botanical name: Vanilla planifolia*
*Part used: fruit and seed*
*Main flavour and aroma compounds: vanillin*
*Character: deep, heady, enveloping richness, sweet and creamy*
*Note: bass*
*Buy: pods*

A highly distinctive, sweet, mellow, calming aroma, over 130 trace compounds have been found in vanilla extract, many of which contribute to the flavour of vanilla. They are also the reason that the taste of real vanilla is beyond comparison with artificial.

Although you'll often hear of vanilla 'beans', what we use is the dried ripe fruit pod of a plant in the orchid family. Around 15–20cm long and 1cm in diameter, each pod contains thousands of tiny seeds which, along with the oil around them, contain most of the fragrance and flavour. The tiny black speckles you see in good-quality vanilla ice cream are the vanilla seeds.

The lengthy drying and curing process explains why good-quality vanilla is expensive. Look for dark brown, 'waxy', pliable pods with a deep aroma; poor-quality vanilla pods are pale, stiff and lack aroma. The flavour is mostly in the seeds and the oil which you scoop from the slit pod, but the pod itself contains plenty of flavour. Whole pods can be infused in warm liquid to impart their flavour, and then reused after washing and drying. The emptied pod can then be dropped into your sugar container to make vanilla sugar.

Vanilla is used mainly in sweet dishes such as ice cream, cookies and cakes. However, adventurous cooks increasingly use it in savoury dishes, where it can subtly lift and smooth other flavours. If you absolutely must; extract is superior to essence and vanilla paste is better again; 1 level teaspoon of paste is equivalent to 1 juicy pod.

# THE SCIENCE OF FLAVOUR

Spices are parts of plants, rich in flavour compounds. They offer a complex, diverse and almost endless palette for us to use as we cook and create flavour combinations. And at the heart of this palette is flavour – a fascinating yet equally complex topic, so I'm going to concentrate on one particular area of flavour: how taste is perceived and how flavour 'works'.

The understanding of flavour and taste perception is becoming increasingly well explored. In simple terms, taste is perceived in the mouth, flavour in the nose. In our mouths are many different types of specialized receptors called sensors that are triggered, or 'tripped', when food hits them, sending information to our brain to help us form an overall picture of the food we're eating. This is our perception of the information provided by the senses. The parts of food that are soluble in saliva are sensed on the tongue – for example, sugars trigger the taste perception of sweetness. Parts of food that are volatile are detected by the nose – more precisely, the nasal epithelium, which gives us our sense of smell. As we eat, all the information sent from these taste-triggers is gathered up and deciphered by our brain. This is how we seamlessly perceive the flavour of food as a whole, which is greater than the sum of all its individual taste parts.

We generally think in terms of five basic taste sensations: salt, sour, sweet, bitter and umami. The tastes of salt and sour have similar recognition mechanisms. Umami and sweet share a receptor unit, and then there's bitter, perhaps the most complicated of tastes, which has over 30 receptors on the human tongue. These five tastes all have biological functions. Sweet is our body's way of rewarding us for consuming calorie-rich carbohydrates. Sourness tells us about the acidity of foods, and is a great indicator of things such as the ripeness of fruit. Umami is our method of recognizing proteins, and we need the ability to recognize salt to maintain equilibrium and balance in our bodies. Bitter compounds are often toxic or medicinal, and this might explain why we've developed a more highly tuned receptor system for bitter substances in terms of self-protection and self-nurturing.

Other 'tastes' are less well understood. The taste receptor for fat has only recently been found in humans. Some fats make food delicious. Fat can enrich texture and mouthfeel while making flavours and aromas interact for longer with the tongue and nose. It's a flavour-carrier. But what most scientists thought was purely a textural, physical sensation seems also to be an actual 'taste', with its own dedicated receptor cells. We all sense fat differently and this difference is closely linked to the type of food we each choose to eat. Indeed, many of our sense levels differ; this is why we have individual tastes and like different foods. Some of these differences can be attributed to genetics. There are also some complex interactions with our exposure to sensations, which allow some people to become 'used to' certain foods, such as chilli.

Kokumi is a taste sensation you've probably never heard of, but have almost certainly experienced. As a mechanism, it's similar to umami in that it recognises the building blocks of protein. If you cook a stew or a curry, then reheat and eat some the next day, you might perceive it to taste better, richer, deeper than when it was first cooked. My Persian Lamb Tagine with Rhubarb-Orange Salad (see page 65), Beef, Carrots & Ale (see page 49), Asian Sticky Beef Ribs (see page 55) and Tarka Dhal (see page 162) are good examples of dishes that display this trait. This is scientifically explained as an increase in kokumi. As proteins and DNA in the food continue to degrade over time, their simple amino acids and nucleotides are more greatly perceived by the tongue, and so the kokumi taste is enhanced. This is handy information if you're cooking a stew, tagine or curry for a dinner party; it's better to make it a day ahead.

Astringency and metallic are other tastes less well understood by science. Metallics are thought of as either 'zapping' the tongue with a taste-hit – a kind of physical reaction to partial oxidation of the receptor cells – or as a sudden increase in the electrical conductivity of our saliva. Astringency is a mix between a taste sensation and a physical reaction: the immediate release of proteins in our saliva when it comes into contact with tannins or similar compounds. Highly tannic red wines, unripe grapes, strong black tea, pomegranates and floral waters are all examples of this. In fact, I use some of these in my recipes to help cut richness, counteract sweetness and create balance.

There is another type of taste perception: a physical reaction called chemesthesis, which is associated with the effects that mint and chilli have on our bodies. This is the chemical response associated with pain, touch and heat receptors. The cooling effect of mint and the heat of chilli have opposite effects on the tongue, and they both affect our perception of temperature. Menthol, a compound in mint, triggers a receptor on the tongue that responds to cool temperatures. It just happens that we have the same receptors all over our skin, so our bodies are tricked into thinking they're cooling off, when in fact this is merely the effect of menthol. Chilli has a similar effect, but its tricky trigger-compound is known as capsaicin. This triggers a receptor on the tongue that elsewhere on our bodies is linked to the perception of heat, so consuming capsaicin makes us think we're heating up. Our body's cells help us regulate our core temperature by sending signals to the brain when hot or cold is received by the sensors on our tongue and body. You could say that menthol and capsaicin act as receptor 'blockers'. Menthol raises the temperature at which the cell will send a cold signal, so that even at room temperature, the food we eat feels cold. The opposite happens when we eat chilli: the taste receptor would normally trigger and send a warning signal to the brain at around 42°C, but eating food containing capsaicin lowers this threshold to around 35°C. The result is that we feel hot from eating food containing chilli, even though the food may be at room temperature.

Chillies are interesting in other ways, too. To digress for a moment, the commonly accepted scale that measures the heat of chillies, the Scoville scale, was devised using a panel of chilli tasters drinking various dilutions of capsaicin in water. The system allots Scoville Heat Units (SHU) to different chillies: the higher the number of units, the hotter the chilli. My favourite chilli, the bird's-eye, rates about 50,000–100,000 SHU and the jalapeño 2500–8000. Trouble is, everyone perceives taste differently, so the scale is very unreliable. A second system, the American Spice Trade Association (ASTA) scale, measures the concentration of heat-producing chemicals more scientifically. Roughly, one capsaicin part per million equals 15 SHU, so 1 ASTA is about the same as 15 SHU.

We're the only animals that deliberately consume chillies for pleasure. Our brains respond to the perceived pain by releasing the pleasant and addictive substances known as endorphins, and this in turn perpetuates our desire to eat chillies. Furthermore, chilli increases our perception of salt, so you can actually reduce the amount of salt you use in dishes by adding chilli.

Incorporating spices in our food has other health benefits, too. Spices improve digestion through increased salivary, gastric and intestinal secretions, bile production and healthy bowel function. Pungent food sensations occur not only in the mouth and nose cavity, but also in the respiratory, gastro-intestinal, cardiovascular and nervous systems, suggesting the possibility of more systemic health effects. To cut to the chase, spices contain many bioactive compounds. On a physiological level, we perceive the flavour of these compounds as exciting, pronounced and vibrant, but these compounds often work in tandem with many of our other bodily functions, which modern medicine is only just beginning to explore. Many spices have antibacterial, antioxidant, anti-inflammatory or other beneficial properties, which is why they have a rich history of use both in food preserving throughout many culinary cultures and in Ayurvedic medicine.

# AYURVEDA

Ayurveda is an ancient Hindu philosophy, more than 3000 years old, the basis of which can be summed up as 'Look after your body and your body will look after itself.' It is the science of life, the science of longevity.

I happen to believe that the basic principles of Ayurveda can benefit our overall well-being. So how do we get our bodies to look after themselves? Mainly through common sense and a little understanding: regular exercise, managing stress levels and, more importantly, thinking about what we eat and how we manage our diets.

Ayurveda is all about maintaining a healthy digestive system. Spices form an integral part of an Ayurvedic diet, and many have proven health benefits; they are traditionally matched with foods not only for their specific taste but also for their digestive properties. Certain meats and vegetables are always paired with certain spices as they have been found over time to help the digestion of the foodstuff. So starchy tubers go with carom, lentils with asafoetida, gourds with coriander – that sort of thing. 'Synergy' is a concept I apply when combining spices in a blend: it derives from two

Greek words meaning 'working together' and means that every spice has its role to play, not just from a flavour perspective, but also from a digestive, soothing or stimulating slant.

Ayurveda explains that if you eat seven different *rasas* (tastes) at every meal, then your body can best assimilate and absorb its nutrients. Generally in the West we recognize five main taste sensations: salt, sweet, bitter, sour and umami. Ayurveda mentions two more: pungent and astringent. Pungent tastes come from foods such as garlic, ginger and asafoetida. Astringency comes from floral waters such as rose, from rhubarb, pomegranates and certain other fruits, and in the form of tannins found in wine and coffee. Think of pungent garlic and astringent red wine, and the benefits they add to the French diet.

To look at this from a Western perspective, it's like when rose bushes are planted between vines. The roses not only attract insects and pests away from the grapes, but they make the vines compete and work harder for soil nutrients. Or think about getting a vaccination before going on holiday: the vaccination contains a little of the infection, which causes the body to jump into action, helping the immune system to fight it off. Similarly, in Ayurveda, the pungent and astringent elements make our bodies work harder from the inside, keeping us strong and healthy, naturally. It's a question of balance and eating a variety of foods at each sitting. Part of the reason Indian cuisine has so many pickles, chutneys and relishes is to help bring all the elements into each meal.

Another principle of Ayurveda divides us into three *doshas*, or body types: *vata*, *pitta* and *kapha*. Determining which dosha you are helps to determine which foods and spices will keep you in the best of health. Further, your dosha can change as you become 'out of balance', overstressed and under-exercised; you can change your diet until balance is restored, bringing you back to your ideal type. This is the essence of food as medicine.

My cousin Guria swears by the traditional remedy of cinnamon mixed with honey to ward off colds and flu, while turmeric in warm milk at night is said to help improve memory. Western medicine is now discovering the beneficial properties of spices. Turmeric has been proven to have anti-cancer and anti-inflammatory properties. Other scientific studies have shown that fenugreek lowers blood-sugar levels and is particularly useful for managing type 2 diabetes.

I won't go into every spice from an Ayurvedic point of view – that'd be a whole book in itself – but here is just one example in the form of coriander. According to Ayurveda, coriander improves digestion and stimulates hunger. It has antibacterial, anti-fungal, anti-spasmodic, carminative (flatulence-relieving) and diuretic properties. It also helps routine function of the stomach, relieves distension, diarrhoea and cold symptoms and may help to lower cholesterol. When steeped in water, the seeds can help regulate overactive peptic acid and relieve morning sickness. Coriander also has a relatively high vitamin B and C content. Sounds a bit like a wonder drug, doesn't it? The point is, eaten as part of a balanced diet, coriander's health benefits shine through. In conclusion, we can all benefit from Ayurveda, simply by eating a balanced diet, with regular meals, regular exercise and lots of spice – obviously!

PORK & BACON

WHEN I MOVED TO IRELAND, PORK (AND PARTICULARLY BACON) JUMPED INTO MY COOKING REPERTOIRE. Green bacon, boiled bacon, smoked ham, gammon, loin chops, rashers … I love them all. The group of spices I use in this chapter are about lifting porcine tastes, enlivening sweet fat with an aromatic buzz and mellowing saltiness.

The Bacon Chops with Glazed Pepper Pineapple and Fenugreek Potatoes is a firm and loving nod to my Irish family, my mother-in-law Rose and her cooking. Next time you poach a joint of bacon or gammon, simply add a mix of green cardamom and turmeric to the water: they balance and counteract the salty cure taste sensations. I've developed this idea in my Bacon Chop recipe, adding the sweetness of pineapple and the crunchy texture of breadcrumbs. My Roast Pork Shoulder Vindaloo is a similar case of stretching hands across the water. The combination of coriander, green cardamom, cloves, fennel, vinegar, garlic, ginger and chillies don't detract from the meat, they compliment, lift and embellish the ignoble swine!

I twist, tweak and muddle green (lightly cured) bacon with the highs of green cardamom, fennel, nutmeg, coriander, white pepper, using them in other elements of the dish – the cooking liquid, marinade or sauce. But there are times when the sweetness of the meat needs no emphasis, for example in my Warm Lentil and Ham Hock Salad, but by accenting the lentils with a little cumin and freshening it all up with peppery watercress and bitter chicory the dish comes together as a whole.

Pork is essentially a sweet-tasting meat: it needs a light touch, but it loves a little 'crazy' – try Szechuan pepper, mace and chilli. In my Pig Plate, star anise, clove and ginger combine with the more traditional juniper to tinge and soften the edges of the choucroute, with green cardamom, black pepper and nutmeg to define and bring together all the different pork flavours.

*Previous page: Fennel adds sweet anise notes, a vibrancy that balances salty sensations and cuts through sweet fat meat.*

# Roast Pork Shoulder Vindaloo

SERVES 4–6

## FOR THE MARINADE

2 tsp black peppercorns
1 tsp coriander seeds
5 green cardamom pods
1 tsp cumin seeds
5 cloves
½ tsp fennel seeds
175ml (6fl oz) cider vinegar
10 garlic cloves, crushed
125g (4½oz) fresh ginger
225g (8oz) onions, roughly
   chopped
1 heaped tbsp tomato purée
2 tbsp rapeseed oil
2 tsp Kashmiri chilli flakes
2 tsp powdered turmeric
½ tsp finely ground cassia
1 tsp sea salt
2 tsp golden caster sugar

## FOR THE PORK

2kg (4lb 8oz) piece of shoulder
   pork, boned and scored
2 tbsp sunflower oil
750ml (1⅓ pints) light chicken
   stock
1 red bird's eye chilli, deseeded
   and finely diced (optional)
30g (1oz) butter, cubed
1 handful coriander leaves,
   chopped
Coconut flakes, toasted

*This wonderfully fragrant, almost sweet-and-sour Goan dish has a peppery perfume. Its name hints at its Portuguese heritage – vindaloo is more about vinegar (vin) and garlic (alho) than pure heat – but the chillies reflect Goa's penchant for a little extra kick.*

1. Finely grind the marinade spices using a mortar and pestle. Put all the marinade ingredients into a food processor and blitz to a paste. (Alternatively, grate the garlic, ginger and onions, then add the remaining ingredients and grind to a paste using a mortar and pestle.) Taste to judge how much bird's eye chilli, if any, you will need to use later.

2. Put the meat in a large mixing bowl and pour the paste over it. Massage the meat with the paste, then cover, put it into the fridge and leave for at least 4 hours or preferably overnight.

3. Preheat the oven to 180°C (gas mark 4). Put a large roasting tin over a high heat. Lift the joint from its marinade, reserving the marinade in the bowl. Sear all sides of the meat to achieve a golden, nutty colour. Remove from the heat.

4. Next, pour the oil over the joint, followed by the marinade, coating the meat all over. Add the stock and the bird's eye chilli, if using, to the roasting tin, then give it a quick stir. Dot the butter over the meat and cover loosely with foil or moistened greaseproof paper. Put on the middle shelf of the oven and roast for 2 hours.

5. Remove the foil, give the cooking liquor a quick stir, then pop the roast back into the oven, uncovered, for another 10 minutes or until the meat and sauce are just coloured. Remove from the oven and put the joint on a board to rest. Stir the sauce, then put it over a high heat until reduced to the consistency of double cream, stirring frequently. Remove from the heat and set aside.

6. Carve generous slices of the pork and put on a warmed serving plate. Coat the slices with the sauce, sprinkle with fresh coriander and coconut flakes, and serve with fragrant basmati rice.

# WARM LENTIL & HAM HOCK SALAD

*This dish takes a little time to make, but it's very simple. Earthy lentils combine with the earthy-citrus notes of cumin. Sweet, tender ham adds texture and contrast, while sun-blush tomatoes, parsley and fresh mint add a clean lift at the end. The use of hot ham stock in the mayonnaise emulsion balances the dish, coating peppery salad leaves for freshness and bite.*

**SERVES 6**

### FOR THE HAM HOCKS
**2 ham hocks or knuckles, about 850g–1kg (1lb 14oz–2lb 4oz) each**
**2 carrots, chopped into chunks**
**1 leek, chopped into chunks**
**1 onion, chopped into chunks**
**3 celery sticks, chopped into chunks**
**3 ripe tomatoes**
**2 garlic cloves, crushed**
**2 tsp cumin seeds**

### FOR THE LENTILS
**350g (12oz) Puy lentils**
**500ml (18fl oz) ham-hock cooking liquor**
**500ml (18fl oz) vegetable stock**
**2 tsp cumin seeds, finely ground**

### FOR THE VEGETABLES
**3 tbsp light olive oil**
**2 shallots, finely chopped**
**1 small carrot, finely chopped**
**2 celery sticks, finely chopped**
**1 garlic clove, crushed**

1. To cook the ham hocks, put all the ingredients in a large saucepan and cover with cold water. Bring up to a simmer over a low heat, partially cover and allow to bubble gently for 4–5 hours until the meat is meltingly tender and soft. Top up the water from time to time to ensure it doesn't go below the level of the meat, skimming away the foam.

2. Leave the hocks in the cooking liquor until cool enough to handle, then remove to a plate. Strain the liquor into a large measuring jug.

3. Put the lentils, cooking liquor, stock and cumin seeds in a large heavy-based saucepan. Bring up to a gentle bubble and cook over a low heat, partially covered, for about 20 minutes until only a couple of teaspoons of liquid run around the pan and the lentils are only just soft. Remove from the heat, cover completely, then set aside and keep warm.

4. Heat the olive oil in a sauté or frying pan, then add the vegetables and garlic and cook over a medium–low heat for a couple of minutes. Tip out onto a plate, set aside and keep warm.

[ *Continued* ]

## FOR THE MAYONNAISE

**150ml (5fl oz) ham-hock
  cooking liquor**
**2 medium egg yolks**
**1 tsp Dijon mustard**
**1 tbsp white wine vinegar**
**250ml (9fl oz) light olive oil**
**Grinding of white pepper**
**Sea salt**

## FOR THE SALAD

**12 sun-blush tomatoes,
  quartered**
**1 handful curly parsley leaves,
  chopped**
**1 small handful mint leaves,
  finely shredded**

## TO GARNISH

**1 large bunch watercress, leaves
  and thin stalks**
**2 heads chicory, sliced
  lengthways into thin shards**

5. To make the mayonnaise, heat the cooking liquor in a small saucepan to a gentle bubble. Put the egg yolks, mustard and vinegar in a food processor and pulse to combine. With the processor on slow, slowly trickle the oil down the spout. With the processor still running, carefully trickle in the hot ham stock, then add the white pepper and salt to taste. (Alternatively, make the mayo in a bowl, using a balloon whisk and plenty of elbow grease.)

6. If not using immediately, allow to cool, pour into a sterilised jar (see page 255) and put a circle of greaseproof paper on the top of the dressing. Cover with a lid and store in the fridge. It keeps for at least two weeks.

7. When ready to serve, remove the jellied skin from the ham hocks and chop into small dice, then pull off the meat, trying to keep it in nice strips.

8. Warm the dressing, if necessary. Put the lentils, vegetables and salad ingredients in a large mixing bowl and add a small handful of the chopped hock skin, together with about 2 tablespoons of the warm dressing – just enough to coat. Gently mix all the ingredients together.

9. In another bowl, combine the watercress and chicory with 1 tablespoon of the dressing.

10. Serve the warm lentils and ham in generous amounts with some dressed salad leaves.

# SLOW-ROAST PORK NECK CHOPS

*The rich roast pork, soft spicy beans and zingy 'llajua' (hot sauce) come together to make a wonderful combination of flavours, textures and heat.*

**SERVES 4–6**

8 pork neck chops, about 125g
(4½oz) each
Sea salt
1 tbsp light olive oil
2 onions, halved and thinly
sliced
1 tsp golden caster sugar
1 tsp white peppercorns
2 tsp fennel seeds
Seeds of 2 black cardamom pods
850ml (1½ pints) chicken stock
200ml (7fl oz) sweet cider,
preferably local
2 strips of lemon zest, pared
with a veg peeler
2 × 400g tins haricot or butter
beans, drained and rinsed
(250g/9oz drained weight)

## FOR THE LLAJUA

5 jalapeño peppers, deseeded and
roughly chopped
½ onion, roughly chopped
1 small handful coriander leaves,
with thin stems
4 ripe tomatoes, roughly
chopped
1 tsp sea salt

1. Preheat the oven to 140°C (gas mark 1). Sprinkle a little salt on both sides of each chop. Add a splash of olive oil to a large flameproof casserole or deep roasting tin and put over a high heat.

2. When hot, add the chops and sear for 1 minute on each side or until the meat is a nice nutty-brown colour (you may need to do this in a couple of batches). Remove from the casserole and set aside.

3. Turn down the heat, add a little more oil, the onions and sugar, and fry gently for 12–15 minutes until they take on a little colour and become really soft.

4. Finely grind the peppercorns, fennel and cardamom seeds using a mortar and pestle. Add the stock to the casserole, followed by the cider, lemon zest and spices, stir well, then put the chops on top of the onions, pouring in any juices. Cover tightly with foil and cook on the middle shelf of the oven for 3½ hours.

5. Meanwhile, make the llajua. Put the chillies, onion and coriander in a food processor or blender and blitz to a smooth paste, then add the tomatoes and salt, and pulse to a chunky consistency. Set aside. (Alternatively, grind everything together using a mortar and pestle.)

6. When the meat is cooked, still moist and tender, remove the foil, take out the chops and keep them warm. Remove and discard the lemon zest.

7. Add the beans to the casserole, put over a medium heat and stir gently to combine them with the cooking liquor. Bring up to a gentle bubble and cook for 3–5 minutes until the beans are warmed through.

8. Take off the heat, pour the beans into a warmed serving dish, pop the chops on top, drizzle with a little of the llajua and serve the remainder in a side bowl.

# BLACK PUDDING SALAD

SERVES 2

## FOR THE DRESSING

1 tsp caraway seeds
½ tsp fennel seeds
½ tsp black peppercorns
1 tsp English mustard powder
2 tbsp red wine vinegar
100ml (3½fl oz) light olive oil
1 tsp sea salt
3 tbsp boiling water

## FOR THE CROÛTONS

1 tsp caraway seeds
½ tsp cumin seeds
4 thin slices sourdough bread
A splash fruity olive oil
1 garlic clove, halved
1–2 pinches sea salt

## FOR THE SALAD

1–2 splashes light olive oil
300–400g (10½–14oz) black
    pudding, sliced on the
    diagonal
1 head each white chicory, red
    chicory and radicchio, leaves
    separated
200g (7oz) watercress
A splash black truffle oil
8 quail eggs
1 pinch sea salt
8 pickled walnuts, sliced into
    rounds, ends discarded

*There are so many types of black pudding, from the almost solid, meaty ones with a very piggy flavour, through the cereal-flecked ones to the delicate, almost mousse-like versions. All are perfect for this recipe. This salad has real earthy notes, ethereal truffle oil, crisp winter leaves, peppery watercress and a delicate touch of fragrant anise.*

1. Finely grind the spices for the dressing using a mortar and pestle. Put all the dressing ingredients into a clean screwtop jar, pouring in the boiling water last, then shake well and set aside.

2. Finely grind the spices for the croûtons and set aside. Drizzle the sourdough slices with a good glug of olive oil, pop them under a hot grill and toast until the edges char. Allow them to cool slightly, then rub with the cut side of the garlic clove and sprinkle with the spices and sea salt. Cut each slice in half lengthways to make dramatic, long triangular 'soldiers'. Set aside on a wire rack.

3. For the salad, heat a small splash of oil in a non-stick frying pan over a medium heat, then add the black pudding. Fry on one side for a few minutes until crisp, then turn over with a spatula and fry the other side. Remove from the pan and set aside to keep warm. Wipe the pan clean with kitchen paper.

4. Put the chicory, radicchio and watercress into a large bowl. Shake the dressing jar, add 2 tablespoons to the bowl and, using your hands, gently mix the leaves, adding a little more dressing if you like. Set aside.

5. Pour another slug of olive oil and a generous splash of black truffle oil into the wiped frying pan. Break the eggs into it and put over a medium–low heat. Gently fry for 2 minutes until the whites are just set, sprinkle with sea salt, then spoon some of the oil over the eggs. Take off the heat.

6. Working fairly quickly, warm the croûtons under the grill, then carefully scatter the dressed leaves over a large serving plate. Remove the croûtons from the heat and pop an egg onto each. Put these, and the pudding slices, among the leaves, scatter the pickled walnuts on top and, finally, drizzle with a little more of the dressing. Serve immediately.

# Bacon Chops with Glazed Pepper Pineapple & Fenugreek Potatoes

*From my first trips to fast-food restaurants around English northern towns in the 1970s, to school lunches and then the occasional 'greasy spoon' café, I developed, loved and nurtured a taste for gammon and pineapple. This is my version: spiced pineapple paired with a breaded bacon chop for texture and satisfying crunch. The potatoes are something Dad taught me more recently, and the bitter fenugreek also works well with the pineapple's sweetness. Prepare the glazed pineapple the day before, as it really benefits from 24 hours marinating.*

**SERVES 6–8**

## FOR THE GLAZED PEPPER PINEAPPLE

**250g (9oz) demerara sugar**
**425g (15oz) tin pineapple slices in syrup, drained and syrup reserved (250g/9oz drained weight)**
**1 red finger chilli, deseeded and chopped into 3 pieces**
**40g (1½oz) fresh ginger, roughly chopped**
**1 thyme sprig, leaves only**
**1 strip of orange zest, pared with a veg peeler**
**1 tsp black peppercorns**
**½ tsp Szechuan pepper**
**½ long pepper spike, smashed**
**½ nutmeg, smashed**
**3 cloves**

1. Put a large heavy-based sauté pan over a medium heat. Add the sugar and 2 tablespoons of the pineapple syrup, give it a quick stir and allow to dissolve gently – about 6 minutes. Meanwhile, pat the pineapple slices dry with kitchen paper and set aside.

2. Once the sugar has dissolved, add the chilli, ginger, thyme, zest and spices and cook for 1–2 minutes, then add the pineapple slices.

3. Cook in the syrup for 2 minutes, turn them over, then cook for another 2 minutes. Take the pan off the heat, leaving the pineapple in the syrup, and set aside overnight, covered with a clean tea towel.

4. Next day, lift the pineapple onto a wire rack. Strain the syrup through a fine sieve into a jug.

*[ Continued ]*

# POTTED PEPPER PORK

*Potted pork is perfect for picnics or starters served with crostini, Melba toast or crusty sourdough bread, plus cornichons and assorted pickles, crunchy radishes and celery. If you're using really good pork, the Calvados and scorched orange zest may seem a little extravagant, but it adds a lovely depth of flavour that works so well with the clove notes.*

### MAKES 700G (1LB 9OZ)

#### FOR THE MIREPOIX

**2 carrots, cut into 8mm (⅜in) dice**

**1 onion, cut into 8mm (⅜in) dice**

**3 celery sticks, halved**

**6 garlic cloves, peeled and gently smashed**

**1 large cooking apple, such as Bramley, peeled, cored and cut into 8 pieces**

#### FOR THE POTTED PORK

**3 Indian bay leaves (tejpatta), very lightly crushed**

**1kg (2lb 4oz) pork belly, rind removed**

**150ml (5fl oz) dry cider, preferably local**

**½ tsp white peppercorns**

**4 cloves**

**1 piece blade mace**

**1 allspice berry**

**1 tsp fine sea salt**

**½ tsp finely ground cinnamon**

**3–4 gratings nutmeg**

**2 tbsp Calvados**

**Zest of ¼ orange, pared with a veg peeler**

**75–100g (2¾–3½oz) unsalted butter, melted**

1. Preheat the oven to 160°C (gas mark 3). Spread all the mirepoix ingredients over the base of a deep baking tray. Sprinkle with the Indian bay leaves, then put the pork belly on top. Add the cider, cover and seal tightly with foil, and slow-roast for 3–4 hours until the meat is meltingly tender. Leave in the tray to cool to room temperature. Finely grind the whole spices using a mortar and pestle; set aside.

2. Transfer the pork to a chopping board. Strain the cooking juices and reserve. Cut off and discard the pork rind, then cut the white fat away from the meat. Carefully remove the thin sinew from the meat and discard. Pull about a quarter of the pork meat into 'single-thread' strips. Roughly chop 2 tablespoons of the white fat into small dice.

3. Discard the bay leaves, celery and garlic. Put the pork threads in a large bowl, and add the diced fat and the braised carrots, onion and apple. Set aside. Put the remaining meat and white fat into a food processor. Pulse until it forms a velvety, airy emulsion. (Alternatively, chop the meat and fat as finely as you can, then put it into a bowl and beat well with a wooden spoon.) Sprinkle the salt, cinnamon, nutmeg and ground spices over the meat, and briefly pulse or stir again. Using a rubber spatula, scrape the emulsion into the bowl of pork threads. Set aside.

4. Put the Calvados and orange zest in a heavy-based saucepan. Warm the alcohol, then set it alight and let it burn for 10 seconds. Put the lid on to extinguish the flame, discard the zest and set aside to cool. Add the Calvados and 4 tablespoons of the reserved cooking juices to the pork. Mix together with your fingers to form a spreadable consistency, adding a little more of the juices, if needed. Season to taste. Transfer to sterilised jars (see page 255) and pour melted butter on top to about 3mm (⅛in). Store in the fridge for two to three days before serving. Bring to room temperature and serve with pickles and toast. Store in the fridge unopened for six months; once opened, use within seven days.

# PIG PLATE

*This dish is a celebration of all things pig, and is something I first tried on a hazy day spent in Paris. Salt-cured cabbage, aka choucroute or sauerkraut, the stalwart of the brasseries, forms the backbone of this beautiful dish and is the foil to a selection of salted, cured or smoked pork cuts and charcuterie. Look for pure pork poaching sausages at your local master butcher, farmers' markets, East European delis or even supermarkets. Buy ready-cooked sauerkraut in jars – it's a tricky thing to make from scratch. This makes a generous quantity, so is ideal for family celebrations, because you can really push the boat out, and have a feast of different cuts garnished with a whole host of vegetables.*

### SERVES 6–10

**1.2kg (2lb 12oz) boneless
    smoked gammon joint**
**1.5kg (3lb 5oz) salted,
    unsmoked pork belly bacon**
**800g (1lb 12oz) pure pork
    sausages: French, German or
    Polish poaching sausages**

### FOR THE COOKING LIQUOR
**2 leeks**
**2 celery sticks**
**1 small handful parsley stalks**
**2 carrots**
**1 large onion**
**1 red chilli, split in half and
    deseeded**
**20 black peppercorns**
**8 green cardamom pods,
    smashed**
**1 whole nutmeg**

1. Put the gammon and belly joints into a large saucepan, cover the meat with cold water and bring to the boil. As the bubbles burst to the surface and a scum forms, take the pan off the heat, pour away the water, then repeat. Do this three times.

2. Cover the joints with cold water as before, but this time add all the cooking liquor ingredients. Bring to the boil, then turn the heat down to a gentle simmer, partially cover and cook for 40 minutes.

3. Add the sausages and cook for another 35 minutes, then lift out all the meat, set aside and keep warm. Strain the cooking liquor into a large jug or bowl. Preheat the oven to 120°C (just under gas mark 1).

4. Finely grind the spices for the choucroute using a mortar and pestle.

5. Put the goose fat into a large cast-iron casserole or heavy-based roasting tin. Add the choucroute, sprinkle in the spices, then add the orange zest, 750ml (1⅓ pints) of the strained cooking liquor, the wine, ginger, celery, carrots and onion quarters. Cover with greaseproof paper, then seal the casserole with a close-fitting lid and foil.

6. Put in the oven and cook for 45 minutes or until most of the liquid has been absorbed into the cabbage. If the vegetables are not quite cooked, add a little more cooking liquor and return to the oven until they're only just able to hold their shape.

## FOR THE CHOUCROUTE

1 small piece blade mace
1 star anise
½ tsp Szechuan pepper
2 juniper berries
½ long pepper spike
3 cloves
¼ cinnamon stick
1½ tbsp goose fat, duck fat or
  bacon dripping
2kg (4lb 8oz) cooked choucroute
  (sauerkraut), drained
  through a colander, pressing
  down with a plate to ensure
  all liquid is removed
Zest of ½ an orange, pared with
  a veg peeler
400ml (14fl oz) good white wine
50g (1¾oz) fresh ginger, peeled
1 celery heart, quartered
10 carrots
3 onions, quartered

7. Remove the vegetables using a slotted spoon and transfer them to a large, warmed oval serving plate, piling them in a mound on one side.

8. Remove the cabbage with a slotted spoon (so that the juices remain in the casserole) and pile it onto the other side of the serving plate. Slice the gammon into generous chunks and place on top of the cabbage. Slice the pork belly into 1cm (½in) thick pieces and add to the plate, placing them on top of the gammon along with the sausages, left whole.

9. Pour a little of the cooking liquor over the vegetables and the meats to moisten them.

10. Take the choucroute and vegetables to the table and serve with a generous quantity of boiled waxy potatoes, a pot of Dijon mustard and a well-chilled Riesling, Pinot Blanc or Pilsner lager. Spectacular!

# BEEF & VENISON

DARK AND RICH, BEEF AND VENISON need spice notes that are going to cut through richness. Chillies do this to good effect and I love using varieties like dried Kashmiri or chipotle chillies: they introduce a smoky, fruity element that's more than just pure heat. In my Chilli Beef Hash, Kashmiri chillies add subtle heat and 'kick' to liven up a favourite family supper.

Try to find beef where the animal has been grass-fed on lush pastures and suitably aged (preferably for no less than 21 days). Ageing brings out an iodine-rich, almost fresh leathery perfumed flavour in the meat (beasts less loved, less carefully raised and slaughtered, tend to produce meat with a 'metallic' edge). Venison is also aged, or hung, before eating, and has a deeper flavour than beef, typically referred to as 'gamey'. And it's these characteristics I pick up on when it comes to spices.

Dark, aged, strong-flavoured meats with hearty, 'meaty' textures can carry off dark, sultry spices. Black cardamom, black pepper, nutmeg and star anise are used in the blend for Beef, Carrots and Ale: the deep, smoky notes add depth to the dish, but also bring a clarity to the richness of the stew.

Black cardamom has a kind of twisted perfume, as does long pepper, and I think these two work really well together. Ginger has a lovely sweet perfume, while still a little 'mottled', sitting in the background to nutmeg's heady dominance. All these spices combine with the rich, warm aromatics of beautiful star anise in my Asian Sticky Ribs, to stunning effect.

Mace is great for defining flavours, with its floral perfume and touch of astringency – just a small amount can make a big difference. I use mace in the Smoked Chilli Sauce of my 'Dog' to help balance and add definition to the smoky aubergine.

*Previous page: The subtly perfumed, slightly astringent qualities of mace help define and lengthen the finish of rich, dark meats.*

# CHILLI BEEF HASH

*Here's a spicy take on a dish we used to have as kids: corned beef hash and baked beans. This is brilliant comfort food and really tasty. I like to use up leftovers for my hash and find that a mix of meats is excellent. Poultry, pork and beef work very well together.*

**SERVES 4**

400g (14oz) waxy potatoes, such as Charlotte

75g (2¾oz) unsalted butter

1 onion, diced

2 tsp cumin seeds

2 tsp Kashmiri chilli flakes

½ tsp sea salt

500g (1lb 2oz) cooked beef brisket, diced and torn, or a mix of leftover cuts

100g (3½oz) fresh mushrooms (porcini, chanterelles or wood blewits work well), roughly chopped

100ml (3½fl oz) good-quality chicken stock

A little sunflower oil

4 eggs

1 handful curly parsley leaves, finely chopped

1. Put the potatoes in a saucepan and cover generously with water. Bring to the boil over a high heat and cook until only just tender. Drain and cut into 2.5cm (1in) pieces. Set aside.

2. Put a heavy-based, non-stick frying pan over a medium–low heat. Add 50g (1¾oz) of the butter and allow to melt, then add the onion and cook gently until soft and translucent.

3. Turn up the heat slightly and sprinkle in the cumin seeds, chilli flakes and salt. Stir to combine, then add the diced potatoes and the meat. Don't stir them, just leave them to cook until they begin to colour slightly.

4. Turn the mix over with a wide spatula or fish slice and scatter in the mushrooms. Add the remaining butter and cook for 5–6 minutes until the potatoes and meat are lightly browned all over.

5. Add the stock, turn up the heat to a simmer and give the mixture a little stir. Allow the stock to bubble and reduce.

6. Meanwhile, heat the oil in another frying pan, crack in the eggs and fry them until they're cooked just as you like. Set aside.

7. Check that the potatoes are cooked, then spoon a generous amount of the hash onto each of four warmed plates. Pop a fried egg on top of each mound of hash, sprinkle with the parsley and serve immediately.

# BEEF-ON-BEEF 'DOG' WITH SMOKED CHILLI SAUCE & GUBBEEN CHEESE

*This is a delicious and simple way to use up leftovers of beef brisket – the addition of my aromatic smoked chilli sauce gives this 'hot dog' the edge. Gubbeen cheese is a semi-soft, washed-rind cheese made by Tom and Giana Ferguson at the Gubbeen Farmhouse in West Cork, Ireland. If you can't get your hands on it, then simply use your favourite melting cheese instead: Comté or a mild Cheddar are perfect.*

### SERVES 4

300g (10½oz) poached brisket
   (see Tip) – or any cooked
   beef or pork leftovers

FOR THE DOG DRESSING
½ tsp black peppercorns
4 cloves
½ star anise
1 tsp Kashmiri chilli flakes
2 tbsp tomato ketchup
1 tsp Worcestershire sauce
2 tsp maple syrup
1 garlic clove
1 coriander sprig, hard stalks
   removed

1. To make the dressing, finely grind the peppercorns, cloves and star anise using a mortar and pestle, then add the chilli flakes. Put all the dressing ingredients into a food processor and pulse until just smooth.

2. Put the brisket on a large plate and use your fingers to break up 250g (9oz) of the meat into large chunks, reserving the remaining 50g (1¾oz).

3. Spoon the dressing over the chunks of brisket, coating the meat well. If you'll be using in it the next hour or so, leave it to marinate at room temperature. If not, cover loosely with greaseproof paper and put it in the fridge for up to 12 hours.

Tip

*To cook brisket, put the brisket joint in a large saucepan and cover with water. Add a few peppercorns and a carrot, then bring to the boil. Reduce the heat and simmer for 2 hours or until the meat is meltingly soft. Serve hot, or drain and leave to cool.*

[ *Continued* ]

## SMOKED CHILLI SAUCE

**2 tsp coriander seeds**
**1 tsp cumin seeds**
**1 small piece blade mace**
**¼ tsp Kashmiri chilli flakes**
**2 firm aubergines**
**1 tbsp light olive oil, plus extra**
**    if needed**
**100g (3½oz) onion, diced**
**2 garlic cloves, finely diced**
**2 tsp black treacle**
**50g (1¾oz) brisket (see above),**
**    pulled into large strips**
**75g (2¾oz) drained tinned**
**    chickpeas, rinsed, lightly**
**    crushed with a fork**
**2 tsp tomato purée**
**Sea salt**

1. Finely grind the coriander and cumin seeds and the mace using a mortar and pestle, then add the chilli flakes.

2. Insert a metal skewer lengthways through each aubergine so you can turn them easily, prick them with a fork, then put them on the open flame of a gas hob or under a preheated grill.

3. When the aubergines are nicely charred all round – this is what gives the aubergine its delicious smoky flavour – cut each one in half, remove the flesh and roughly chop it up. Discard the skins.

4. Heat the oil in a frying pan over a medium heat and sauté the onion for 1 minute, then add the aubergine flesh, the garlic and the ground spices and cook for about 5 minutes until it's all lovely and soft.

5. Add the black treacle to the pan followed by the brisket, the chickpeas and the tomato purée; cook for 2 minutes, adding a little more oil if required, then set aside and allow to cool before adjusting the seasoning.

## TO FINISH

**4 soft hot-dog rolls**
**¼ head iceberg lettuce, finely**
**    shredded**
**½ red onion, thinly sliced**
**150g (5½oz) Gubbeen cheese**
**    (or your favourite), grated**
**1 small handful coriander leaves,**
**    roughly chopped**

1. To assemble your dog, bring the marinated brisket back to room temperature if necessary. Preheat the grill to its hottest setting.

2. Slice open a roll and gently pull it apart, leaving a 'hinge', then put onto a baking tray or grill pan.

3. Pop a little lettuce on the butterflied roll, then spread a couple of spoons of the Smoked Chilli Sauce evenly along the roll. Add some of the marinated brisket, and top with the onion and cheese. Repeat for all the rolls.

4. Put the tray under the very hot grill and glaze the hot dogs until they're just coloured: about 30 seconds to 1 minute.

5. Finish with some chopped fresh coriander and serve immediately. One 'dog' may not be enough!

# BEEF, CARROTS & ALE

*This is an unbelievably rich, unctuous, 'eat-with-a-spoon' beef dish. I love using beef shin for this recipe; it's one of my favourite cuts for slow cooking. The naturally gelatinous meat adds beautiful body and general oomph! If you use stewing beef, ask your butcher for a couple of marrow bones to throw into the cooking pot for extra flavour. You will need to start two days in advance to allow for the long marinating time – or better still, three days, so you can reheat the stew for maximum flavour development. Served with Coconut Mashed Roots (see page 51), it's a total comfort treat!*

**SERVES 4–6**

1kg (2lb 4oz) beef shin steaks, cut roughly in half, keeping the central bone in one half, or stewing beef, plus 1–2 marrow bones, sawn in half by the butcher

FOR THE MARINADE
1 tsp black peppercorns
½ star anise
3 cloves
½ tsp fennel seeds
2 tsp Garam Masala blend (see page 267)
1 tsp chilli flakes
1 litre (1¾ pints) stout – use a dark, rich local brand
3 small thyme sprigs
1 garlic bulb, cloves peeled

FOR THE STEW
2 tbsp plain flour
1 tsp sea salt
2 tbsp rapeseed oil
200g (7oz) button onions or shallots, peeled

1. Finely grind the peppercorns, star anise, cloves and fennel seeds using a mortar and pestle, then add the Garam Masala and chilli flakes. Take out 2 teaspoons of the spice mix to use later.

2. Put all the marinade ingredients into a non-metallic bowl and add the beef. Cover with greaseproof paper, weigh it down with a small plate to make sure everything is submerged, then cover the bowl with clingfilm and put it into the fridge. Leave for 40–48 hours to marinate. After 24 hours, gently move the meat around, then re-cover.

3. To make the stew, mix the flour, the reserved 2 teaspoons spice mix and the salt in a small bowl. Remove the meat from the marinade, dry well with kitchen paper, then lightly coat with the flour mixture and put it on a plate. Set aside.

4. Put a heavy-based flameproof casserole over a medium heat. Add the oil. Shake any excess flour from the meat. When the oil is hot, fry the beef in a couple of batches so that each piece is nicely caramelised on each side. Preheat the oven to 160°C (gas mark 3).

5. Remove the meat to a clean plate. Turn down the heat slightly, then add the onions and celery, stir and cook for 30 seconds. Add the carrots, turnips, meat and marrow bones, if using, and all the marinade, bring to a gentle simmer (no more than a bubble or two), then cover with foil, pop on the lid and put into the oven to cook for 3–3½ hours until tender.

[ *Continued* ]

2 celery sticks, cut into chunky
    batons
2 large carrots, peeled and cut
    into chunks
700g (1lb 9oz) small turnips,
    peeled and halved, or 1 large
    turnip, peeled and diced into
    3cm (1¼in) cubes
1 tbsp red wine vinegar
1 handful curly parsley leaves,
    chopped

6. Remove the casserole from the oven. Using a slotted spoon, carefully remove the meat, celery, turnips, carrots and onions on to a platter and skim any surplus fat from the cooking liquor.

7. Put the casserole over a high heat and reduce the liquid to about half, until the gravy is rich and unctuous. Add the wine vinegar, stir, then put all the meat and vegetables back into the sauce. (If making this the day before you serve it, leave to cool, cover and keep in the fridge overnight. Reheat the stew when the mash is nearly ready.) Sprinkle on the parsley, give it a quick stir and leave it to rest while you make the Coconut Mashed Roots.

# COCONUT MASHED ROOTS

**SERVES 4–6**

500g (1lb 2oz) swede, chopped
    into chunks
500g (1lb 2oz) carrots, chopped
    into chunks
500g (1lb 2oz), or about 3 floury
    potatoes, such as Maris Piper,
    peeled
400ml (14fl oz) coconut milk
50g (1¾oz) salted butter
2 heaped tsp black peppercorns,
    coarsely ground
Sea salt

1. Put the swede and carrots into a saucepan, add warm, salted water to cover, and boil for 35 minutes or until soft. Drain, set aside and allow to steam-dry.

2. Put the potatoes into a second saucepan. Just cover with warm, salted water and boil for 25 minutes or until soft. Drain, set aside and allow to steam-dry.

3. Put the coconut milk, butter and peppercorns into a third saucepan, bring to a gentle bubble and reduce to about 150ml (5fl oz) – this will take about 35 minutes.

4. Combine all the ingredients, mash to a chunky texture and serve hot.

# ROAST RUMP WITH A TAMIL CRUST

*This is a roast joint of meat like no other! I've taken a southern Indian influence to add a little extra dimension to what is an economical, wonderful cut of meat for a Sunday (or any day) roast. The buttery crumb and cooking juices add an extra depth of flavour. You will need to start a day ahead to allow for marinating. Don't forget to keep any leftovers for my Chilli Beef Hash on page 45.*

### SERVES 4

**1.5kg (3lb 5oz) beef rump, aged for at least 21 days, with a nice dark hue**
**3 onions, halved through the root, then each half sliced into 4 wedges**
**Rapeseed oil, for frying**

### FOR THE MARINADE
**3 tsp coriander seeds**
**2 tsp cumin seeds**
**1 star anise**
**5 cloves**
**1 tsp dried rose petals**
**2 tsp finely ground cassia**
**1 tsp Kashmiri chilli flakes**
**75g (2¾oz) fresh ginger, roughly chopped**
**6 garlic cloves, roughly chopped**
**1 handful mixed soft herbs, such as parsley, coriander, dill, roughly chopped**
**75ml (2½fl oz) rapeseed oil**
**125ml (4fl oz) lemon juice**
**2 tbsp lime juice**
**3 tsp sea salt**

1. First grind the coriander seeds, cumin seeds, star anise, cloves and rose petals to a fine powder using a mortar and pestle. Add the cassia and chilli flakes. Put the ginger, garlic, herbs, oil, spice blend, lemon and lime juices and salt into a food processor and blend to a smooth paste.

2. Trim the meat, then, using the point of a knife, make lots of jabbed incisions over both sides. Put the joint into a large non-metallic bowl and coat it in the marinade paste. Rub the marinade in all over. Cover the bowl with clingfilm and leave it in the fridge for 24 hours. Turn the meat over at least three or four times during this marinating time.

3. When you're ready to cook, allow the meat to come to room temperature (it will take about 40 minutes). Preheat the oven to 200°C (gas mark 6).

4. Put a large roasting tin over a medium–high heat, add the onion wedges and a little oil, and fry gently for 5 minutes, tossing them around occasionally, until they're just beginning to soften.

5. Remove the meat from the bowl and shake or scrape off any excess marinade. Reserve the marinade. Put the joint on top of the onions, then put the tin in the oven.

6. Roast for about 50–55 minutes for rare (50–55°C core temperature if using a meat thermometer), or up to 1¼ hours for medium (60–65°C core temperature). Use a slotted spoon to remove the meat and onion wedges from the tin and put them on a warmed plate. Cover with foil and set aside to rest for 20–25 minutes.

## FOR THE SAUCE

**40g (1½oz) jaggery or dark
muscovado sugar**
**4 tbsp red wine vinegar**
**10g (¼oz) flat-leaf parsley,
finely chopped**
**Sea salt**

## FOR THE CRUMB

**40g (1½oz) unsalted butter**
**100g (3½oz) fresh breadcrumbs**
**40g (1½oz) Parmesan cheese,
finely grated**
**½ tsp cayenne pepper**
**1 small handful flat-leaf parsley,
very finely chopped**

7. Meanwhile, make the sauce in the roasting tin over a medium–low heat: add the reserved marinade, the jaggery or muscovado sugar and the vinegar to the meat juices. Bring to a gentle simmer and whisk everything together, incorporating all the cooked, sticky bits. Cook for a couple of minutes, stirring continuously. Check the seasoning, then add the parsley and any cooking juices from the resting meat and stir through; set aside.

8. To make the crumb, put a heavy-based frying pan over a medium heat and add the butter. When it's just beginning to foam, add the breadcrumbs and fry gently for a few minutes until golden, then add the Parmesan, cayenne and parsley; set aside.

9. To serve, warm a large serving platter. Put the meat on a carving board and carve it into chunky slices. Put the slices onto the warm platter, scatter with the onion wedges and sprinkle over the crumb. Pour the sauce into a small, warmed jug and let everyone help themselves.

# ASIAN STICKY BEEF RIBS

*I love getting a bit of a charred crunch along with the succulent, fall-off-the-bone action, a kick of chilli and a big hit of deep, glorious flavour, matched by an equally rich yogurt and coriander dipping sauce. Ideally you need to marinate everything the night before – but it's worth it!*

**SERVES 4–6**

2kg (4lb 8oz) beef short ribs
   (cut as racks)

FOR THE MARINADE

3 star anise
1 cinnamon stick
Seeds of 2 black cardamom pods
1 tbsp black peppercorns
½ nutmeg, grated
½ tsp long pepper spike, finely
   grated (optional)
60g (2¼oz) fresh ginger, peeled
   and finely grated
3 garlic cloves, lightly smashed
75g (2¾oz) soft brown sugar
Zest and juice of 1 orange
2 red finger chillies, cut into thin
   discs, seeds and all
1 tsp sea salt
1 lemongrass stalk, bruised,
   then halved lengthways
1 tsp unsweetened cocoa powder
1 tbsp freshly made espresso
   coffee
125ml (4fl oz) tamari or light
   soy sauce
100g (3½oz) black treacle
2 tsp fish sauce
125ml (4fl oz) rice wine vinegar
4 tbsp white wine vinegar
125ml (4fl oz) water
125ml (4fl oz) dry sherry
1 tbsp sunflower oil

1. Finely grind the star anise, cinnamon, cardamom seeds and black peppercorns using a mortar and pestle. Add the grated nutmeg and long pepper, if using.

2. Put the spices and all the remaining marinade ingredients into a large non-metallic bowl and stir thoroughly to combine. Add the ribs, cover and leave in the fridge for at least 4 hours or overnight. Turn the ribs over once or twice during this time so that everything is well coated.

3. The next day, preheat the oven to 160°C (gas mark 3). Put the ribs into a roasting tin, pour over the marinade, then cover tightly with foil and put onto the middle shelf of the oven to cook for 3 hours.

4. After 3 hours, the racks should be floppy. If they're not, return them to the oven for another 20 minutes or so.

5. Remove the racks from the roasting tin and set them aside on a plate.

6. Pour all the juices through a sieve into a saucepan, put over a medium heat, bring up to a bubble, then gently reduce to a syrupy consistency – a bit like runny honey. Set aside and keep warm.

7. Preheat your grill to high. Put the racks under the grill and cook until they start to sizzle. Remove them from the heat, brush generously with the reduced marinade, then pop them back under the grill until they start to spit, char and caramelise slightly.

[ *Continued* ]

## FOR THE DIPPING SAUCE

**200ml (7fl oz) full-fat yogurt**
**100ml (3½fl oz) crème fraîche**
**Juice of 1 lime**
**2 tsp tamari or light soy sauce**

## TO GARNISH

**1 small handful coriander leaves**
**1 red finger chilli, deseeded and
    diced**
**2 spring onions, thinly sliced on
    the diagonal**

8. In a small bowl, mix all the dipping sauce ingredients, pour into a serving dish and set aside.

9. Cut the racks into individual ribs. Pour the remaining marinade onto a warmed serving platter and put the ribs on top. Sprinkle the fresh coriander, chilli and spring onions over the ribs and sauce, and serve immediately.

## Tip

*To get ahead of the game in a party situation, complete all the steps up to and including number 6, then wrap and chill in the fridge for up to two days. Come party time, allow the meat to come to room temperature, then zoom straight into step 7.*

# VENISON TARTARE

*Steak tartare has to be one of my all-time top meaty dishes. There's just something about being presented with a plate of 'raw', seasoned, hot, textured red meat, crisp, salted frites and fresh green leaves. Although quite easy to put together at home, it's a bit tricky to get absolutely right. The key thing is to take a little time and care.*

*Use fillet tail or rump trimmed of all excess fat and sinew. You can use a hand mincer and mince the meat only once on a coarse blade, but at home I just chop with a sharp, heavy knife. Either way, it shouldn't be too chunky or lumpy; the meat should 'melt' while still retaining a little texture and bite. In any case, try not to get flustered, but get the seasoning just as you like it.*

## SERVES 4

**750g (1lb 10oz) fillet tail or rump venison, trimmed of fat and sinew**

**1 red finger chilli, deseeded and finely diced**

**2 tsp finely chopped chives**

### FOR THE DRESSING

**4 medium egg yolks (use the egg whites to make meringues, see page 206)**

**40g (1½oz) soured cream**

**A drizzle peppery virgin olive oil**

**4 small shallots, finely diced**

**2 tsp thick, black Indian tamarind paste**

**2 tsp very finely grated and chopped fresh horseradish**

**2 tsp fine capers, drained and roughly chopped**

**1 tsp coarsely ground black peppercorns**

**½ tsp dried chilli flakes**

**Seeds of 1 black cardamom pod, finely ground**

**Sea salt**

1. First make the dressing. Put the egg yolks, cream, olive oil, shallots, tamarind paste, horseradish and capers in a shallow bowl. Mix them together with a fork.

2. Season with the pepper, chilli flakes, cardamom and a light touch of salt, and mix well again.

3. Put the well-trimmed venison on a chopping board and, using a sharp, heavy knife, chop it very finely. Add the chopped venison to the dressing, then sprinkle in the fresh chilli and chives.

4. Next, take two forks and gently but firmly bring the dressing into the meat so that it combines really well, while being careful not to overwork it. Check the seasoning and adjust it if necessary.

5. Serve immediately, with french fries and a green salad. You could use ring moulds to give it a bit of shape, if you like.

# LAMB & MUTTON

WHETHER IT'S YOUNG LAMB OR RICHLY flAVOURED MUTTON, THE MEAT OF SHEEP IS IN ITSELF AROMATIC, A WORTHY MATCH FOR SPICES. Use spices to emphasise the floral sweetness in younger meats, or to cut through and 'warm' the more pungent flavours of hogget and mutton. What is the difference between lamb, hogget and mutton? When 7 months or younger, you will find reference to spring, 'suckling' or milk-fed lamb: these have a really tender, sweet-tasting flesh. Up to 12 months, the meat is correctly called lamb. An animal slaughtered at 12 to 24 months would be termed hogget; older than that, it becomes mutton. Interestingly, mutton in India also refers to goat meat.

Lamb is the sweetest meat, with a rich fat. In the West, the fat is offset with strong, astringent herby flavours such as rosemary or mint. I think spices are a wonderful alternative. Cardamom, nutmeg, allspice and cassia all offer heady perfume, and these are some of the spices in the tagine spice blend that I use for the 'Park Railings' (the name refers to the appearance of the ribs of a breast of lamb), while the ginger, turmeric and sweet paprika of the blend add earthy notes to help ground the richness of the dish.

The meat you'll use for the Spiced Lamb Cutlets and Winter Salad will more than likely be hogget, even though it may be labelled lamb at the butcher's and on supermarket shelves. And that's totally fine. Hogget has firm flesh and rich flavour. The spices and flavours in this recipe echo the breadth of flavours in the meat, from the bass notes of cumin to the highs of allspice, the tangy sensations of pomegranate molasses and the floral perfume of rose.

Then there's mutton, with its more pronounced pungent note and aged protein structure. I reflect those pungent notes in my choice of spices. Star anise, fennel and cumin – and anardana to add tangy punch – work particularly well in my Poached Mutton Shoulder, with lemon zest and red wine to bring much-needed astringency and even more wonderful perfume to the deep, rich notes of the glorious mutton.

*Previous page: Dried pomegranate seeds (anardana in Hindi) add a subtle sweet–sour element and glorious crunchy texture.*

# LAMB 'PARK RAILINGS' WITH WALLY-WALLY PICKLE

### FOR THE 'PARK RAILINGS'

1 whole lean breast of lamb,
    900g–1.1kg (2–2¼lb)
    trimmed of cartilage and
    excess fat, outer skin removed
1 tbsp Tagine spice blend (see
    page 266)
½ tsp sea salt
1 garlic bulb, halved
3 medium eggs
Light olive oil, for shallow-frying

### FOR THE WALLY-WALLY PICKLE

250g (9oz) fresh mayonnaise
150g (5½oz) French gherkins,
    finely chopped
2 tbsp chopped shallots
1 tbsp Dijon mustard
2 red finger chillies, deseeded
    and finely chopped
1 tbsp chopped tarragon leaves
2 tbsp chopped mint leaves
2 tsp fennel seeds, finely ground
1 tsp black peppercorns, finely
    ground
½ tsp finely ground cassia
2 tsp black mustard seeds,
    cracked

### FOR THE BREADCRUMBS

400g (14oz) dried breadcrumbs
1 tbsp Tagine spice blend (see
    page 266)
Zest of 2 lemons
1 tsp sea salt

*My version of a classic modern British bistro dish is a nod to my mate, chef Mark Broadbent. 'Park railings' refers to the ribs in the breast of lamb. I serve them with a zingy dipping mayo that I call Wally-Wally Pickle – wally being an old East End slang name for gherkins.*

1. Preheat the oven to 180°C (gas mark 4). Rub the lamb breast with the Tagine spice blend, then put it into a roasting tin, add 100ml (3½fl oz) water, the salt and garlic, and cover tightly with foil. Cook on the middle shelf of the oven for 2 hours or until soft and melting.

2. Remove from the oven, leave to cool for 2–3 minutes, then carefully remove the meat from the roasting tin. Put the breast on a baking tray, then put another baking tray on top and gently press down on the meat. Put a couple of food tins on the tray to weigh it down and leave to cool completely, then put it in the fridge to chill for 4–6 hours.

3. Meanwhile, combine all the pickle ingredients in a bowl, then set aside in the fridge. (Stored in a sealed jar in the fridge, it will keep for two weeks.)

4. Mix all the spiced breadcrumb ingredients in a non-metallic bowl, then spread out on a tray ready for breadcrumbing the lamb. Remove the lamb breast from the fridge, put onto a chopping board and cut into 'park railings' about 1.5cm (⅝in) wide by 7.5–10cm (3–4in) long.

5. Lightly whisk the eggs and pour onto a large dinner plate. Dip each 'park railing' in the egg wash, then roll it in the spiced breadcrumbs so that it's nicely covered all over. Do this twice for each 'railing'.

6. Put a large sauté pan over a medium–high heat, add a splash of oil and fry the lamb for about 5 minutes until golden brown and crisp, cooking the 'railings' in batches and draining them on kitchen paper as you go. Serve immediately, on a warmed serving plate, with the Wally-Wally Pickle in a bowl. Perfect for film nights!

# LAMB BIRYANI KA KESAR

1kg (2lb 4oz) stewing lamb, diced

1 tbsp ghee, sunflower oil or unsalted butter

## FOR THE MARINADE

5 large garlic cloves, crushed

60g (2¼oz) fresh ginger, grated

125ml (4fl oz) natural yogurt

1 green bird's eye chilli, deseeded and finely chopped

2 onions, diced

2 tbsp golden caster sugar

1 tbsp sea salt

2 tsp powdered turmeric

2 tsp black peppercorns, finely ground

1 tsp chilli flakes

2 tsp Garam Masala blend (see page 267)

½ tsp freshly grated nutmeg

Zest and juice of ½ lemon

1 handful mint leaves, chopped

## FOR THE RICE

330g (11½oz) aged basmati rice

3 tsp cumin seeds

3 cloves

Seeds from 3 green cardamom pods

Seeds from 1 black cardamom pod

½ tsp finely ground mace

10 saffron threads

2 tsp sea salt

*This is my version of an Indian classic; 'ka kesar' means 'with saffron'. From the glorious Nizam Hyderabadi palaces to the Moghul territories of Lucknow, Delhi and Agra across to Kashmir, Lahore and Karachi and back to Persia, biryani has many regional variations. Lamb, hogget, mutton – even goat – are all traditional. The key is undoubtedly the beauty of the basmati rice and a slow, 'dum' cooking method. 'Dum' refers to cooking in a sealed pot; traditionally the pot is sealed with dough but here we use a tight-fitting lid.*

1. Combine all the marinade ingredients in a non-metallic bowl and mix well. Add the meat, cover and set aside for at least 4 hours (or preferably overnight) in the fridge.

2. Put the ghee in a large heavy-based saucepan or flameproof casserole with a tight-fitting lid. Put over a medium heat, add the meat and all its marinade and cook for 25 minutes. Set aside.

3. Wash the rice thoroughly and drain it. Finely grind the whole spices, except the saffron, using a mortar and pestle. Put 1.2 litres (2 pints) water into a large saucepan, add all the spices, the rice, saffron and salt, and bring to the boil. Cook, uncovered, for 10 minutes.

4. To assemble the dish, strain the remaining water from the rice into the meat mixture, stir thoroughly and then level the meat out evenly.

5. Spread the rice in an even layer over the meat. Cover the pan and cook over a high heat for 5 minutes.

6. Turn down the heat to its lowest setting and cook gently for 30 minutes, keeping the lid on and not stirring at all. (Alternatively, pop the casserole into the oven, preheated to 180°C (gas mark 4).)

7. Remove the dish from the heat and leave it to rest for 5 minutes before taking it to the table, lifting off the lid with a flourish, and allowing everyone to get the full, fragrant Eastern aroma. Biryani made simple!

# PERSIAN LAMB TAGINE WITH RHUBARB & ORANGE SALAD

*The wonderfully sticky texture of this dish has its roots in Arabic Bedouin tradition, but I've taken influences from Persia for its perfumed flavour and nutty crunch. The tangy rhubarb and orange salad helps cut through the sweet richness of the tagine. I'm really pleased with it and I'm sure you will be, too.*

**SERVES 4–6**

20g (¾oz) unsalted butter
1 tbsp light olive oil
2 onions, cut into
    chunky dice
2 tsp sea salt
1kg (2lb 4oz) stewing lamb, cut
    into 7cm (2¾in) chunks
2 tsp black peppercorns, finely
    ground
1 tsp powdered turmeric
2 tsp finely ground cinnamon
15g (½oz) fresh ginger, finely
    grated
250g (9oz) dates, stoned
1 tbsp runny honey

1. Add the butter and oil to a large heavy-based flameproof casserole and put over a medium heat. Add the onions and salt. Stir and fry gently for 10–12 minutes until the onions are soft and nutty-brown.

2. Add the meat, the spices and ginger. Stir to combine everything, then pour in 700ml (1¼ pints) water and stir again.

3. Turn up the heat, bring to the boil and allow to bubble, uncovered, for 30 seconds. Turn down the heat to a gentle simmer, cover and allow to bubble gently until meltingly soft: about 1½ hours.

4. Take off the lid, add the dates and honey, stir and continue to cook at a gentle bubble, uncovered, stirring occasionally, for another 30–40 minutes, or until the meat is tender and the sauce is sticky and unctuous.

[ *Continued* ]

## FOR THE RHUBARB & ORANGE SALAD

2 small oranges
1 green eating apple
Olive oil, for drizzling
450g (1lb) rhubarb, cut on the
    diagonal into 7.5cm (3in)
    batons
Juice of 1 lemon
1 tbsp runny honey
¼ preserved lemon, finely diced
    (optional)
Seeds of 2 green cardamom
    pods, finely ground
1 small handful mint leaves,
    bigger leaves torn

## FOR THE GARNISH

1 tsp butter
Splash olive oil
1 small handful blanched
    almonds
1 small handful pistachio nuts,
    shelled
2 tsp orange blossom water
1 small handful flat-leaf parsley
    leaves
1 small handful mint, big leaves
    torn, small leaves left whole

5. Meanwhile, make the salad. Preheat the oven to 200°C (gas mark 6).

6. Using a bowl to catch the juice, cut a thin slice off the top and bottom of each orange, then sit it on its freshly cut flat surface and slice off its skin and pith. Turn each orange onto its side and slice it into thin discs, retaining the juice. Remove any pips and discard.

7. Core and peel the apple and cut it in half. Put it flat-side down on a chopping board and cut it into thin slices, about 3mm (⅛in) thick. Put the apple slices onto a baking tray, coat lightly with olive oil and roast for 10 minutes.

8. Take the tray out of the oven, add the rhubarb, drizzle with a little more oil, the lemon juice and honey and return to the oven for another 12 minutes or until the rhubarb is just soft but still holds its shape. Take the fruit from the oven and leave it to cool on the tray.

9. Arrange the orange slices on a serving platter, put the apple slices and rhubarb on and around them, then mix the reserved orange juice with the roasting juices, drizzle over the salad, and sprinkle with the preserved lemon pieces, if using. Sprinkle on the ground cardamom and the mint. Cover the plate with clingfilm and put it in the fridge until it is time to serve.

10. Meanwhile, make the tagine garnish. Melt the butter and oil in a small frying pan over a medium heat. Add the nuts and fry gently until lightly brown, tossing and stirring them as you go. Remove the nuts from the pan, set aside and keep warm.

11. Take the casserole off the heat, sprinkle on the orange water and stir, then scatter with the garnish herbs, then the nuts. Take straight to the table and serve with the Rhubarb and Orange Salad.

# OLIVE'S IRISH STEW SKEWERS

*Irish stew is a bit of an institution where I live on the Emerald Isle, and everybody has their own preferred recipe – normally 'Mammy's'. This is my take, based on my wife Olive's favourite all-time supper. It's worth trying to find the best local lamb, potatoes and carrots you can, because the simplicity of the cooking brings focus to the ingredients. You'll need four long metal skewers to assemble the dish.*

### SERVES 4

**4 large carrots**
**4 waxy potatoes, such as Charlotte, peeled**
**6 lamb chump chops, fat trimmed and reserved, cut into chunky dice**
**3 tsp sea salt**
**A splash rapeseed oil**
**350ml (12fl oz) chicken stock**
**2 thyme sprigs, leaves only**

### FOR THE COATING SAUCE
**2 tsp white peppercorns, finely ground**
**5 gratings nutmeg**
**5 gratings long pepper**
**¼ tsp finely ground mace**
**2 tbsp runny honey**
**2 tsp cider vinegar**
**1 big handful curly parsley leaves, chopped**

1. Put the carrots and potatoes in separate saucepans, cover generously with water and boil until only just soft. Drain and cut into chunky dice. Season the lamb with 2 teaspoons of the salt. Set aside.

2. Put the lamb fat trimmings in a large flameproof casserole and melt them over a medium heat. Add the lamb, turn up the heat and fry, adding a little oil if needed. It might be best to do this in batches so that you don't overcrowd the casserole and stew the meat.

3. When the meat has a nutty-brown colour, add the stock, bring up to a bubble, then add the thyme and turn down the heat. Cover and simmer gently for 2 hours or until the meat is tender.

4. Once the meat is cooked, remove it from the casserole with a slotted spoon, put on a plate and set aside.

5. To make the coating sauce, mix all the spices together and add them, the honey and the vinegar to the casserole. Turn up the heat and reduce to a thick, double-cream consistency, then add the parsley. Stir through and set aside.

6. Preheat your grill to its highest setting (or light the barbecue, if the weather's right). Take a skewer, and slide alternate pieces of meat, carrot and potato along its length until there's no more room. Repeat for the other three skewers, then pour the plate juices into the sauce and stir to combine. Coat the skewers generously all over with the sauce and put them on a grill pan or barbecue.

7. Allow to bubble and char very slightly, then turn and repeat. Remove and serve immediately with sliced bread and butter and a cup of tea or wine, depending on your mood!

# MEATBALLS WITH RAS EL RELISH

*I love meatballs. They're quick and simple to make and are an economic use of cheaper cuts of meat. They can be sandwiched in sourdough or flatbread with mayonnaise and relish, served in a ragù with spaghetti or couscous, used with salad, or dressed in a curried sauce.*

**MAKES ABOUT 20**

### FOR THE MEATBALLS
**1 tsp allspice**
**2 tsp cumin seeds**
**1 tsp fennel seeds**
**2 tsp black peppercorns**
**1 tsp Mixed Spice blend (see page 266)**
**1 pinch dried rose petals**
**4–6 tbsp natural yogurt**
**1 red finger chilli, deseeded and finely diced**
**1kg (2lb 4oz) minced lamb**
**2 tsp rose water**
**2 tbsp chopped mint leaves**
**1 heaped tbsp roughly chopped curly parsley leaves**
**½ tbsp roughly chopped coriander leaves**
**2 tsp sea salt**
**1 tbsp sunflower oil**

1. Finely grind the allspice, cumin, fennel and peppercorns using a mortar and pestle. Mix the spices together in a large mixing bowl then add the remaining meatball ingredients, except the oil, and mix together thoroughly. If the mixture feels a little dry and doesn't hold together when you squeeze it, just add a little more yogurt. Cover and leave in the fridge overnight or for at least a couple of hours.

2. Preheat the oven to 180°C (gas mark 4). Divide the spiced meat mixture into approximately 55g (2oz) mounds. Roll each one into a meatball shape.

3. Put the oil in a heavy-based ovenproof sauté pan or flameproof casserole over a high heat, then gently add the meatballs and lightly brown on all sides. Be careful: these little fellas are likely to break up and you may need to do this in a couple of batches to ensure they cook more evenly. After 4–5 minutes, when they're a light nutty-brown colour, put the pan in the oven for 15–20 minutes until they're cooked through.

4. Remove the pan from the oven and carefully spoon out the meatballs. Serve immediately with the Ras el Relish.

### FOR THE RAS EL RELISH
**150g (5½oz) dark muscovado sugar**
**175ml (6fl oz) cider vinegar**
**400g (14oz) tin chopped tomatoes**
**85g (3oz) dried dates, chopped**
**15g (½oz) fresh ginger, grated**
**1 tsp ras el hanout (see page 266)**
**2 tsp pomegranate molasses**

1. Put the sugar and vinegar in a large saucepan over a medium heat and cook until the sugar dissolves into the liquid, swirling the pan around occasionally.

2. Add the tomatoes, dates, ginger and ras el hanout, and stir carefully. You'll be able to gauge when the relish is ready as it will begin to look like warm jam.

3. Remove from the heat, add the pomegranate molasses and serve immediately.

# SPICED LAMB CUTLETS & WINTER SALAD

*This Persian-inspired dish is quick to make, pretty healthy and contains all sorts of taste and flavour sensations: hot and sour dressing; crunchy walnuts; fresh, clean mint; succulent, satisfying lamb … all brought together in one delicious spicy, colourful plate.*

**SERVES 2**

**6 lamb cutlets, trimmed of excess fat**
**A little olive oil**
**A little sea salt**

FOR THE DRESSING
**85g (3oz) walnuts**
**150–200ml (5–7fl oz) good-quality chicken stock**
**3 tbsp pomegranate molasses**
**1 tbsp golden caster sugar**
**Zest and juice of ½ lemon**
**½ tsp allspice berries**
**1 tsp cumin seeds**
**2 tsp coriander seeds**
**75ml (2½fl oz) light olive oil, plus extra to drizzle**
**1 red onion, diced**
**½ tsp sea salt**
**¼ tsp freshly grated nutmeg**
**2 tsp chilli flakes**
**2 tsp rose water**
**1 handful mint leaves, finely sliced at the last minute**

FOR THE WINTER SALAD
**Chicory, watercress, radicchio or frisée lettuce**

1. Preheat a griddle pan until it's nice and hot. Rub a little olive oil (not too much) onto the cutlets, then put on the griddle for 60 seconds. Turn 60 degrees and cook for another 60 seconds.

2. Turn over and repeat so that you get an attractive bar mark, then remove from the griddle, sprinkle both sides with salt and keep warm on a plate, loosely covered with greaseproof paper.

3. To make the dressing, put the walnuts in a heavy-based frying pan and lightly toast for 2–3 minutes. Tip into a clean tea towel, gather up the corners and rub vigorously to remove the skins. Lightly crush the walnuts.

4. To make the pomegranate syrup, put a small saucepan over a medium–high heat. Add the chicken stock, pomegranate molasses, sugar and lemon juice. Cook for 3 minutes or until it reduces and becomes slightly syrupy.

5. Finely grind the allspice, cumin and coriander seeds using a mortar and pestle. Put a frying pan over a medium heat, add the olive oil, onion, salt and all the spices, and sauté gently for 30 seconds. Add the walnuts and cook for a maximum of 2–3 minutes, so that the onions still have a little bite, but no raw flavour. Add the pomegranate syrup to the frying pan, stir and cook for 1 minute over a gentle heat.

6. Remove the pan from the heat, add the lemon zest and any meat juices from the cutlet plate, then add a generous slug of olive oil, the rose water and the fresh mint leaves.

7. Put the cutlets on a warmed plate. Dress the winter salad with some of the dressing, seasoning to taste, and serve with the cutlets. Spoon the remaining dressing over the lamb cutlets.

# Eat-Me-with-a-Spoon Masala

*This dish is an absolute peach of a comfort recipe, even if I do say so myself! Cooked this way, the meat on a lamb shank becomes so soft, so tender and delicious, it not only falls off the bone but it can be eaten with a spoon. The asafoetida is the secret ingredient that makes all the difference. My friend Jim, from cookery school, was always trying to add secret ingredients to everything he made. This one's for you, sir: 'Sláinte!'*

**SERVES 4**

4 large meaty lamb shanks (about 400–450g/14oz–1lb)

40g (1½oz) unsalted butter, diced

500g (1lb 2oz) onions, thinly sliced

50g (1¾oz) garlic cloves, finely chopped

60g (2¼oz) fresh ginger, finely chopped

2 tsp fennel seeds

Scant ¼ tsp asafoetida resin

3 tsp Garam Masala blend (see page 267)

500ml (18fl oz) Greek yogurt

400g (14oz) tin chopped tomatoes

100ml (3½fl oz) chicken stock

2 tbsp dry vermouth

2 tbsp runny honey

1 tbsp red wine vinegar

1. Preheat the oven to 140°C (gas mark 1). Wrap a 5cm (2in) wide strip of foil around the end of the shank bones, and tie the foil cap securely with kitchen string.

2. Melt the butter in a deep flameproof casserole over a medium heat and gently fry the onions for 5 minutes or until they're soft. Add the garlic, ginger, fennel seeds, asafoetida and 2 teaspoons of the Garam Masala, and stir well to combine. Add the yogurt, tomatoes and stock, and stir well.

3. Put the shanks upright in the sauce, cover with foil and the lid and put into the oven for 4 hours, or less if the shanks are a little skinny. When finished, the meat should be meltingly tender.

4. Carefully take the shanks out, trying to make sure they hold their shape, and set aside on a warmed plate.

5. Put the casserole over a medium heat, add the vermouth, honey, vinegar and the remaining 1 teaspoon of the Garam Masala and cook for 5 minutes, stirring well to combine, until the sauce is glossy and smooth.

6. Put a lamb shank on each of four warmed dinner plates and remove the foil caps. Coat each shank generously with the sauce and serve with a creamy mash, green vegetables, such as kale or sautéed spinach, and a squeeze of lemon juice.

# POACHED MUTTON SHOULDER

*In this hearty, warming dish, I've combined French technique with spicy temperament for a totally indulgent meal. Just be aware that it takes a little time to cook, so get prepared ahead of time.*

**SERVES 4–6**

- 2.5kg (5lb 8oz) mutton shoulder on the bone, outer membrane removed, tied with kitchen string to hold its shape
- 24 dry-cure bacon lardons, about 50g (1¾oz)
- ½ star anise
- 2 tsp fennel seeds
- 1 tsp cumin seeds
- 175g (6oz) unsalted butter, at room temperature
- 2 garlic cloves, finely chopped
- Zest of 1 lemon
- Scant ¼ tsp finely ground mace
- 4 tsp dried pomegranate seeds
- 250g (9oz) smoked streaky bacon, cut into chunky strips
- 8 shallots
- 5–6 small white turnips, cut into roughly the same size as the shallots
- 3 carrots, chopped into chunks on the diagonal
- 375ml (13fl oz) red wine, such as Beaujolais or Pinot Noir
- At least 400ml (14fl oz) ham or chicken stock
- 1 tbsp red wine vinegar
- 1 big handful curly parsley leaves, finely chopped
- 1 tbsp capers, drained
- Sea salt

1. Preheat the oven to 140°C (gas mark 1). Make 24 incisions all over the joint with the point of a sharp knife, then poke the lardons snugly in.

2. Finely grind the star anise, fennel and cumin seeds using a mortar and pestle. In a small bowl, mix the butter, garlic, lemon zest, all the spices and the pomegranate seeds. Spread this mixture all over the joint, coating it generously. Set aside.

3. Take a large flameproof casserole or deep roasting tin that will hold the joint comfortably and put it over a medium heat. Gently fry the smoked bacon until softened, then add the shallots, turnips and carrots and continue to sauté gently for 5 minutes to colour them a little. Remove from the heat.

4. Put the joint in the casserole on top of the vegetables, add the wine, then add enough stock to come about 2.5cm (1in) or so up the joint. Cover tightly with foil and the lid. Cook in the oven for 6 hours or until meltingly soft.

5. Uncover the casserole and turn up the heat to 200°C (gas mark 6). Cook for another 15 minutes to crisp, then remove the joint to a warmed serving plate. Scoop up the bacon and vegetables with a slotted spoon, arrange around the meat, then set aside and keep warm.

6. Strain the juices through a sieve into a saucepan and skim to remove most of the fat. Put over a medium heat, bring to a rapid boil and reduce by half – about 15 minutes. Add the vinegar, parsley and capers, then taste and adjust the seasoning, if necessary. Spoon a little of the sauce over the mutton, then pour the remainder into a jug.

7. Take the joint to the table, carve and serve with boiled new potatoes and the sauce.

# HOGGET & SQUASH BAKE

*As the nights start to close in and the north wind brings its inevitable chill, this simple, all-in-one roast dish makes perfect warming comfort food – ideal for eating by an open fire on a cold autumnal evening. The mix of seasonal squashes, hearty chunks of meat and thick tomato sauce fired up with a blend of fragrant spices, lemon zest and thyme will warm the cockles of anyone's heart. Hogget is another term for lamb that's between 12 and 24 months old; the flesh is firmer, the flavour richer, so ask your butcher if he or she can get hold of some slightly older lamb.*

**SERVES 4**

2 tsp coriander seeds
8 cloves
1 small piece blade mace
1 tsp Szechuan pepper
1 heaped tsp chilli flakes
1 tsp finely ground cinnamon
4 tbsp olive oil
1 garlic clove, crushed
Zest of ½ lemon
1½ tsp sea salt
8 gigot (leg) bone-in lamb chops
    (steaks), about 2.5cm (1in)
    thick
900g (2lb) cherry tomatoes
650g (1lb 7oz) butternut squash
    flesh (about 1.2kg (2lb 12oz)
    before peeling), peeled,
    deseeded and chopped into
    1.5cm (⅝in) chunks
4 thyme sprigs
1 handful mint, chopped into
    ribbons

1. Preheat the oven to 190°C (gas mark 5). Finely grind the whole spices using a mortar and pestle, then mix in the chilli flakes and cinnamon.

2. Pour the oil into a large non-metallic bowl and add the spices, garlic, lemon zest, salt, lamb chops, tomatoes, squash and thyme.

3. Using your hands, mix everything around in the bowl, then take out the chops, put them onto a plate, cover and set aside.

4. Carefully pour the spiced squash and tomato mixture into a large roasting tin, scraping in every last scrap. Gently spread the mixture into an even(ish) layer and bake in the oven for 15 minutes.

5. Give everything in the dish a thorough, but gentle, stir, then take the chops from the plate, put them on top of the squash mixture, cover with a sheet of foil and put back into the oven for another 15 minutes.

6. Remove the foil and continue to cook for another 10 minutes. When the chops have taken on a nutty-brown colour, take the tin out of the oven.

7. Carefully remove the stalky twigs of thyme, sprinkle the fresh mint on top, then stir to combine all the flavours. Serve immediately with your favourite crusty bread, couscous or soft-set polenta.

# BIRDS

Ranging across a broad spectrum of flavours, from subtle, sweet poussin through to the earthy, gamey flavours of guinea fowl, pheasant and pigeon, when it comes to spicing, this chapter is all about playful, happy, uplifting spice notes. Soft citrus, teasing exotic aromatics, the faintest hint of menthol from green cardamom to cut through and lift the perfume of the spice blend.

For the Spatchcocked Jerk Poussin I've gone for a strong jerk seasoning of black pepper and clove, brightened with allspice, coriander and nutmeg, then combined with a hot and tangy sauce of Scotch Bonnet chilli, ginger for length of finish and grapefruit for playful citrus zest and balance. Opposing flavours working in harmony with one another, their taste profiles bridged by spice.

Peached Chicken with Lemongrass and Herbs sets off along a well-trodden path of Southeast Asian flavours, combining lemongrass, coriander, ginger and star anise, but the unexpected addition of Gewürztraminer wine (appropriately, *Gewürz* is the German word for spice) results in a wonderful cooking liquor to serve as a sauce or use as the base of a comforting broth. The freshness of herbs and fruitiness of orange zest accent the sweet flesh of chicken.

Pheasant is often referred to as an 'Indian chicken'. In my Pot-roasted Pheasant I've chosen spices for their light, happy, citrus, perfumed characters: green cardamom, juniper, Szechuan pepper. Green cardamom for high, 'pingy' notes, cubeb for mid–high notes of subtle bitterness and camphor, grounded with star anise and rounded out by cassia; all compliment the unique taste of pheasant.

In the main, I try to convey a light, happy mood in all the dishes in this chapter, from the everyday to the exotic. Visualising colours I associate with foods helps me build a better dish: for birds of all types it's deep golden yellows, light greens, nutty browns, warm oranges, reds and purples. In the Spiced Wood Pigeon Salad I've included purple-red beetroot, nuts and green artichokes, all brought together by the black cardamom in the dressing, giving it an edge and helping define the dish as a whole.

*Previous page: Black cardamoms add smoky notes and accentuate the perfume of the darker, more gamey meats.*

# SPATCHCOCKED JERK POUSSIN

*I love jerk chicken. It brings back happy memories of the Notting Hill Carnival, moving from one smoky grill stall to another to choose corn, slaws and the hallowed jerk. I use poussins here because I think their sweet, tasty meat works so well with the citrus and spicing. Orange is the traditional citrus for a jerk marinade, but I have chosen grapefruit, partly inspired by 'Ting', a well-known Jamaican soft drink based on grapefruit juice.*

## SERVES 4

### FOR THE TING & TING SAUCE

**1 grapefruit**
**2 tbsp sunflower oil**
**1 bunch spring onions, thick green parts removed, whites finely chopped**
**3 garlic cloves, diced**
**1 tsp Kashmiri chilli flakes**
**30g (1oz) fresh ginger**
**1 Scotch bonnet chilli, deseeded and roughly chopped**
**200g (7oz) tin chopped tomatoes**
**1 tbsp tomato purée**
**75g (2¾oz) dark brown sugar**
**1 tsp white wine vinegar**
**1 tsp sea salt**

### FOR THE SPATCHCOCKED POUSSIN

**1 tbsp coriander seeds**
**2 tsp black peppercorns**
**¼ tsp cloves**
**½ cinnamon stick**
**3 allspice berries**
**¼ nutmeg, freshly grated**
**2 tsp thyme leaves**
**½ tsp dried oregano**
**2 tsp sea salt**
**2 poussins, backbones and wingtips removed**
**2 tbsp sunflower oil**

1. To make the sauce, using a sharp knife and working over a bowl to catch the juice, slice off the grapefruit skin and pith. Cut out the segments of half the grapefruit, leaving the membrane behind, and set aside. Squeeze the juice from the remaining half grapefruit and add to the bowl.

2. Put a large saucepan over a medium heat, add the oil and cook the spring onions until soft. Add the garlic, chilli flakes, ginger and chilli, stir and fry gently for 1 minute. Add the grapefruit, 4 tablespoons of the juice and the remaining sauce ingredients, turn up the heat and bring to a bubble, then turn down the heat and simmer for 5 minutes until the sauce has thickened slightly.

3. Remove from the heat and blitz in a food processor or with a stick blender. Cover loosely and set aside. Preheat the oven to 180°C (gas mark 4).

4. Grind the coriander seeds, peppercorns, cloves, cinnamon and allspice using a mortar and pestle, then add the nutmeg, thyme, oregano and salt.

5. Put the poussins in a roasting tin, breast-side up. Apply a little pressure to the birds with the palm of your hand until you hear a crack, then arrange them as flat as possible. Using a sharp knife, score the legs and breasts with three incisions on each.

6. Mix the seasoning blend with the oil to make a thick paste, then use it to coat the birds, massaging the paste all over the meat.

7. Cover loosely with foil and roast for 35 minutes.

8. Remove from the oven, take off the foil and pour the sauce all over the birds, then return to the oven and roast for another 20–25 minutes, until they're cooked; test by piercing the thickest part of a thigh with a skewer; the juices should run clear, not pink. Serve with buttered grilled corn-on-the-cob and some pepper-spiced rice.

# CHICKEN MARRAKESH

*This pan-fried chicken breast with spiced butter is a brilliant combination of warming flavours and pure, fresh spice. It's also a quick way to make a meal a little different while keeping things really simple and light. Spiced chicken, zingy mayonnaise and crisp green salad ... what's not to like?*

**SERVES 4**

4 chicken breasts, skin on
A little rapeseed oil

FOR THE SPICED BUTTER
200g (7oz) unsalted butter, at
    room temperature
2 tsp ras el hanout (see page
    266)
½ tsp lemon zest
1 tbsp flat-leaf parsley leaves,
    finely chopped

1. Mix all the spiced butter ingredients together in a small bowl. If not using immediately, lay a square of clingfilm on your work surface, put the butter mix at one end, then carefully roll it up into a sausage shape. Twist each end like a sweet wrapper and put it into the fridge. When you need it, simply slice a thin disc of butter off the end, remove the clingfilm and off you go.

2. Using a sharp knife, slice along the length of the thickest part of each breast to form a pocket, taking care not to slice right through.

3. Divide 100g (3½oz) of the spiced butter into four pieces (keep the remainder, wrapped in clingfilm, in the fridge for up to four weeks). Spread one piece of butter into the pocket of each breast and secure with a skewer.

4. Put a griddle, sauté pan or frying pan over a medium heat. Rub a little oil over the skin of each breast and, when the pan is good and hot, put the chicken pieces into the pan, skin-side down, and fry gently for about 5 minutes – don't move the chicken in the pan at this stage.

5. Turn the chicken pieces over, cover and turn down the heat to low. Allow to cook in the vibrant-coloured, buttery juices until the chicken is done; to test, pierce the thickest part with a skewer; the juices should run clear, not pink. This will take about 5–8 minutes.

[ *Continued* ]

## ALGIER AÏOLI

**2 fat garlic cloves, crushed**
**Sea salt**
**2 medium egg yolks**
**300–450ml (10–16fl oz) fruity olive oil**
**Juice of at least 1 lemon and zest of ½ lemon**
**1 tsp Garam Masala blend (see page 267)**

1. While the chicken is cooking, make the aïoli and the vinaigrette. Crush the garlic with a little salt until it forms a paste. In a bowl, whisk the egg yolks and garlic paste together until thick.

2. Whisking continuously, pour in half the olive oil in a thin stream, then add a little of the lemon juice and some more oil. Continue beating, adding alternately more lemon juice and more oil until you have a thick mayonnaise.

3. Adjust the salt to taste and add the Garam Masala and lemon zest. Mix and set aside.

## FOR THE VINAIGRETTE

**1 garlic clove, halved**
**1½ tbsp best-quality Dijon mustard**
**150ml (5fl oz) grapeseed or sunflower oil**
**3 tbsp fruity olive oil**
**1 tsp good-quality white wine vinegar**
**½ tsp golden caster sugar**
**Fine sea salt and finely ground black pepper**

1. To make the vinaigrette, rub the inside of a large screwtop jar very firmly with the cut edge of the garlic clove.

2. Add all the dressing ingredients, then pour in 50ml (2fl oz) boiling water (the water goes in last to prevent the jar from cracking).

3. Screw the lid on tightly and shake very, very vigorously until everything emulsifies – a minute or so should do it.

## FOR THE GREEN SALAD

**4 Baby Gem lettuce hearts**
**1 large bunch of chives, tarragon and chervil**

1. Divide the lettuce leaves among four plates. Spoon the vinaigrette generously over the leaves, then scatter the herbs on top.

2. Put the chicken breasts on the plates and serve with warmed flatbread and a ramekin of Algier Aïoli.

# POACHED CHICKEN WITH LEMONGRASS & HERBS

SERVES 4–6

## FOR THE SEASONING

1 tsp white peppercorns
1 tsp coriander seeds
Seeds of 4 green cardamom pods
1 large coriander sprig
1 large tarragon sprig
1 large chervil sprig
15g (½oz) fresh ginger, finely
   chopped
1 garlic clove, finely chopped
½ tsp sea salt
1 tbsp light olive oil

## FOR THE CHICKEN

1 oven-ready chicken, about
   1.8kg (4lb)
100ml (3½fl oz) Alsace
   Gewürztraminer or Riesling
85g (3oz) piece of fresh ginger,
   cut into three
1 lemongrass stalk, crushed and
   roughly chopped
A few coriander stems
Zest of 1 orange, pared into
   strips with a veg peeler
1 red chilli, halved and deseeded
1 leek, chopped into chunks
2 celery sticks, chopped into
   chunks
1 onion, halved
1 garlic bulb, halved horizontally
5 star anise
15 black peppercorns

*Poaching is a brilliant and far too often overlooked cooking method, perfect for lovingly imparting delicate flavours to every type of ingredient, from the commonplace to the rare. Rant over – let's cook! This poaching method may seem a little controversial, but it produces the best, most delicate chicken. It's one of the first chicken recipes I ever made. It is excellent served with Pistachio & Rose Pilau (see page 156) and some steamed greens.*

1. First, grind the white pepper, coriander seeds and cardamom seeds together using a mortar and pestle. Then, blitz or finely chop all the seasoning ingredients with the spices in a food processor so that you have a lovely thickish paste. (If you don't have a food processor, chop the herbs finely and grate the ginger and garlic, then mix together in a small bowl.) Carefully insert this paste under the chicken's skin from the front and rear cavities right down into the legs. Try not to split the skin. This may take 15 minutes or so, but it makes the dish spectacular.

2. Dislocate the leg joints, then put the chicken in a large saucepan or stockpot. Add the wine, ginger, lemongrass, coriander stems, orange zest, chilli, leek, celery, onion, garlic, star anise and peppercorns. Pour in enough water to cover the chicken.

3. Cover the pan and bring to the boil. Cook for 5 minutes at a rolling boil, then turn off the heat and leave the chicken in the liquid until it's cool enough to handle – about 2 hours.

4. Remove the chicken from the stock, put on a large warmed serving platter and strain the liquid into a clean pan, skimming off any excess fat. Discard the flavourings and vegetables. Bring the cooking liquor to the boil and reduce to 300ml (10fl oz), then pour into a warmed sauce boat.

5. Carve the bird and serve, ensuring that each guest has both dark and brown meats, pouring some of the sauce over the meat.

# SOFA CHICKEN

*Love this dish! Spiced, floured and fried chicken, perfect for sofa sloths – and a perennial favourite of my friends and family. I prefer using boned thigh meat as it's quicker to cook and easier to chomp into. Whole thighs and drumsticks are great too, but will take a little longer to cook through – about 7–10 minutes. You can skip the buttermilk-bath stage if you're in a hurry, but it does make an excellent and notable difference.*

## SERVES 4

**500g (1lb 2oz) boned and
  skinned chicken thighs, cut
  into long lozenges, gristle
  and sinew removed
Groundnut oil, for deep-frying**

### FOR THE BUTTERMILK BATH
**250ml (9fl oz) buttermilk
1 vanilla pod, split lengthways
½ tsp Kashmiri chilli flakes**

### FOR THE CRISP CRUMB
**150g (5½ oz) potato starch or
  cornflour
250g (9oz) instant polenta
Zest of ½ unwaxed lemon, grated
1 tsp sweet paprika
½ tsp smoked paprika
1 tsp cayenne pepper
¼ tsp chopped thyme leaves
½ tsp amchoor
1 tsp fine sea salt**

### FOR THE SPICED SALT
**2 tsp black peppercorns
2 tsp coriander seeds
1 tsp fennel seeds
Seeds of 1 green cardamom pod
2 tsp sea salt**

1. Put the buttermilk in a large bowl, scrape in the vanilla seeds and add the vanilla pod and chilli flakes. Add the chicken, cover and put in the fridge for at least 6 hours or overnight.

2. When it's time to cook, put all the crisp crumb ingredients in a bowl and mix well. Lift the chicken out of the buttermilk bath and into the crumb bowl. Toss until well coated, then set aside on a wire rack.

3. Grind all the spices for the spiced salt using a mortar and pestle.

4. Pour the groundnut oil into an electric deep-fat fryer set to 170°C. (Or fill a large saucepan one-third full of oil and put it over a medium heat. After about 4–5 minutes drop a piece of white bread into the oil; if it takes 3 seconds to turn golden brown, it's the right heat for the chicken. If not, adjust the heat accordingly.)

5. Using kitchen tongs, pick up individual chicken pieces and gently lower them into the hot oil. Don't crowd the chicken – cook in two or three batches. Deep-fry until crisp and golden, allowing about 4–6 minutes, depending on the thickness of the chicken; check by slicing into one of the thicker pieces; the juices should run clear, not pink.

6. Remove from the pan, sprinkle liberally with the spiced salt and serve immediately. They go really well with Chilli Jam (see page 262) and a rich garlic mayo.

# HYDERABADI CHICKEN WITH SPICED CASHEW BUTTER

*When it comes to chicken, buy the best you can afford. To me, the breed and age of the chicken matter more than whether it's free-range or organic, but you must choose according to your own criteria. This recipe is a bit of a take on a chicken curry, so whichever chicken you choose for it, enjoy!*

**SERVES 4**

### FOR THE SPICED CASHEW BUTTER

**175g (6oz) cashew nuts**
**½ tsp black peppercorns**
**½ tsp cumin seeds**
**¼ tsp cloves**
**1 tsp powdered turmeric**
**½ tsp finely ground cassia**
**1 heaped tsp sea salt**
**2 tbsp desiccated coconut**
**1 small handful curly parsley leaves, finely chopped**
**1 red bird's eye chilli, deseeded and finely diced**
**30g (1oz) fresh ginger, very finely grated**
**½ tsp very finely grated lemon zest**

### FOR THE CHICKEN

**1 oven-ready chicken, about 1.4kg (3lb)**
**1 tbsp rapeseed oil**
**16 small shallots or pickling onions**
**12 whole garlic cloves, skin on**
**150ml (5fl oz) chicken stock**
**2 tbsp crème fraîche**
**30g (1oz) unsalted butter, cubed and chilled**

1. To make the cashew butter, put the cashews in a saucepan, cover with water and boil for 15 minutes. Drain, reserving 2 tablespoons of the cooking water. Put the nuts and reserved cooking water in a food processor or blender and blitz until smooth. Finely grind the whole spices using a mortar and pestle. Add all the spices, the salt, coconut, parsley, chilli, ginger and lemon zest to the nuts and pulse to form a thick paste. (Or chop the ingredients finely, then grind together using a mortar and pestle). Reserve 50g (1¾oz) of the cashew butter in a small bowl.

2. Wipe the chicken with kitchen paper and remove any excess fat. Put the chicken on a clean work surface. Carefully lift the skin of the bird away from the flesh, starting at the neck end, then gently push the cashew butter under the skin, using your fingers. Rub any remaining butter over the legs and breasts.

3. Tie the legs neatly to the body using kitchen string. Preheat the oven to 180°C (gas mark 4). Put the oil in a large flameproof casserole over a medium–high heat. Add the shallots and garlic, and cook for 4–5 minutes to colour slightly. Remove from the heat. Add the stock and the chicken. Cover with foil, then with the lid. Cook in the oven for 1 hour 20 minutes, or until the thigh-meat juices run clear when pricked with a skewer. Remove the bird from the casserole, cover loosely with foil and keep warm.

4. Skim off any excess fat from the juices. Put the casserole over a medium–high heat and reduce the cooking liquor by half. Remove from the heat, add the crème fraîche and stir well to combine, then put back on the heat and continue to reduce until the sauce just coats the back of a spoon. Add the reserved cashew butter and the cubed butter and whisk to combine until glossy. Serve the chicken with the sauce and pilau rice.

# POT-ROASTED PHEASANT

*I came up with this recipe when I was asked by Richard Corrigan to appear on his Channel 4 programme,* Cookery School. *I was showing the students how to cook with spices. This dish is my play on the classic pheasant-and-grape combination. Clementines make a beautiful fruity addition to the bird, while cardamom brings together the flavours of both. This recipe was classed as 'super advanced' for the programme, due to the number of elements and steps, but just take it easy when preparing it and you'll be fine.*

### SERVES 4

3 clementines
1 tsp juniper berries
1 tsp cubeb pepper
1 tsp fennel
Seeds from 2 green cardamom
    pods
¼ tsp Szechuan pepper
1 star anise
1 tsp finely ground cassia
75g (2¾oz) unsalted butter
2 oven-ready young hen
    pheasants, at room
    temperature
Sea salt and finely ground black
    pepper
10 thick slices streaky dry-cured
    unsmoked bacon
1 tbsp rapeseed oil
100g (3½oz) pancetta, chopped
    into lardons and blanched for
    about 3 minutes
6 small shallots, peeled
2 tbsp Armagnac
100ml (3½fl oz) dry white wine

1. Preheat the oven to 180°C (gas mark 4). Using a veg peeler, remove the zest from the clementines in strips. Boil a small pan of water, add the zest strips and boil for 1 minute to blanch them. Drain. Using a sharp knife, with a plate to catch the juice, slice off the top and bottom of a clementine, then slice off the pith. Cut out the segments, leaving the membrane behind. Squeeze the juice out of the membrane into a bowl and add the juice from the plate. Repeat with the remaining clementines. Set aside.

2. Grind all the spices together using a mortar and pestle. Mix a quarter of the spice blend with the butter. Season the birds well inside and out with salt and pepper, then cover generously with the spiced butter.

3. Lay the bacon slices over the breast meat, then truss to secure the bacon in place. Put a large flameproof casserole over a medium heat and pour in the oil. Brown the bacon-wrapped pheasants all over, then remove them from the casserole and set aside.

4. Put the pancetta and shallots into the casserole and cook until lightly browned. Remove from the heat and put the pheasants in the casserole, breast-side down.

5. Pour the Armagnac into a small saucepan, heat until hot, then set it alight and pour it over the birds. When the flames have subsided, pour in the wine and stock, sprinkle in the remaining spice blend, the clementine juice and strips of clementine zest.

6. Cover the casserole with foil, then with its lid, and put on the middle shelf in the oven. Cook for 40 minutes.

*[ Continued ]*

75ml (2½fl oz) chicken stock
2 tbsp Mandarine Napoléon or
   Grand Marnier
40g (1½oz) unsalted butter,
   cubed and chilled
A drizzle best-quality cider
   vinegar or lemon juice

7. Remove the casserole from the oven. Remove the lid and foil (keep the foil), and turn the birds breast-side up.

8. Return to the oven, uncovered, for another 10–20 minutes, then check to see if the birds are cooked: the legs will move easily when gently tugged. Remove the birds from the casserole, cover with the reserved foil and set aside to rest for 10–12 minutes. Turn down the oven to 160°C (gas mark 3).

9. Using a slotted spoon, remove the lardons and shallots from the casserole and keep warm. Remove and discard the zest.

10. Strain the cooking juices from the casserole, pour into a jug, skim off any excess fat and set aside.

11. Put the casserole over a medium heat, add the orange liqueur and stir well to deglaze and loosen the browned cooking residue. Set the liqueur alight, ensuring that you burn off all the alcohol.

12. Now pour the juices back into the casserole, bring up to a vigorous bubble, and reduce the sauce until it clings slightly to the back of a spoon. Add the cold, cubed butter and vinegar to taste, and whisk well. Check the seasoning, then set the sauce aside until you are ready to serve.

13. Meanwhile, remove the trussing string and the bacon from the birds. Put the bacon on a baking tray and put it in the oven to crisp for about 5 minutes. Preheat the grill.

14. Carve the birds – remove and joint the legs, then neatly cut the breasts from the carcasses – and put them in a roasting tin. Flash the jointed birds under the hot grill for 30 seconds.

15. Pour the cooking juices from the 'flashed' roasting tin through a sieve into the sauce. Finish the sauce by gently reheating it and adding the clementine segments. Only just warm it through to make sure you retain the integrity and freshness of the segments. Serve the jointed pheasant on warmed plates, with the crisp bacon, shallots and lardons, and a little of the sauce with a few clementine segments; serve the remaining sauce separately.

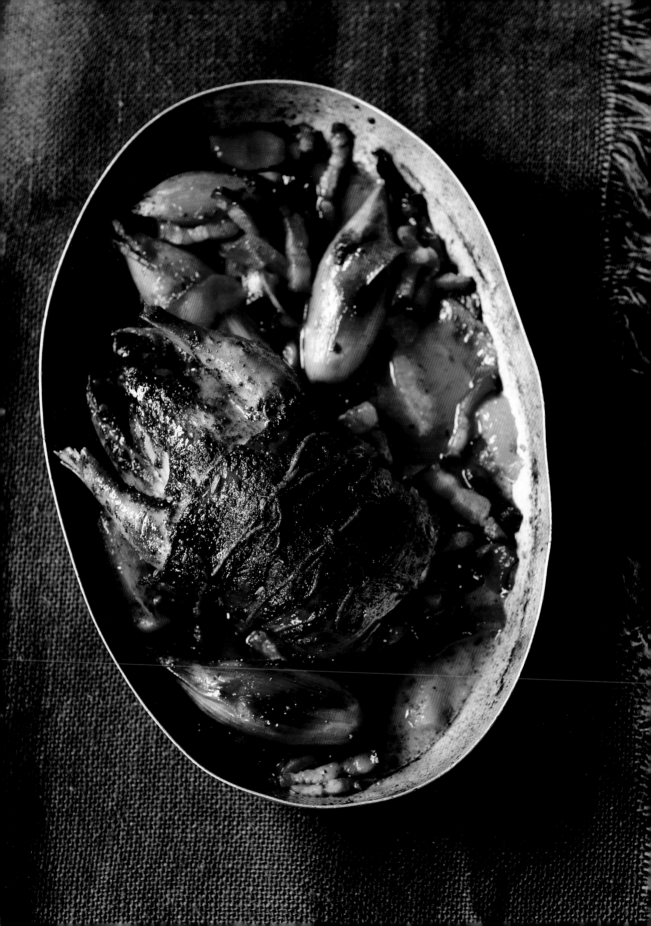

# Persian Quail

*This is one of my favourite quick dishes – brilliant for entertaining or festive occasions. I love quail, and it goes so well with the Persian-style 'fesenjan' (pomegranate and walnut) sauce.*

**SERVES 2 AS A MAIN,
4 AS A STARTER**

## FOR THE QUAIL

1 small pinch saffron threads
1 small handful pistachio nuts,
    roughly chopped
1 small handful dried cherries
1 small handful sultanas
1 tbsp anardana, finely ground
2 tbsp Grand Marnier or Cointreau
4 gratings nutmeg
1 tbsp dried rose petals, chopped
4 oven-ready quail
30g (1oz) unsalted butter
A little light olive oil
½ butternut squash, peeled and
    cut into 2cm (¾in) dice
1 tbsp runny honey

## FOR THE SAUCE

1 tsp black peppercorns
1 small piece blade mace
Seeds of 2 green cardamom pods
1 tsp finely ground cinnamon
200g (7oz) walnuts
½ tsp powdered turmeric
A splash light olive oil
2 banana shallots, finely diced
1 garlic clove, finely chopped
1 tsp sea salt
100ml (3½fl oz) pomegranate
    juice
4 tbsp pomegranate molasses
300ml (10fl oz) chicken stock
Juice of 1 lime

1. Preheat the oven to 200°C (gas mark 6). Soak the saffron in 2 tablespoons warm water in a large bowl, then stir in the nuts, cherries, sultanas, anardana, liqueur, nutmeg and rose petals to make the stuffing. Cover and set aside for 15 minutes. Fill the cavities of the birds with the stuffing, then truss the legs with kitchen string. Heat the butter and oil in a large frying pan over a medium heat until foaming, then add the birds and brown lightly on all sides, turning and basting as they cook. You may need to do this one bird at a time. Transfer the birds to a snug-fitting, deep roasting tin. Put the frying pan to one side.

2. Cover the roasting tin tightly with foil, then roast the quail for 10–15 minutes – no more – just until the juices run clear when a thigh is pricked with a skewer. Remove from the oven, set aside and keep warm.

3. To make the sauce, finely grind the peppercorns, mace and cardamom using a mortar and pestle, then add the cinnamon; set aside. Put the walnuts in a heavy-based frying pan and lightly toast for 2–3 minutes. Tip into a clean tea towel, gather up the corners and rub vigorously to remove the skins. Put the nuts and turmeric into a food processor or blender and pulse to a rough texture. (Or grind using a mortar and pestle.) Set aside.

4. Put the oil in a wide saucepan over a medium heat. Add the shallots and fry gently until soft and translucent. Add the garlic, the spice blend, walnuts and the salt. Stir well, then add the pomegranate juice, molasses and stock, stir again and increase the heat. Once the sauce has begun to bubble, turn down to a simmer and reduce to the thickness of double cream. Remove from the heat and add the lime juice. Stir and adjust the seasoning if necessary, then set aside and keep warm.

5. Preheat the grill. Heat a little more oil in the frying pan over a medium heat. Add the butternut squash and fry for 8 minutes or until there's just a little give in the flesh. Add the honey, stir to coat, then put briefly under the grill to colour. To serve, remove the string from the quail, add a spoonful of the squash and coat the meat generously with the sauce.

# ROAST GUINEA FOWL

*This dish helped me win a chef's version of* Come Dine with Me *on Ireland's RTÉ channel's* Afternoon Show – *brilliant fun. I then went home for Christmas and cooked it as a Boxing Day dish for 12 members of our family. With hindsight, it probably wasn't the best idea in terms of my workload, but it was really well received from a taste point of view. For that reason, I've since refined the recipe to cut out a little of the 'fuss and bother'. Enjoy it with Puy lentils and my Clementine, Date & Chilli Chutney (see page 258).*

**SERVES 4**

### FOR THE SPICED BUTTER
**Seeds of 5 black cardamom pods**
**1 tsp black peppercorns**
**1 tsp sea salt**
**2 tbsp chopped tarragon leaves**
**1 tsp Grand Marnier or**
**Cointreau (optional)**
**250g (9oz) unsalted butter, at**
**room temperature**

1. First, make the spiced butter. Finely grind the cardamom seeds and peppercorns using a mortar and pestle. Put into a small bowl and add the salt, tarragon, liqueur (if using) and butter. Mix well.

2. Preheat the oven to 180°C (gas mark 4). Remove the wishbones from the birds to make it easier to carve them (or you can ask your butcher to do this if you prefer). Season the birds inside and out with a little salt, then gently lift the skin of each bird away from the flesh, starting at the neck end, and smear a quarter of the spiced butter between the meat and the skin. Try not to split the skin.

3. Lay the bacon rashers over the breast meat, then tie the bacon in place with kitchen string.

4. Pour the oil into a large flameproof casserole over a medium heat. Lightly fry the birds all over until the bacon browns, then arrange them in the casserole, breast-side down.

5. Pour in the wine and stock, cover with foil, then with the lid and cook on a middle shelf in the oven for 25 minutes.

6. Remove from the oven and remove the lid and foil (keep the foil). Turn the birds breast-side up.

7. Put the casserole back into the oven, uncovered, for 25–30 minutes. The exact cooking time depends on the size of the birds and how you like them cooked. Check to see if they're done by gently tugging the legs; they should move easily when the birds are ready.

## FOR THE BIRDS

**4 oven-ready young guinea fowl**
**Sea salt**
**16 thick slices streaky bacon**
**1 tsp rapeseed oil**
**200ml (7fl oz) dry white wine**
**150ml (5fl oz) chicken stock**
**3 tbsp Armagnac**
**50g (1¾oz) unsalted butter,**
**    cubed and chilled, plus a little**
**    extra at room temperature**
**16 seedless grapes, preferably**
**    peeled (but this isn't**
**    absolutely necessary)**

8. Remove the birds from the casserole, set aside and cover with the reserved foil. Turn up the oven to 220°C (gas mark 8).

9. Strain the cooking juices through a sieve into a jug, skim off any excess fat and set aside.

10. Pour the Armagnac into the casserole and gently heat it, then tip the casserole away from you slightly and carefully light the Armagnac with a match. Once the flames have died away, pour the cooking juices back into the casserole, bring up to a vigorous bubble, add the cold cubed butter, whisk and reduce for a moment.

11. Add the grapes and only just warm them through to make sure you retain the integrity and freshness of the fruit. Check the seasoning, adjust if necessary, then set aside.

12. Remove the trussing string and the bacon from the birds. Put the bacon on a baking tray and put it in the oven for a couple of minutes to crisp, then take it out and set aside.

13. Carve the birds, removing the legs first, then neatly cut the breasts from the carcasses and put in a roasting tin. Cover with greaseproof paper.

14. Put the roasting tin into the hot oven for 2 minutes, then joint the legs, trim the breasts and slice them on the diagonal; serve on warmed plates, with the crisp bacon and the grapes in their sauce.

# Spiced Wood Pigeon, Artichoke, Beetroot & Chicory Salad with Cobnut Dressing

*This salad is all about rich, bold, gamey notes of the pigeon, offset by the perfume of green cardamom, Szechuan pepper and juniper. There are lots of elements – including hot potato fritters, crisp leaves and creamy dressing – but once the prep work is done it's really more about presentation. I like pigeon cooked medium-rare. Give it a go – and don't be afraid of the pink!*

**SERVES 4**

### FOR THE ARTICHOKES
**A splash light olive oil**
**4–6 globe artichoke hearts, each cut into 6 slices, through their poles**
**Juice of ½ orange**
**1 garlic clove, crushed**
**1 pinch sea salt**
**1 small thyme sprig**

### FOR THE BEETROOT
**6–8 beetroots, unpeeled**
**Sea salt**
**½ tsp black peppercorns, finely ground**
**A splash rapeseed oil**

### FOR THE PIGEON
**5 juniper berries**
**½ star anise**
**1 tsp fennel seeds**
**Seeds of 4 green cardamom pods**
**½ tsp Szechuan pepper**
**2 tsp finely ground cassia**
**1 tsp smoked paprika**
**1 thyme sprig, leaves only**

1. Preheat the oven to 180°C (gas mark 4). Put a heavy-based sauté pan over a medium heat. Add a splash of oil, then gently fry the artichoke slices for 2 minutes. Add the orange juice, garlic, salt and thyme, and continue to sweat until just soft. Drain and set aside, discarding the garlic.

2. To prepare the beetroots, spread a thin layer of sea salt over the base of a small roasting tin, put the beetroots on top and roast in the oven for 35–40 minutes until they're just tender. Leave them to cool. Peel and cut them in half through the poles, then cut each half into segments. Pop them into a small bowl, add a touch of salt, the pepper and a drizzle of rapeseed oil. Set aside. Leave the oven on.

3. Finely grind the whole spices for the pigeon using a mortar and pestle. Tip all the spices into a bowl with the thyme and orange zest. Flatten each bacon rasher with the back of a knife while gently stretching it, then slice in half lengthways. Add the pigeon breasts to the spice mixture and roll them around until well coated, then wrap each breast in a piece of bacon, making sure the meat is fully covered.

4. Add a splash of olive oil to a sauté or frying pan and gently fry the pigeon breasts for 1–1½ minutes on each side, then remove and set aside on a large baking tray.

5. To make the potato fritters, coarsely grate the potatoes into a bowl of cold water. Wash and rinse the potatoes thoroughly with running water, then drain well and put into a clean tea towel. Twist and squeeze the towel firmly to remove all the water.

Zest of ½ orange
4 slices dry-cured streaky bacon
8 wood pigeon breasts

## FOR THE POTATO FRITTERS
2 waxy potatoes, such as
    Charlotte, peeled
1 tsp sea salt
1 tsp Quatre Épices blend (see
    page 266)
1 tbsp light olive oil
30g (1oz) unsalted butter

## FOR THE SALAD & DRESSING
100g (3½oz) fresh cobnuts or
    hazelnuts, shelled
3 tbsp rapeseed oil
Seeds of 1 black cardamom pod,
    finely ground
1 tsp Dijon mustard
2 tbsp crème fraîche, plus extra
    if needed
½ tsp sea salt
1 small head white chicory
1 small head radicchio
1 small piece fresh horseradish
    root, peeled

6. Transfer the potato to a bowl, season with the salt and Quatre Épices, and stir to combine. Divide the mixture into eight equal heaps.

7. Put the oil and butter in a non-stick frying pan over a medium heat. Put four potato heaps in the pan and gently press down with a fish slice until they are about 8cm (3¼in) in diameter. Fry for 3–4 minutes on each side until crisp and golden. Drain on kitchen paper and set aside. Repeat with the remaining four potato heaps.

8. For the salad, gently dry-roast half the nuts in a non-stick frying pan over a medium heat until they are just slightly coloured, then set aside.

9. Drop the remaining nuts into a food processor or blender, add the rapeseed oil, black cardamom seeds, mustard, crème fraîche and salt, and blitz to a very smooth paste. (Alternatively, grind everything together well using a mortar and pestle). Pass this paste through a sieve and add a little more crème fraîche to achieve a pleasant dropping consistency.

10. Carefully separate the leaves of the chicory and radicchio.

11. To serve, put the baking tray with the wrapped pigeon breasts into the oven for 2–3 minutes, turning once, then remove, cover loosely with foil, and leave to rest for 3 minutes. Meanwhile, pop the potato fritters into the oven to warm through for 4–5 minutes.

12. Arrange the salad leaves, artichokes and beetroots on four large warmed plates, then drizzle the salad with the dressing and sprinkle with the roasted nuts. Slice the pigeon breasts on the diagonal, arrange them attractively in the salad, then grate a little horseradish finely over each salad. Put two potato fritters next to the pigeon and serve.

# Duck, Pork & Beans with Spiced Crumb

*On trips to France, I used to love buying those jars of cassoulet packed full of beans, various meats and herbs, almost set with duck fat. I came up with this recipe after a little trial and error, using spices to lift the earthy duck and beans and mute the saltiness of the pork. You'll notice I don't add any salt, simply because it doesn't need it with all that pork, but if you have a particularly salty palate, then be my guest!*

**SERVES 4**

1kg (2lb 4oz) salted pork belly
2 pig trotters, split
3 duck legs
2 star anise
2 black cardamom pods
4 green cardamom pods
1 leek, halved
2 carrots, halved
½ head celery, cut into 3 chunks
1 onion, quartered
1 large bunch curly parsley, with stalks
10cm (4in) cassia stick
12 white peppercorns
4 cloves
6 pieces of beef bone marrow, 6–10cm (2½–4in) long (ask your butcher to chop them)

1. Put the pork belly into a large flameproof casserole, cover with cold water, and put over a high heat. Bring to the boil, then reduce the heat and simmer gently for 8–10 minutes. Pour away the water, add the trotters and duck legs, cover with cold water and repeat. Meanwhile, lightly crush the anise and cardamom pods in a mortar and pestle. Set aside.

2. Pour away the water, put the meat in a colander under a tap and rinse well, then put the pork belly and trotters back into the casserole. Add the leek, carrots, celery, onion, parsley, crushed anise and cardamom and all the remaining spices, followed by the duck legs. Cover well with cold water, put over a high heat, cover and bring to the boil. Turn down to a gentle simmer and cook, partially covered, for 2½ hours or until the meats are really tender.

3. Remove from the heat, take out the meats and leave until cool enough to handle. Strain the vegetables through a colander over a bowl to retain the cooking liquor. Discard the vegetables and spices.

4. Once cooled, strip the trotter meat and gelatinous skin from the bones. Shred the meat onto a plate. Keep the bright-looking pieces of fat and skin – but not any hairy bits or bony, grey fat – and dice them finely. Set aside on a separate plate from the shredded meat.

5. Cut away the rind from the pork belly and remove any dull-looking fat, keeping only the bright bits. Roughly cube and shred the belly meat, and add it to the trotter meat. Dice the retained fat and add it to the plate of trotter fat.

## FOR THE BEANS

½ star anise
Seeds of 2 green cardamom pods
3 cloves
2 × 400g (14oz) tins chopped
  tomatoes
1 garlic bulb, halved horizontally
1 thyme sprig, leaves only
400g (14oz) tin haricot beans,
  drained (250g/9oz drained
  weight)

## FOR THE SPICED CRUMB

½ bunch curly parsley, roughly
  chopped, stalks and all
8 garlic cloves
2 tbsp light olive oil
125g (4½oz) coarse fresh
  breadcrumbs
2 tsp Quatre Épices blend (see
  page 266)
2 tbsp goose fat or olive oil

6. Finely grind the spices for the beans using a mortar and pestle. Put the beans in a large saucepan, add the gelatinous skin of the trotter, the diced fat, tomatoes, garlic, thyme leaves and spices.

7. Add 400ml (14fl oz) of the reserved meat cooking liquor, then put over a medium heat, stir and bring to a gentle simmer. Cook for 20–25 minutes until it has reduced by one-third. Take off the heat and set aside.

8. Preheat the oven to 200°C (gas mark 6). To make the crumb, put the parsley and garlic into a food processor and blend to a purée. Add the olive oil, pulse briefly, then pour the paste into a small bowl. (Alternatively use a mortar and pestle.) Add the breadcrumbs, Quatre Épices and goose fat to the bowl and mix everything together with your fingers.

9. Arrange the pork belly chunks and trotter meat in a 30 × 20 × 9cm (12 × 8 × 3½in) gratin dish, or a 26 × 22cm (10½ × 8½in) cast-iron oval casserole.

10. Remove the skin from the duck legs, and cut them in two across the joints. Put them into the dish, then spoon over the beans. Gently sink the bone marrow into the beans and sprinkle the spiced crumb generously over everything.

11. Cook on the middle shelf of the oven for 20–30 minutes until golden and bubbling. Serve while still bubbling, with plenty of Dijon mustard.

FISH

WHEN I THINK OF SPICING fish, MY THOUGHTS TURN fiRST TO ZINGY, UPLIFTING NOTES, PERFUMED HEAT, CITRUS FRESHNESS. But there's a host of spice possibilities to match the wealth of flavours and textures found in white fish, oily fish such as salmon, tuna and mackerel, and smoked fish. Sweet, delicate sea-fresh white fish needs a light touch, with attention to the high notes, to heighten its flavour without overpowering. The darker, more pronounced flavours of the oily fish work well with the gnarled nuttiness of mustard seeds, the sweet-sourness of tamarind, the pungency of pepper.

For white fish I often use the perfumed notes of cardamom, nutmeg, star anise, long pepper. My Crisp Haddock Cobbler, with its rich sauce and scone topping, needs the slightly more robust but nonetheless fragrant spices in my Garam Masala. Ceviche has chilli heat and a citrus bite, with cumin to help ground and pull back the acidic notes of the citrus fruits.

When it comes to oily fish, the gloves are off as far as subtlety goes! Tamarind, chilli, mustard and ginger perk up the Mackerel Skewers, creating a touch of the exotic and wonderful balance. In my Crammed Beach Fish, I use Garam Masala in the accompanying Aïoli, preferring a fragrant ras el hanout blend and plenty of fresh herbs to help cut the richness of the fish.

In the Bengal Fry-Up, I've combined smoked haddock with the beautiful Bengali Panch Phoron blend. Panch translates from Hindi as 'five' and Phoron as flavour or spice: it's the Indian five-spice blend, often used with fish and seafood. The nutty heat of the mustard seeds, subtle nutty pepperiness of kalonji, earthiness of cumin, bittersweet fenugreek and sweet anise of the fennel seeds, cajole and caress the smoky fish to flavour perfection.

*Previous page: Aji lemon chillies have the most amazing pineapple-citrus flavour, a good level of heat and beautiful colour.*

# PARSNIP & SALT COD CHOWDER

*Salt cod and parsnips used to be considered poor man's food. I've devised this velvety smooth, creamy spiced soup to showcase both ingredients because, regardless of status, they work so well together.*

**SERVES 4–6**

**250g (9oz) salt cod fillet**

### FOR THE SPICE BLEND
**1 tsp black peppercorns**
**5 cloves**
**2 tsp coriander seeds**
**1 tsp cumin seeds**
**Seeds of 3 green cardamom pods**
**1 tsp powdered turmeric**
**2 tsp finely ground cassia**

### FOR THE VEGETABLES
**100ml (3½fl oz) rapeseed oil**
**3 tbsp light olive oil**
**1 shallot, diced**
**½ garlic clove, crushed**
**175g (6oz) floury potatoes, such as Maris Piper, peeled and diced**
**700g (1lb 9oz) young parsnips (no woody hearts), peeled and cut into 5mm (¼in) slices**
**150ml (5fl oz) whole milk, plus extra if needed**
**100ml (3½fl oz) single cream**

### FOR THE GARNISH
**3 tbsp Greek yogurt**
**1 spring onion, thinly sliced**
**3 plain papads (poppadoms), cooked according to the pack instructions, cracked into interestingly shaped shards**

1. Soak the salt cod in cold water for 12 hours, changing the water once. Rinse the fish under cold running water. Put 500ml (18floz) water in a saucepan over a medium heat, bring to the boil, add the fish and poach it very gently for 20–30 minutes until cooked though.

2. Meanwhile, prepare the spice blend. Finely grind the peppercorns, cloves, coriander, cumin and cardamom seeds in a mortar and pestle. Add the turmeric and cassia. Set aside.

3. Using a slotted spoon, lift out the fish, then carefully remove the skin and bones and gently break apart into generous-sized flakes. Set aside. Strain the cooking liquor through a fine sieve, reserving 400ml (14fl oz).

4. Put the rapeseed oil in a small saucepan and add one-third of the spice blend. Cook over a medium heat for 2–3 minutes until the oil is just warm. Remove from the heat and leave to cool. Strain through muslin into a bowl (do not be tempted to squeeze the cloth). Set aside.

5. Put the olive oil in a large saucepan over a medium heat. Add the shallot, garlic, potatoes and parsnips, then partly cover and fry gently for 15 minutes until they're just soft, stirring from time to time. Add the remaining spice blend and cook for another 1 minute. Add the reserved cooking liquor and 400ml (14fl oz) water, increase the heat and bring to the boil. Reduce the heat and cook gently, covered, for 15–20 minutes until the potatoes and parsnips are completely soft. Blitz in a food processor until really smooth, then pass through a fine sieve and pour back into the saucepan. Put the pan over a medium heat, add the salt cod flakes, milk and cream, and bring to a gentle simmer for 3–4 minutes to heat through.

6. Add the yogurt, stir well, then check the seasoning. Adjust the consistency, if necessary, by adding a little water or milk. Ladle the chowder into deep warmed bowls. Drizzle with the spiced oil and sprinkle with spring onion. Serve with a plate of papad shards for your guests to add at will.

# CRISP HADDOCK COBBLER

*Soft-fleshed fish, perfumed cobbler scones, creamy sauce and crispy, spiced topping... what's not to like? I've kept the flavours simple here, turning the spotlight on the topping so that the beautiful, multi-layered Garam Masala shines through and doesn't confuse. There's a generous amount of sauce, so you may need to pop a tray under the baking dish to save your oven from bubbling spillages.*

**SERVES 4–6**

**1kg (2lb 4oz) haddock, skinned and cut into 3cm (1¼in) dice**
**425ml (¾ pint) whole milk**
**1 pinch sea salt**
**Ground black pepper**

FOR THE SAUCE
**35g (1¼oz) unsalted butter, at room temperature**
**30g (1oz) plain flour**
**125ml (4fl oz) single cream**
**2 heaped tsp Dijon mustard**
**½ tsp sea salt**
**1 large handful curly parsley, no thick stalks, finely chopped**

1. Preheat the oven to 220°C (gas mark 7). Put the fish in a saucepan, and cover with the milk. Add the salt and pepper to taste and put over a medium heat. Bring up to a bubble, then poach gently for 5 minutes. Take off the heat, remove the fish pieces from the milk with a slotted spoon and set aside to cool. Reserve the cooking liquor.

2. For the sauce, put a large saucepan over a medium heat, add the butter and allow to melt. Add the flour and whisk to form a roux, then cook for 30 seconds.

3. Pour 400ml (14fl oz) of the reserved cooking liquor and the cream into a jug, then pour it bit by bit into the pan, whisking all the time to combine well with the roux. Once all the liquid has been added, keep whisking and allow the sauce to cook until you see the first bubbles appear, then continue to cook for another 2 minutes.

4. Next, add the mustard and salt, and stir well to combine. Cook gently for 5 minutes, with only the odd bubble or two popping up, stirring occasionally. Add the parsley, stir, then cover the surface with greaseproof paper and set aside.

5. Lay the fish in a 30 × 25 × 4.5cm (12 × 10 × 1¾in) roasting tin or ovenproof dish. Pour in the sauce, coating the fish. Set aside to cool completely.

## FOR THE TOPPING

**50g (1¾oz) fresh breadcrumbs**
**1 tbsp olive oil**
**30g (1oz) Parmesan cheese,**
 **finely grated**
**½ tsp cayenne pepper**

## FOR THE COBBLER SCONES

**200g (7oz) plain flour**
**30g (1oz) cornflour**
**3 tsp baking powder**
**½ tsp sea salt**
**2 tsp Garam Masala blend (see**
 **page 267)**
**150g (5½oz) unsalted butter,**
 **cubed and chilled**
**150–175ml (5–6fl oz) whole**
 **milk**

6. Put all the topping ingredients in a bowl and mix well. Set aside.

7. To make the cobbler scones, sift the flours and baking powder into a mixing bowl. Add the salt and Garam Masala and stir to combine. Rub the chilled butter into the flour with your fingertips until it looks like breadcrumbs. Then, using a fork to stir, pour in a little milk at a time until you have a batter with a thick dropping consistency (like fruit cake batter).

8. Drop random blobs of the scone mixture over the fish, then pop the tin or dish into a large roasting tin to catch any bubbling sauce that overflows as it cooks. Cook on a high shelf in the oven for 15 minutes or until the topping has risen.

9. Pull the tin out of the oven slightly, scatter the surface with the crumb topping, then put the tin onto a middle shelf and continue to bake for 12–15 minutes until the crumbs are golden brown and the sauce bubbles up through the cobblers. Serve with some fresh, crisp leaves.

# CEVICHE & CORN

*I have loved ceviche, especially this Peruvian version, ever since my younger brother and his wife returned from their South American honeymoon and introduced me to this zingy classic – small pieces of delicate fish marinated with aji chillies, lime and onion, served with corn. My brother now grows these chillies, so we can enjoy their lemony, pineapple-type perfume.*

**SERVES 4**

1 red onion, finely sliced into rings
350g (12oz) sea bass fillet

## FOR THE FENNEL SALAD

1 fennel bulb, with lots of green,
     feathery fronds
Juice of ½ orange
Juice of ½ lemon
1 tsp sea salt
¼ tsp amchoor (optional)

## FOR THE CEVICHE MIX

½ tsp each black peppercorns,
     white peppercorns, coriander
     seeds, cumin seeds
¼ tsp Szechuan pepper
1–2 gratings nutmeg
1 tsp sea salt
2 fresh aji lemon chillies (or
     1 tsp aji paste or 1 Scotch
     bonnet chilli), deseeded and
     finely chopped
Juice of 3 limes and ½ orange

## FOR THE CORN

100g (3½oz) unsalted butter
1 tsp cumin seeds
2 tsp ground black pepper
1 tsp chilli flakes
1 tsp sea salt
2 sweetcorn cobs, halved

1. To make the salad, trim the ends of the fennel bulb, reserving the fronds. Shave the bulb thinly lengthways on a mandolin or use a sharp knife to slice it as thinly as you can. Put the shavings in a large glass bowl, add the orange and lemon juices and sprinkle in the sea salt and amchoor powder, if using. Gently mix everything together, then cover with clingfilm and chill in the fridge.

2. Put the red onion slices into a bowl of cold water for 5 minutes, then remove them, shake them and put them onto kitchen paper to dry. Set aside.

3. To make the ceviche mix, finely grind the peppercorns, coriander and cumin seeds and the Szechuan pepper in a mortar and pestle, then mix in the nutmeg and salt. Finely chop the reserved fennel fronds and add to the mix, together with the chillies.

4. Remove the skin and oily, dark flesh from the fish. Put the fish on a plate and coat with a generous layer of the ceviche mix. Leave to stand for 1 minute, then add the lime and orange juices and set aside for 15 minutes.

5. To cook the sweetcorn, first preheat the grill. Mix the butter with the spices and salt and spread over the corn. Put the corn into a grill pan and grill for 10 minutes or until slightly charred all over.

6. To serve, put the corn on a serving plate and spoon the buttery juices from the grill pan over it. Gently squeeze the fennel salad to remove the excess dressing, then put it on a serving plate. Arrange the onion rings on a third plate. Slice the fish as thinly as possible, then gently scoop up the fish and pop it on the onion. Serve with a shot glass of the ceviche marinade, the *leche de tigre* (tiger's milk) for those who dare!

# SALMON, POTATO & FENNEL FISHCAKES WITH ORANGE, FENNEL & RED ONION SALAD

*Earthy potatoes, sweet, moist salmon invigorated with hits of anise-perfumed fennel. Floral, sour capers, bites of fragrant crunch, celery and shallot… These fishcakes have a fresh, palate-pleasing lightness, especially when served with a simple salad. Here snap-crunchy fennel bulb combines with the cool, sweet acidity of ripe, juicy orange.*

**SERVES 4**

### FOR THE FISHCAKES
**350–400g (12–14oz) floury potatoes, such as Rooster or Maris Piper, unpeeled**
**A splash olive oil**
**¼ fennel bulb, finely chopped**
**½ celery stick, finely chopped**
**2 shallots, finely chopped**
**3 tsp fennel seeds, coarsely ground**
**2 tsp black peppercorns, coarsely ground**
**1 tsp sea salt**
**750g (1lb 10oz) salmon fillet, skinned**
**2 spring onions, finely sliced on the diagonal**
**3 fennel bulb-top fronds, chopped**
**2 tsp baby capers, drained**
**1 medium egg, lightly beaten, plus extra if needed**
**50g (1¾oz) fresh breadcrumbs, plus extra if needed**

1. Preheat the oven to 190°C (gas mark 5). Put the potatoes in a saucepan and cover generously with water. Bring to the boil and cook for 20 minutes or until tender. Drain and peel, then put back in the pan and smash with a potato masher. Meanwhile, heat 1 tablespoon oil in a frying pan over a medium heat and add the fennel, celery and shallots. Cook for 8–10 minutes until just soft but still a little crunchy. Set aside.

2. Put a square of greaseproof paper, a little larger than the piece of fish, in a sturdy roasting tin. Give the paper square a random drizzle of olive oil, then sprinkle over half the fennel seeds, peppercorns and salt. Lay the salmon on top of the spices.

3. Sprinkle the fish with a little more oil, then with the remaining salt and spices. Put the tin on the middle shelf of the oven and bake for 8 minutes. Remove the fish from the oven and set aside to cool to room temperature, then gently flake the fish into generous pieces and set aside.

4. In a large bowl, gently mix together the mashed potatoes, the cooked vegetables, spring onions, fennel fronds, capers, egg and breadcrumbs. Check the seasoning and adjust if necessary. Add the salmon, taking care not to overwork the mixture. It should be just moist but not wet. If necessary, adjust the consistency with more egg or breadcrumbs.

## FOR COATING AND FRYING

**3–4 tbsp plain flour**
**4 medium eggs, lightly beaten**
**with ¼ tsp sea salt**
**200g (7oz) dried breadcrumbs**
**Sunflower oil, for shallow-frying**

5. Generously fill an 8–10cm (3¼–4in) diameter ring mould with salmon mixture so that it's compact but not squashed. Turn it over and the cake should drop out. (Alternatively, use a greased teacup. Fill the cup half-full with salmon mixture, press it down gently, turn the cup over and shake the cup; the fishcake should drop out. Tidy it up with a knife.) Repeat to make seven more fishcakes. Rest the fishcakes in the fridge for 30 minutes to firm up.

6. Dredge the fishcakes lightly in flour, then coat them in the beaten egg, then in the breadcrumbs. Repeat the process, then rest the cakes in the fridge until needed.

7. When ready to serve, preheat the oven to 200°C (gas mark 6). Shallow-fry the fishcakes until lightly golden on both sides, then transfer to a baking tray and cook in the oven for 5 minutes. Drain on kitchen paper.

## FOR THE SALAD

**1 fennel bulb, with lots of green,**
**feathery fronds**
**2 red onions**
**2 oranges**

## FOR THE DRESSING

**2 tbsp balsamic vinegar**
**Sea salt and finely ground white**
**pepper**
**6 tbsp fruity olive oil**

1. To make the salad, put some of the fennel fronds to one side. Finely slice the fennel bulb lengthways; this is best done using a mandolin if you have one – just be really careful of your fingertips!

2. Put the slices of fennel into ice-cold water to crisp up. Slice the onions in the same way.

3. Using a small sharp knife, and a bowl to catch the juice, cut a thin slice from the top and bottom of an orange, then slice off its skin and all the pith. Cut the segments neatly away from the membrane. Remove any pips and discard. Repeat with the other orange.

4. To make the dressing, dissolve a little salt in the vinegar, add a little pepper, 2 tablespoons of the reserved orange juice and the olive oil, and whisk until it emulsifies. Taste and adjust the seasoning.

5. In a large bowl, toss all the salad ingredients together with the dressing, taking care not to damage the orange segments.

6. To serve, put a fishcake or two on each plate and gently pile the fennel salad alongside. Chop the reserved fennel fronds and sprinkle them over the top.

# ROAST HERBED SALMON WITH CARDAMOM SAUCE

*I use green cardamom in this recipe to cut through the rich fish and creamy sauce, while at the same time adding a gentle perfume to brighten up the whole, delicious experience.*

**SERVES 4**

4 × 175g (6oz) centre-cut
  salmon fillets, nice and thick
  and evenly sized
Dijon mustard, for brushing
Sea salt

### FOR THE CRUST
A little light olive oil
40g (1½oz) shallots, finely diced
1 garlic clove, finely diced
40g (1½oz) fresh breadcrumbs
15g (½oz) Parmesan cheese,
  grated
2 tbsp black peppercorns, finely
  ground
50g (1¾oz) soft herbs, a mix
  of parsley, chives, dill and
  chervil, finely chopped

### FOR THE SAUCE
6 green cardamom pods
100ml (3½fl oz) double cream
200ml (7fl oz) chicken stock
50g (1¾oz) unsalted butter,
  cubed and chilled
½ tsp white peppercorns, finely
  ground

1. Preheat the oven to 200°C (gas mark 6). Put a little olive oil in a sauté pan over a medium heat and cook the shallots for 3 minutes or until they become translucent. Add the garlic, breadcrumbs and a little more olive oil so that the crumbs are moist but not wet. Cook gently for 2 minutes until golden brown. Remove from the heat, then tip into a bowl to cool. Add the Parmesan, 1 teaspoon of the black pepper and the herbs, and mix well.

2. Put the fish fillets on a plate, skin-side down. Season with a pinch of salt and 1 teaspoon of the black pepper, brush with a little Dijon mustard, then apply the breadcrumb crust until about 5mm (¼in) thick, gently pressing the edges with a palette knife so that they're even, tidy and tight. (Any leftover herb crust can be frozen for another day.)

3. Put a sheet of greaseproof paper on a baking tray. Brush it with a little olive oil, season with sea salt and 2 teaspoons of the black pepper and put the fillets on it so that they are evenly spaced. Cook on the middle shelf of the oven for 8 minutes or until the crust is only just golden.

4. Meanwhile, prepare the sauce. Gently smash four of the cardamom pods. Put the cream and smashed cardamom pods in a small pan over a medium heat and bring to a gentle bubble. Cook for 2 minutes, then take off the heat and leave to cool. Strain through a sieve. Remove the seeds from the other two pods and grind to a fine powder.

5. Pour the chicken stock into a saucepan, bring to the boil, then turn down the heat and simmer to reduce by half. Add the strained cream and bring to a simmer. Whisking constantly, add the cold butter and bring to a brisk boil. As the sauce starts to thicken, whisk in the white pepper and check the seasoning. Serve the salmon fillets on warmed plates, with the sauce drizzled around the fillets, sprinkled with the cardamom powder.

# Seven-Pepper Tuna with Chickpea Chips

*This is a beautiful, and healthy, recipe. Tuna has a lovely firm texture, the aubergine adds smokiness and a creamy texture and the chickpea chips, influenced by southern French cuisine, are crunchy and add a subtle sweetness to the whole wonderful eating experience. Sashimi-grade tuna is best for this recipe: it should be bright red with a firm flesh. But you could also use four tuna steaks, as long as the steaks are quite thick so that the meat remains rare after searing.*

## SERVES 4

### FOR THE CHICKPEA CHIPS
**200g (7oz) gram (chickpea) flour**
**2 tsp sea salt**
**1 tsp fenugreek seeds, finely ground**
**½ tsp fennel seeds, finely ground**
**½ tsp rosemary leaves, finely chopped**
**Sunflower oil, for deep-frying**

### FOR THE SMOKED AUBERGINE
**2 firm aubergines**
**2 tsp coriander seeds**
**1 tsp cumin seeds**
**1 tsp black peppercorns**
**A splash light olive oil**
**2 garlic cloves, crushed**
**1 tsp Kashmiri chilli flakes**
**1 tsp sea salt**

1. Preheat the oven to 180°C (gas mark 4). To make the chickpea chips, put all the ingredients, except the oil, in a bowl and add 300ml (10fl oz) hand-hot water. Mix well, then put in the fridge and chill for 10 minutes.

2. Line a 20cm (8in) square baking tray with greaseproof paper. Pour the batter evenly into the tray and bake for 20–25 minutes until the mixture is cooked and set. Leave to cool, then remove from the tray and put it in the fridge to chill.

3. When cold, cut into chips about 1cm (½in) wide and 10cm (4in) long. Put back into the fridge until you are ready to fry them.

4. To make the smoked aubergine, insert a metal skewer through each aubergine so that you can turn them easily, prick them with a fork, then put them over the open flame of a gas hob or under a preheated hot grill until charred. Cut each one in half, remove the flesh and roughly chop it. Discard the skins.

5. Finely grind the coriander and cumin seeds and peppercorns using a mortar and pestle. Set aside.

6. Heat the olive oil in a frying pan over a medium heat. Add the garlic, all the spices, the salt and chopped aubergines, and fry gently until the mix is nicely soft, then mash gently and set aside to cool.

## FOR THE PEPPER CRUST

**2 tsp black peppercorns**
**1 tsp white peppercorns**
**½ tsp green peppercorns**
**½ tsp cubeb pepper**
**½ tsp Szechuan pepper**
**¼ tsp finely grated long pepper**
**¼ tsp finely ground allspice**
**    (Jamaican pepper)**
**1 tsp sea salt**

## FOR THE TUNA

**1 tbsp olive oil**
**500g (1lb 2oz) yellow-fin tuna**
**    loin, at room temperature**

7. To make the pepper crust, coarsely grind the black, white and green peppercorns with the cubeb and Szechuan peppers using a mortar and pestle. Add the long pepper, allspice and sea salt and mix well.

8. Rub the olive oil over the tuna, then roll it evenly, using a little pressure, in the pepper mix so that it has a nice crust all over.

9. Put a griddle pan over a high heat until it's very hot, then sear the tuna on all sides for about 30–45 seconds on each side. Don't overcook the beautiful tuna, or it will go grey, become solid and taste like cardboard.

10. To fry the chickpea chips, heat the sunflower oil in an electric deep-fat fryer set to 170°C. (Or fill a large saucepan one-third full of oil and put it over a medium heat. After about 4–5 minutes drop a piece of white bread into the oil; if it takes 3 seconds to turn golden brown, it's the right heat. If not, adjust the heat accordingly.). Fry the chickpea chips for 2 minutes or until they crisp up. Drain on kitchen paper.

11. To serve, slice the tuna into four steaks. Serve with the hot chickpea chips and the cool smoked aubergine. My Sizzled Tomatoes (see page 182) also go well with this recipe.

# Lemongrass & Tamarind Mackerel Skewers with Tomato Chilli Relish

*I was given this idea by a friend of mine, a brilliant chef called Vivek Singh. It works perfectly on the barbecue, under a grill or in the oven and is guaranteed to bring a real 'wow factor' to fresh mackerel.*

**SERVES 4**

4 whole mackerel, scaled, gutted
    and fins removed
4 long lemongrass stalks

FOR THE PASTE
5 dried Kashmiri chillies
2 tsp fennel seeds
1 heaped tsp powdered turmeric
1 tsp black mustard seeds
1 onion, roughly chopped
4 garlic cloves
40g (1½oz) fresh ginger
1 green chilli
10 curry leaves, fresh or dried
2 tbsp thick, black Indian
    tamarind paste
4 tbsp sunflower oil
1 tsp sea salt
1 tsp golden caster sugar

FOR THE RELISH
400g (14oz) tin chopped
    tomatoes
½ green bird's eye chilli,
    deseeded and diced
½ tsp sea salt
1 tsp golden caster sugar

1. Put the Kashmiri chillies for the paste into warm water to soak for 20 minutes while you prepare the fish. Using a sharp knife, carefully score both sides of each fish to create three short, diagonal cuts on each side. With the back of a chopping knife, splat or bruise the lemongrass stalks slightly and insert one into the mouth of each fish, leaving about 5cm (2in) or so sticking out for good effect.

2. Drain the Kashmiri chillies and pat dry. Grind the fennel seeds using a mortar and pestle. Add the turmeric and mustard seeds and mix well. Put these and the other paste ingredients into a food processor and blitz to a thick, fragrant paste. (If you don't have a food processor, grate the onion, garlic and ginger, and chop the chillies and curry leaves finely. Then add the ingredients to a small bowl and stir well to combine.) Remove the paste from the bowl and divide into three equal parts. Set aside.

3. Use two-thirds of the paste to coat the fish on both sides. Set aside for 20 minutes. Preheat the oven to 180 °C (gas mark 4). Put the coated fish onto a baking tray, put in the oven and bake for 6 minutes. Turn the fish over, then bake for another 6–8 minutes until cooked through.

4. To make the relish, put the remaining third of the spicy paste into a saucepan over a medium heat, stirring frequently. As the paste begins to sizzle, allow it to cook for 1 minute or so, stirring frequently, then add the tomatoes, chilli, salt and sugar, then stir again. Allow it to reduce to a soft dropping consistency, then set aside.

5. Serve each fish with a large dollop of the tomato relish on the side. A green salad and a baked potato make simple accompaniments.

# CRAMMED BEACH FISH

*These fish are not just stuffed, they are crammed full of flavour, texture and pure spice in a wonderful, easy-to-make dish. The key to success is to use only the freshest of fish. The breadcrumb stuffing has a touch of garlic and vibrant spices, with a little citrus fruit to add balance and freshness. Ideally, use Japanese panko breadcrumbs, but other crisp dried breadcrumbs will do at a pinch.*

**SERVES 4**

**8 sardines or 4 mackerel, cleaned and filleted (see Tip)**

### FOR THE STUFFING
**4 tbsp olive oil, plus extra for grilling**
**75g (2¾oz) baby spinach**
**50g (1¾oz) shallots, finely chopped**
**75g (2¾oz) panko (dried) breadcrumbs**
**1 garlic clove, crushed**
**¼ tsp grated nutmeg**
**½ tsp finely ground star anise**
**Zest and juice of ½ orange**
**Sea salt and finely ground black pepper**

### FOR THE SPICED AÏOLI
**2 medium egg yolks**
**2 fat garlic cloves, crushed**
**Sea salt**
**300–450ml (10–16fl oz) fruity olive oil**
**Juice of at least 1 lemon**
**1 tsp Garam Masala blend (see page 267)**
**Zest of ½ lemon**

1. First, prepare the stuffing. Put a small pan over a medium heat, add 1 tablespoon olive oil and the spinach. Cook for 30 seconds, then remove the pan from the heat, leave the spinach to cool and then chop it finely.

2. Combine the spinach and the remaining stuffing ingredients in a bowl and mix gently. Check and adjust the seasoning, then stuff the sardines evenly, being careful not to overfill the fish. Set aside.

3. Preheat the barbecue or grill to medium–hot. Rub a little oil over the fish and grill or barbecue for 1 minute on each side. You want to char the skin nicely, without burning.

4. If you're using a barbecue, move the fish to a tray and put the tray on the barbecue. Cover the tray with a large lid and leave to cook and smoke for no more than 3 minutes – the flesh should be just cooked. If you are using a grill, continue cooking until just cooked through. Serve on a large wooden board or tray, with the salad, tabbouleh and aïoli.

1. In a bowl, lightly whisk the egg yolks with the crushed garlic and a little salt until thick.

2. Pour in the olive oil in a thin stream, whisking continuously. Add a little of the lemon juice and some more oil, and continue beating, adding alternately more lemon juice and oil until you have a thick mayonnaise.

3. Adjust the salt to taste. Add the Garam Masala and the lemon zest, mix well and set aside.

[ *Continued* ]

## FOR THE TABBOULEH

500g (1lb 2oz) fine couscous
1 tbsp olive oil, plus extra
    to drizzle
2 red onions, finely chopped
½ garlic clove, crushed
200g (7oz) tin chickpeas,
    drained and rinsed
    (125g/4½oz drained weight
1 tbsp ras el hanout (see page
    266)
Juice of ½ orange
1 large handful each of flat-leaf
    parsley, coriander and mint,
    all finely chopped
Sea salt and finely ground black
    pepper

1. Put the couscous in a heatproof bowl. Heat 1 tablespoon oil in a heavy-based frying pan over a medium–low heat and cook the red onions and garlic gently until soft.

2. Add the drained chickpeas and the ras el hanout. Continue frying gently for 1 minute, then pour in the quantity of boiling water specified on the couscous pack to make a delicious spicy stock. Immediately pour the boiling stock over the couscous and quickly fork through to mix.

3. Cover with clingfilm and allow to steam for 10 minutes, then fluff up with a fork, add a generous drizzle of olive oil and the orange juice. Check and adjust the seasoning if necessary.

4. Finally, when you're ready to serve, add the herbs.

---

## FOR THE VINAIGRETTE

1 garlic clove, halved
1 heaped tbsp Dijon mustard
150ml (5fl oz) grapeseed
    or sunflower oil
3 tbsp fruity olive oil
1 tsp good-quality white wine
    vinegar
½ tsp golden caster sugar
Fine sea salt and finely ground
    black pepper

## FOR THE GARDEN SALAD

1 head butter lettuce
1 large bunch chives, tarragon
    and chervil leaves

1. To make the vinaigrette, rub the inside of a large screwtop jar firmly with the cut edge of the garlic clove.

2. Add all the vinaigrette ingredients, then pour in 50ml (2fl oz) boiling water (the water goes in last to prevent the jar from cracking).

3. Screw the lid on tightly and shake vigorously until it emulsifies – a minute or so should do it.

4. Put the lettuce leaves in a serving bowl. Spoon the dressing generously over the leaves, then scatter the herbs over the top.

Tip

*To fillet the fish, chop off the fish's head neatly and slightly on the diagonal, then put the fish on a board, belly-side down, and press gently along the spine. Turn the fish so the belly-side is facing up and gently ease the spine, with the ribs attached, away from the flesh. Snip it off with scissors just before the tail, leaving the tail in place.*

# Bengal Fry-Up

*Eastern and Western influences come together to make a perfect brunch or breakfast treat, inspired by kedgeree. Its heart is a generous slice of lightly poached smoked haddock, in a wilted salad of spring onions and meaty braised shiitake, all topped with the luxury of a slow-fried free-range duck egg.*

**SERVES 4**

2 bunches spring onions, trimmed and halved to about 7.5cm (3in) long
Sea salt
85g (3oz) unsalted butter
Light olive oil, for frying and greasing
200g (7oz) fresh shiitake mushrooms, sliced 5mm (¼in) thick
2 tsp Panch Phoron blend (see page 266)
1 garlic clove
2 lemon thyme sprigs, leaves only
4 × 125g (4½oz) centre-cut, naturally smoked haddock fillets, at room temperature
4 duck eggs

1. Put a saucepan over a medium heat and add the spring onions, 2 tablespoons water, a pinch of salt and 20g (¾oz) of the butter. Cook until they're just soft, then set aside.

2. Heat 1 tablespoon oil in a large non-stick frying pan, add the mushrooms, Panch Phoron, garlic and thyme, and heat gently for 25 minutes or until the mushrooms soften slightly and (most importantly) give off some of their succulent juices. Add the wilted spring onions. Stir well, but gently, then set aside to allow the flavours to mingle. Keep warm.

3. Preheat the oven to 200°C (gas mark 6). Lay a sheet of greaseproof paper on a baking tray and lightly grease it. Put the haddock fillets on top, put a knob of butter on top of each, then put the tray in the oven for 7–10 minutes until the fish is just cooked but still very slightly translucent.

4. Put a large knob of butter (about 1 tablespoon) in each of two small non-stick frying pans (or one large one), add a splash of light olive oil and put over a low heat. Carefully break two eggs into each pan, trying to keep the yolks intact. Season with a little sea salt, then very, very gently fry the eggs until the whites are just set and the yolks are golden, rich and runny – about 6–8 minutes.

5. Using a slotted spoon, divide the mushrooms and spring onions among four warmed plates, and drizzle the succulent cooking juices evenly around them. Put a haddock fillet on top of each mound, followed by a fried duck egg. I like to spoon a little of the haddock cooking juices over the top. Enjoy with some crusty, buttered white sourdough toast.

# Shellfish & Squid

SEA-FRESH SWEET flESH – WITH ATTITUDE! THE CRAB'S CLAWS, THE MUSSEL'S TIGHTLY SHUT SHELL, THE LIGHTNING SPEED OF A SQUID. I think of clean heat, delicate yet distinct perfume, astringent warmth, all the peppery flavours: black, cayenne, white and Szechuan to get some real intrigue going. Freshness is important here – fresh pepper, freshly ground or cracked – as the high note perfume is what it's all about and is what works so well with citrus and chilli.

Shellfish sometimes need coaxing out of their shells with earthy, floral and peppery tones. My Crab Cakes use turmeric for earthiness, saffron and mace provide floral perfume, while white peppercorns, Szechuan and cayenne pepper and carom bring peppery notes aplenty. The fresh chillies, shallots and herbs add freshness and the pickle accompaniment contributes a sweet tang.

I adore squid and mussels, the sweet meat, soft flesh with just a touch of resistance as you bite into it, crying out for flavour. Mouclade is a traditional mussel dish from the Vendée region of France. In this region, mussels are harvested and cream produced – and in days gone by, spices were traded. My version uses a fragrant south Indian blend of spices. I spent a fantastic summer there on the Atlantic Coast, and I discovered that the perfect accompaniment to the mild curry spice, cream and sweet mussel flesh is a glass of chilled Pineau des Charentes, another local speciality.

Squid, at first sight, appear quite docile beasts, but when they strike they do so with speed and unnerving accuracy. The spicing for these cephalopods needs to reflect this side to their character, as well as bring delicate perfume. My Italian-inspired Old-School Squid Salad combines black pepper with nutmeg and Kashmiri chillies, spiked with lemony coriander, fresh mint and saffron aïoli.

*Previous page: Kashmiri chillies offer subtle fruity flavour with a hint of smoky edge, gentle but definitive heat and ruddy red beauty.*

# CRAB CAKES WITH PICKLE

## FOR THE PICKLE

150g (5½oz) small onions, very
    thinly sliced
150g (5½oz) golden caster
    sugar
1 tsp sea salt
1 tsp powdered turmeric
100ml (3½fl oz) cider vinegar
400g (14oz) cucumber, very
    thinly sliced

## FOR THE CRAB CAKES

1 small pinch saffron threads
1 tbsp lemon juice
20g (¾oz) unsalted butter
1 small leek, finely diced
1 tsp white peppercorns
½ tsp Szechuan pepper
2 tsp coriander seeds
900g (2lb) fresh white crabmeat
1 tbsp finely chopped tarragon
    leaves
1 small handful fresh chives,
    thinly sliced
Zest of ½ lemon
Scant ¼ tsp finely ground mace
½ tsp cayenne pepper
½ tsp carom seeds
1 green finger chilli, deseeded
    and finely diced
2 shallots, finely diced
2 tsp sea salt

## FOR BINDING & FRYING

3 medium eggs, lightly beaten
150g (5½oz) fresh breadcrumbs
1 knob unsalted butter
Sunflower oil, for frying

*These cakes are light, meaty and fresh-tasting, with no potato to make them stodgy. The cucumber and turmeric pickle is simple, but it adds another flavour dimension.*

1. In a large bowl, mix all the pickle ingredients together, except the cucumber, until the salt and sugar have dissolved, then fold in the cucumber slices. Cover the bowl with clingfilm and set aside in the fridge for at least 4 hours.

2. For the crab cakes, put the saffron in a small bowl and add the lemon juice. Heat the butter in a frying pan over a medium heat and gently fry the leek until just soft, but not coloured, then remove from the heat. Add the saffron and lemon juice. Set aside to cool.

3. Line a baking tray with greaseproof paper. Finely grind the peppercorns, Szechuan pepper and coriander seeds using a mortar and pestle. Put all the crab cake ingredients, including the leek and saffron mixture, in a mixing bowl and gently fold to combine. Add the eggs for binding and fold to combine. Add the breadcrumbs, a little at a time, until the mixture is just stiff enough to hold its shape. Form the mixture into golf-ball-sized cakes, put each one on the lined tray and gently press to flatten slightly. Preheat the oven to 170°C (gas mark 3).

4. Put the butter and a little oil in a large frying pan over a medium heat. Lightly fry the crab cakes on both sides, in batches. These have a delicate texture so you'll need a gentle touch as you cook them. Set aside.

5. Pop the crab cakes onto a baking tray and warm through in the oven for 5 minutes. Take the pickle from the fridge and give it a gentle stir. Serve the crab cakes immediately, with a forkful of the pickle.

# BENGALI GRILLED SEAFOOD WITH CRISP OKRA

*This makes a brilliant starter for a posh dinner party. It's a bit of a showstopper, with its beautiful colours, textures and spices. I first made it when I was (apparently) showing people 'how to be fabulous' at home by making a supper for a well-known Irish crystal company. Fab demos aside, this is a seafood dish that rocks!*

**SERVES 4 AS A STARTER**

FOR THE CHILLI OIL
DRESSING
**10g (¼oz) Kashmiri chilli flakes**
**100ml (3½fl oz) grapeseed oil**
**½ garlic bulb**

1. Put the chilli flakes in a bowl and pour over boiling water to cover. Wait for 5 minutes, then squeeze and pat dry with kitchen paper.

2. Put the softened chilli flakes, oil and garlic in a small saucepan and warm through over a very low heat for 5 minutes.

3. Leave to infuse for at least 24 hours in the fridge, then strain through a fine sieve or muslin.

**8 raw king prawns, shell on, deveined**
**150g (5½oz) baby squid, cleaned and sliced, tentacles left whole**
**1 green bird's eye chilli, deseeded and roughly chopped**
**2 tsp Panch Phoron blend (see page 266)**
**Generous splash grapeseed oil**
**300g (10½oz) live mussels, scrubbed and de-bearded**
**Sea salt and freshly ground black pepper**

1. Put the prawns and squid in a bowl with the chilli and Panch Phoron blend, mix together, then toss together with the grapeseed oil. Leave for 10 minutes to marinate.

2. Heat a griddle pan until very hot, shake some of the oil off the prawns, then pop them onto the griddle and sear for no more than 2–3 minutes on each side. Remove from the heat and set aside.

3. Discard any mussels that do not close when the shell is tapped. Put the mussels on the griddle. They're ready when the shells open. Remove from the heat and set aside. Discard any mussels that remain closed.

4. Wipe the griddle with kitchen paper, then grill the squid over a high heat for no more than 30 seconds on each side. Remove from the heat and set aside.

5. Season the shellfish and squid with a little salt and pepper to taste.

*[ Continued ]*

## FOR THE CRISP OKRA

**200g (7oz) okra**
**300g (10½oz) gram (chickpea) flour**
**2 tsp Panch Phoron blend (see page 266)**
**1 tsp amchoor (optional)**
**1 pinch sea salt**
**1 pinch freshly ground black pepper**
**200ml (7fl oz) whole milk**
**About 1.2 litres (2 pints) sunflower oil, for deep-frying**

1. Trim the stalks from the okra, then cut them lengthways into even slices.

2. Put the flour, Panch Phoron blend, amchoor powder, salt and pepper in a bowl and mix together. Pour the milk into another bowl, and dip the okra into it, then dredge through the flour mixture until lightly dusted, not gloopy.

3. Pour the sunflower oil into an electric deep-fat fryer set to 170°C. (Alternatively, pour the oil into a large saucepan until one-third full and heat it over a medium heat. After about 4–5 minutes, drop a cube of white bread into the hot oil. If it takes 3 seconds to turn golden brown, it's the right heat. If not, adjust the heat accordingly.) Fry the okra in small batches for about 3 minutes until crisp and golden, then drain on kitchen paper and set aside. This can be done up to 1 hour in advance.

## FOR THE CORIANDER & POMEGRANATE DRESSING

**1 pomegranate**
**3 tbsp rapeseed oil**
**2 tbsp orange juice**
**Zest of ½ orange**
**1 dash Worcestershire sauce**
**1 large pinch Garam Masala blend (see page 267)**
**A splash mirin (sweet Japanese rice wine)**
**1 pinch sea salt**
**1 tsp coriander seeds, lightly crushed**
**2 mild fresh red chillies, halved, deseeded and very thinly sliced on the diagonal**
**2 spring onions, very thinly sliced on the diagonal**

## TO SERVE

**Coriander leaves**
**2 lemons, halved**

1. For the pomegranate and coriander dressing, first cut the pomegranate in half and, holding it over a bowl to collect the seeds and juice, bash it until the seeds fall out. Pick out and discard any of the bitter white pith. Squeeze the halves to extract more of the juice. Mix all the ingredients together just before serving.

2. To serve, put two prawns on each warmed plate, then add the squid and mussels around them. Drizzle the dressing generously over the squid and shellfish. Delicately (and decoratively) drop 1 teaspoon of the chilli oil in 'drops' onto each plate. Serve a small handful of the fried okra on top of the seafood or on the side. Scatter coriander leaves over the seafood and serve with a lemon half on each plate.

# Cajun Popcorn Shrimp with Hot Pepper Mayo

*I used to snack on this delicacy when I worked the restaurant floor as a busboy for 51-51, a Cajun-Creole restaurant in London, back in the eighties. Here's my version.*

**SERVES 4 AS A SNACK**

### FOR THE HOT PEPPER MAYO
**150g (5½oz) best-quality mayonnaise**
**Juice of ½ lemon**
**½ tsp black peppercorns, finely ground**
**¼ tsp Szechuan pepper, finely ground**
**1 tsp cayenne pepper**
**9 gratings long pepper**

### FOR THE POPCORN SHRIMP
**Sunflower oil, for deep-frying**
**ice cubes**
**1 medium egg**
**250g (9oz) plain flour**
**1 tsp cayenne pepper**
**1 tsp sea salt**
**1.5kg (3lb 5oz) raw prawns, shelled, deveined and chopped into 2.5cm (1in) chunks (aka the 'popcorn shrimp')**
**Cornflour, for dusting**

1. Mix all the mayo ingredients together in a bowl, pour into a small serving dish, cover with clingfilm, then set aside in the fridge.

2. Pour the sunflower oil for the popcorn shrimp into an electric deep-fat fryer set to 170°C. (Alternatively, pour the oil into a large saucepan until one-third full and heat it over a medium heat. After about 4–5 minutes, drop a cube of white bread into the hot oil. If it takes 3 seconds to turn golden brown, it's the right heat for the prawns. If not, adjust the heat accordingly.)

3. Take two mixing bowls, one slightly larger than the other. Pop some ice cubes into the larger bowl and cover with cold water. Put the smaller bowl on top of the ice, nestling it into the iced water. In another small bowl, mix the egg with 200ml (7fl oz) ice-cold water.

4. Add the flour, cayenne and salt to the smaller bowl over the ice, mix well, then pour in the egg–water mix and only just combine the mixture with a fork. Don't worry at all about the few lumps; in fact they'll help to form the crisp, cooked batter.

5. Pop the prawn pieces onto a plate, dust them in cornflour, then dip them into the batter and coat well, allowing any excess batter to drain off. Gently lower them into the hot oil. Don't crowd the pan; cook in three or four batches if necessary. Deep-fry for a few minutes until crisp and golden, then drain on kitchen paper. Serve immediately in a large serving dish with the hot pepper mayo.

# MOUCLADE

*This fragrant French dish of steamed mussels is traditionally made with spices, cream, shallots and a generous helping of parsley on top. It's perfect for a late-summer supper, with crusty bread to mop up the juice. 'Moucle' is the name for 'mussel' in the Vendée region of France. The spices, a reminder of the centuries-old spice trade between the port of La Rochelle and the Orient, give this dish its unique flavour, fragrance and inspiration. Make the sauce first, then add the mussels to cook them off.*

**SERVES 4**

### FOR THE SAUCE
2 tbsp unsalted butter
2 banana shallots, finely diced
1 garlic clove, crushed
2 heaped tsp Mouclade spice
    blend (see page 267)
1 tbsp plain flour
125ml (4fl oz) light chicken
    stock
125ml (4fl oz) dry white wine or
    dry cider, preferably local
150ml (5fl oz) crème fraîche
Sea salt
½ tsp thyme leaves

### FOR THE MUSSELS
1.5kg (3lb 5oz) live mussels
    or clams, scrubbed and de-
    bearded
1–2 squeezes fresh lemon juice
1–2 grindings black pepper
1 small handful flat-leaf parsley,
    chopped

### TO SERVE
sourdough bread
1 garlic clove, halved
butter for spreading
mixed bitter salad leaves
    (dandelion, sorrel, parsley –
    whatever's to hand)

1. To make the sauce, put half the butter in a large heavy-based saucepan. Put it over a medium heat and when the butter has melted add the shallots and garlic and cook for 3 minutes or until just soft.

2. Add the Mouclade spice blend and the flour and cook for 2 minutes, stirring continuously.

3. Add the stock and wine, stir well, then turn up the heat and allow to bubble until the liquid has reduced by half. Add the crème fraîche, salt to taste, the remaining butter and the thyme leaves and stir.

4. Discard any mussels that do not close when the shell is tapped. Add the mussels to the pan and cook, uncovered, for 3–4 minutes. Their lovely juices will mix with the sauce, making it the same sort of consistency as vanilla custard. Discard any mussels that remain closed.

5. Add the lemon juice and black pepper to taste and, finally, a handful of parsley.

6. Slice the sourdough bread into thick wedges. Rub the cut edge of the garlic clove over the bread, then toast the bread under a hot grill and spread generously with butter.

7. Fill a large warmed platter with the delicious saucy mussels, and serve immediately with the sourdough toast – and plenty of napkins or kitchen paper. Add a bitter, aromatic leaf salad of dandelion, mustard leaves, lovage, sorrel, parsley, coriander and a splash of vibrant colour from nasturtium flowers.

# OLD-SCHOOL SQUID SALAD

SERVES 4

## FOR THE GREMOLATA

100ml (3½fl oz) olive oil
3 fat garlic cloves, crushed
1 small handful flat-leaf parsley,
    finely chopped
Zest of 1 lemon

## FOR THE SAFFRON AÏOLI

1 floury potato, such as Maris
    Piper, unpeeled
5 saffron threads
1 garlic clove
A little sea salt
1 medium egg yolk
A splash fruity olive oil
Juice of 1 lemon

## FOR THE SQUID

500ml (18fl oz) sunflower oil,
    for deep-frying
100g (3½oz) potato flour
2 tsp black peppercorns, finely
    ground
1 tsp coriander seeds, ground
2 tsp peperoncini or Kashmiri
    chilli flakes
1–2 gratings nutmeg
½ tsp sea salt
400–500g (14oz–1lb 2oz) fresh
    squid, cleaned and thinly
    sliced, tentacles left whole
200ml (7fl oz) whole milk
1 head radicchio
1 small handful mint leaves,
    chopped
1 red chilli, deseeded and diced

*One of my first meals in an Italian restaurant in London was a salad like this – a taste of the sea from Liguria. Over time, I found that the best way to get crisp squid is to use potato flour for dredging. And as with every type of fish, try to buy the freshest possible squid from your fishmonger; it really does make a difference.*

1. Combine all the gremolata ingredients in a bowl. Set aside for 30 minutes.

2. Meanwhile, for the aïoli, put the potato in a saucepan and cover generously with water. Boil for 20 minutes or until tender. Drain and leave until cool enough to handle, then peel and leave until cool. Put the saffron in a small bowl and add 1 teaspoon warm water.

3. Chop the garlic with a pinch of salt until it forms a paste. In a small bowl, combine the potato, egg yolk, garlic paste and saffron, gently working them into a smooth paste, then drizzle in the olive oil until the aïoli has a lovely velvety texture. Add the lemon juice and sea salt to taste. Set aside.

4. To cook the squid, pour the sunflower oil into an electric deep-fat fryer set to 180°C. (Alternatively, pour the oil into a large saucepan until one-third full and heat it over a medium heat. After about 4–5 minutes, drop a cube of white bread into the hot oil. If it takes 3 seconds to turn golden brown, it's the right heat. If not, adjust the heat accordingly.)

5. Mix the potato flour, spices and salt in a bowl.

6. Dip the squid in the milk, gently shake off the excess, then coat in the seasoned flour mix. Deep-fry 6–7 squid pieces at a time until crisp and golden, about 3–4 minutes. Lift out using a slotted spoon and drain well on kitchen paper. Repeat until all the squid has been fried.

7. Arrange the radicchio on a large platter and dress the leaves with a generous drizzle of the gremolata. Scatter the crisp fried squid on top, followed by the mint and chilli. Serve immediately.

# Seafood Gumbo with 'Dirty' Dumplings

*The first restaurant I ever worked in as a busboy was when I moved to London at 18. It was called 51-51, a Cajun-Creole restaurant with a brigade made up mostly of chefs from Louisiana. There was one big, stocky guy called Yves, who was brilliant. New Orleans was his home town and I couldn't always understand his thick, deep-Southern accent, but he would occasionally show me how to cook a few dishes. 'The secret is a dark roux, buddy – y'get it, see?' A proper good guy, an excellent cook, and he made some really great food. Hopefully, this recipe would gain his approval and give you a taste of what gumbo is all about.*

**SERVES 4**

500g (1lb 2oz) raw large
    prawns, deveined and shelled
    (retain the shells and heads)
Sunflower oil, for frying
500g (1lb 2oz) andouille or
    smoked sausage, cut into
    2.5cm (1in) thick discs
300g (10½oz) okra, sliced into
    rounds
70g (2½oz) unsalted butter
65g (2¼oz) plain flour
1 large onion, cut into 1cm
    (½in) dice
3 garlic cloves, roughly chopped
3 celery sticks, diced
4 spring onions, finely sliced
1 green pepper, deseeded and cut
    into 8 chunks
Sea salt
2 thyme sprigs, leaves only

1. Put the prawn shells and heads into a large saucepan, pour in 1.5 litres (2¾ pints) water, then bring to the boil. Reduce the heat and simmer for 45 minutes, then remove from the heat and set aside. Strain the stock.

2. Add a splash of oil to a heavy-based sauté or frying pan and fry the sausage in batches until light brown, then drain on kitchen paper.

3. Add a little more oil to the pan, then put in the okra and fry gently over a low heat, stirring frequently, for 20 minutes or until they're browned and somewhat dry-looking.

4. Meanwhile, to make the roux, melt the butter in a large saucepan over a medium–low heat, add the flour and cook gently, whisking frequently, for 20–30 minutes until it turns a dark-caramel/milk-chocolate colour.

5. Add the onion to the roux and cook for 1 minute. Next, add the garlic, celery, spring onions, green pepper and salt to taste, stir well and cook for 1 minute.

6. Add the prawn stock to the saucepan, pouring it over the roux and vegetables. Stir well, then add the sausage and thyme leaves. Bring to the boil, then turn down the heat to a simmer. Add the cooked okra, and continue to cook, uncovered, at a gentle bubble for 1 hour.

250g (9oz) shelled fresh or
    defrosted frozen crab claws,
    or 500g (1lb 2oz) crab claws
    in their shells
2 tsp black peppercorns, finely
    ground
1 tsp cumin seeds, finely ground
5 cloves, finely ground
½ tsp powdered turmeric
1 tsp hot paprika
1 tsp oregano leaves, or ½ tsp
    dried oregano
1 handful curly parsley, finely
    chopped

## FOR THE DIRTY DUMPLINGS

250ml (9fl oz) whole milk
200g (7oz) stale baguette or
    crusty bread, cut into 2cm
    (¾in) dice
1 small handful curly parsley,
    finely chopped
2 tsp black peppercorns,
    coarsely ground
1 tsp cumin seeds, coarsely
    ground
5 gratings nutmeg
½ level tsp cayenne pepper
1 thyme sprig, leaves only
1 pinch sea salt
1 medium egg, lightly beaten
1 tbsp plain flour, plus extra if
    needed
Unsalted butter, for frying

7. Add a little more stock if necessary to maintain a double-cream consistency, then add the raw prawns and crab claws and cook for another 5–10 minutes. Remove from the heat. Add the spices, oregano and half the parsley, stir well but gently, then set aside and keep warm.

8. Meanwhile, boil the milk for the dumplings and set aside. Put the bread in a bowl. Add the milk and parsley and mix well to combine. Set aside for 15 minutes, or until the milk is absorbed.

9. Add the spices, thyme, salt and egg. Then add the flour, a little shake at a time, and mix well to achieve a sticky, not wet, texture. (Try not to use too much flour, as you'll run the risk of the dumplings becoming claggy.)

10. Dampen your hands, then roll out 12–16 small dumplings between your palms.

11. Put the butter in a frying pan over a medium heat, then fry the dumplings until they're golden brown all over. Drain on kitchen paper.

12. Ladle the gumbo into warmed serving bowls, add the remaining chopped parsley and pop three or four dumplings into each bowl, then serve immediately.

EGGS & CHEESE

EGGS AND CHEESE, STAPLES OF EVERY HOUSEHOLD FRIDGE, need light, subtle spicing. Their intrinsic flavours can so easily be diminished if the spices you choose are used with a heavy hand: with cheese and eggs, less is more.

Cheese needs spice notes to cut through fat and dense textures – such as nutmeg, peppers, mace – and to calm saltiness, such as peppers and chillies. But can spices that work perfectly with blue cheese work similarly well with hard cheese, soft cheese, pasteurised or raw, 'sweet' cheeses or those with more lactic bite? The answer is both yes and no. We're essentially pairing spice characteristics with the types of milk protein (casein), salt and lactic tastes.

I firstly think about the type of milk used for the cheese: is it goat's, sheep's or cow's? Sheep's milk cheese tends to be sweeter, so cardamom and cloves work well. Goat's cheeses have a more pronounced and lactic flavour so try cumin, nutmeg and peppers. Cow's milk cheeses vary wildly, but when cooking with hard, salty cheeses, turn to chilli, clove, cubeb and tamarind. These form your flavour foundation. To address the fat content of the cheese, use mace and nutmeg to accentuate or mask.

In my Cheese and Onion Flaky Puff Pie I use a combination of green cardamom, black pepper, clove and nutmeg to balance the mix of cow's milk cheeses. Ardrahan and Comté are semi-hard, while Lancashire and Gruyère are hard, but all these cheeses have sweetness as well as lactic bite. Cardamom accentuates the sweetness, clove the natural fruitiness, nutmeg and pepper add definition.

When it comes to eggs, I try to use only organic or corn-fed and certainly free-range. Before cooking, try to start with eggs at room temperature. A cooked egg should have a glorious dark yellow yolk and sweet white surround. Egg's rich sweetness can be earthed with a little cumin, warmed with ginger, balanced with turmeric or clove, or lifted with green cardamom or nutmeg. I also love eggs with Garam Masala, cayenne or chillies. So much depends on the other ingredients of the dish. My Lunchbox Frittata with spinach is simply spiced with nutmeg, which adds sweetness to astringent vegetables, and at the same time cuts the richness and cleans up the finish of creamy, buttery eggs.

*Previous page: A subtle use of cloves can accent fruity tastes, add perfume and depth, yet also 'clean up' a rich finish. But beware: too much and the flavour's wrecked, bordering on the medicinal.*

# EGG & BACON PIE

*This pie is perfect for late breakfasts, picnics and food-on-the-run-type meals. My wife, Olive, once won a competition for hers; here's my version. When making the pastry, remember to work fast but with a light touch and keep everything as cool as possible; if the butter melts, the pastry will be tough. This makes a very short, delicate dough: aim for dough that is slightly drier and more difficult to control than you might want. If it tears as you line the dish, simply patch it up. If the raw pastry is too wet, it will shrink from the sides of the dish as it cooks.*

**SERVES 6–8**

### FOR THE SHORTCRUST PASTRY
¼ tsp cubeb peppercorns
3 cloves
Seeds of 1 green cardamom pod
½ tsp black peppercorns
175g (6oz) plain flour
1 pinch fine sea salt
115g (4oz) unsalted butter,
    cubed and chilled
1 medium egg

### FOR THE FILLING
5 large eggs
1 tbsp light olive oil
8 rashers dry-cured streaky
    bacon, rind removed, cut into
    strips about 2cm (¾in) wide
125ml (4fl oz) whole milk, plus
    extra for brushing
125ml (4fl oz) double cream
1 pinch sea salt
5 gratings nutmeg
1 small handful curly parsley,
    finely chopped

1. To make the pastry, finely grind the spices using a mortar and pestle. Sift the flour, spices and salt into a large mixing bowl (discarding any large pieces of spice) and rub in the butter using your fingertips until you have a breadcrumb-like texture. Lift the mix high above the bowl as you work to keep everything as aerated as possible.

2. Mix the egg with 1 tablespoon of cold water. Using a cold metal fork, add a little of the egg–water mixture to bring the pastry together, until it just begins to holds its shape. Cover in clingfilm and put in the fridge for 25 minutes. Cut the pastry in two. Roll out one half thinly and use it to line a 24cm (9½in) pie dish about 3cm (1¼in) deep. Roll out the other half so that it's ready to form a lid. Preheat the oven to 200°C (gas mark 6). Put a baking sheet on a high shelf of the oven to preheat.

3. To make the filling, boil three of the eggs for 6 minutes, then immerse them in a bowl of cold water until cool. Peel and chop them into quarters. Heat the oil in a frying pan and fry the bacon strips. Drain on kitchen paper and set aside.

4. Beat together the milk, cream, salt and the remaining two eggs. Put the bacon and chopped boiled eggs into the lined pie dish, then pour in the milk mixture. Grate in the nutmeg and sprinkle with the parsley.

5. Dampen the edges of the pie and put the remaining pastry on top. Trim to fit and press the lid to the base to seal. Make a hole in the centre to allow steam to escape, then brush the top with a little milk. Put the pie on the heated baking sheet and bake for 10 minutes.

6. Turn down the heat to 180°C (gas mark 4) and bake for another 25–30 minutes until the pastry is golden. Serve immediately, or allow to cool completely and serve with Sizzled Tomatoes (see page 182).

# Egg Curry

*This is a dish Mum used to make for us as a treat – it evokes such good memories. I've spiced things up a little to include influences from southern India, adding coconut, fennel and tamarind. Do try to make sure the egg yolks are still a little runny.*

**SERVES 6**

1 tsp cumin seeds
3 cloves
½ tsp finely ground mace
1 tsp black peppercorns
Seeds from 2 green cardamom
    pods
1 tsp fennel seeds
1 tsp powdered turmeric
1 tsp chilli flakes
½ tsp finely ground cassia
1 handful flaked almonds
6 eggs
60g (2¼oz) unsalted butter,
    ghee or sunflower oil
300g (10½oz) onions, diced
3 fat garlic cloves, crushed
20g (¾oz) fresh ginger, grated
1 tsp sea salt
400g (14oz) tin chopped
    tomatoes
400ml (14fl oz) coconut milk
1 handful coriander, leaves only

FOR THE RAITA

200ml (7fl oz) full-fat yogurt
100ml (3½fl oz) crème fraîche
2 tsp thick, black Indian
    tamarind paste
30g (1oz) fresh ginger, peeled
    and finely grated
Zest of 1 lime
1 small pinch finely ground
    cloves

1. Mix all the raita ingredients together in a small bowl and put it in the fridge.

2. Finely grind the first six spices using a mortar and pestle, then add the turmeric, chilli flakes and cassia, and mix well. Dry-fry the almonds lightly in a frying pan over a medium heat; set aside.

3. Put the eggs in a pan of cold water, bring to the boil and simmer very gently for 4 minutes. Drain and refresh under cold running water for 3 minutes or so. Crack the eggshells and peel the eggs. Set the eggs aside on kitchen paper to dry.

4. Put a large heavy-based pan or flameproof casserole over a medium heat, add the butter and heat for a moment. Add the onions, stir and cook for a couple of minutes, then add the garlic and ginger, stir and cook until the onions are soft.

5. Add the spice mix and salt, stir, then add the tomatoes. Stir again, turn down the heat slightly and simmer gently for 1 minute or so.

6. Add the coconut milk, stir, turn up the heat and bring to the boil, then allow the mixture to bubble gently for 1 minute before turning the heat back down to low and simmering, uncovered, until the sauce has the consistency of double cream and can coat the back of your stirring spoon with a glossy covering. This will take about 10–15 minutes.

7. Turn off the heat. Cut the eggs in half lengthways, put them onto warmed dinner plates, spoon over lashings of the beautiful sauce, then sprinkle with the fresh coriander and toasted almonds.

8. Serve immediately with Pistachio & Rose Pilau (see page 156) and a dollop of the raita on the side.

# FULL IRISH BREAKFAST

*Breakfast is renowned among chefs as one of the hardest sessions – particularly cooked breakfasts. With all the ingredients here, trying to get everything ready on a plate so it's all warm and freshly cooked is quite an art. I used to do the odd breakfast shift at Ballymaloe and this recipe is one of the easier ones to get right. Good luck!*

**SERVES 4**

4 tsp white peppercorns, finely ground
10 gratings nutmeg
Light olive oil, for frying
200g (7oz) closed-cap mushrooms, sliced 2cm (¾in) thick
Sea salt
1 lemon, halved
4 ripe tomatoes, halved horizontally
1 thyme sprig, leaves only
A little golden caster sugar (optional)
4 discs black pudding, sliced 4cm (1½in) thick with a serrated knife
4 discs white pudding, sliced 4cm (1½in) thick with a serrated knife
8 rashers dry-cured bacon

1. Preheat the oven to 100°C (gas mark ¼). Preheat the grill to medium. Mix the peppercorns with the nutmeg.

2. Put 1 tablespoon oil in a large heavy-based sauté pan over a high heat. Add just enough of the mushrooms to cover the base of the pan. Toss them around gently in the oil. Add a pinch of salt, a pinch of the spice mix and a generous squeeze of lemon juice. As soon as the mushrooms become glossy and opaque, turn them out onto a large plate. Repeat until all the mushrooms are cooked. Set aside.

3. Put the tomatoes, cut-side up, on a grill pan, sprinkle with the thyme leaves, a pinch of salt and a sprinkle of sugar, if you like, and put under the grill for 5–7 minutes until they char slightly. Remove from the heat and set aside.

4. Wipe the sauté pan clean with kitchen paper and add 1 tablespoon oil. Fry the slices of black pudding on both sides for 2–3 minutes until browned and crisp. Transfer to a baking tray, cover with foil and put in the oven to keep warm. Fry the white pudding in the same way.

5. Wipe the pan again, then fry the bacon in a little oil on both sides to lightly crisp. Transfer it to the baking tray with the puddings (but do not cover with the foil) and put the tray back in the oven.

**4 large eggs**

**4 slices sourdough bread, 3cm (1¼in) thick**

**½ garlic clove**

**Extra virgin olive oil, for drizzling**

**A pot of Chilli Jam (see page 262)**

6. Add 5 tablespoons oil to a second large heavy-based frying pan. Crack the eggs carefully into the oil and put over a high heat. As soon as you hear the first spit and the eggs just start to undulate, turn off the heat, put on a lid and leave to rest. After 4 minutes or so, check to see that the white has set; the yolk should still be golden yellow. If not, give the pan another short blast of heat. Using a fish slice, cut the white around each yolk to separate the four fried eggs.

7. Meanwhile, toast the bread and rub the cut side of the garlic over one side of each slice. Turn up the grill to high. Drizzle a little extra virgin olive oil onto the toasted bread. Arrange the toast, the black and white pudding, bacon, a tomato half and a spoonful of mushrooms on each of four plates. Put a plate (or two if they'll fit), under the grill for 30–45 seconds, remove and put an egg on the toast. Sprinkle it with a pinch of the spice mix, add a dollop of Chilli Jam by the bacon slices and serve immediately.

# LUNCHBOX FRITTATA

*This fabulous omelette is packed full of flavours. It's superb hot or cold, and great as a snack, picnic item or light supper. Serve it with Sizzled Tomatoes (see page 182): the tomato dressing adds a wonderful tang that complements the rich combination of eggs and soft cheese.*

**SERVES 2**

**6 tbsp olive oil**
**85g (3oz) baby spinach**
**250g (9oz) waxy potatoes, such as Charlotte, peeled and sliced into very thin discs**
**2 large onions, thinly sliced**
**1 large pinch sea salt**
**6 eggs**
**½ nutmeg, freshly grated**
**125g (4½oz) Cashel Blue or other blue cheese**
**3 spring onions, thinly sliced on the diagonal**

1. Heat 1 tablespoon of the oil in a small frying pan and quickly cook the spinach. Cool and press in a tea towel to remove the excess water. Set aside.

2. Heat the remaining oil in a large heavy-based frying pan over a medium heat. Add the potatoes and fry for 3 minutes.

3. Add the onions, sprinkle with the salt, cover and cook for 15 minutes or until soft, stirring from time to time.

4. Crack the eggs into a bowl. Sprinkle in the nutmeg and beat well.

5. Tip the onion and potato mix into the beaten eggs and mix well. Crumble in the cheese, add the spinach and spring onions, and stir gently to combine.

6. Pour the mixture back into the pan and cook over a gentle heat until it begins to set. Shake the pan from time to time so that the omelette does not stick to the base.

7. Remove from the heat and turn the omelette over by putting a plate on top of the pan, then carefully turn the pan upside-down so that the omelette lands on the plate. Slide it back into the pan and cook it for only a few minutes more, until it looks firm but is still slightly moist inside.

8. Remove from the heat, rest for a few minutes, then slide it onto a large, clean serving plate.

# EGGS AKOORI

*This recipe was first shown to me by a Parsi chap we were staying with on a visit to Goa. It's perfect on warm, buttery toast in the morning after a long night, and is a kind of Indian version of scrambled eggs, firmer set, with a kick of chilli. It's totally up to you how softly set or firm you like your eggs, but whichever way you choose, this is simple and beautiful.*

**SERVES 4**

8 medium eggs
60g (2¼oz) unsalted butter,
    cubed and chilled
2 onions: 1 chopped,
    1 thinly sliced
20g (¾oz) fresh ginger, finely
    grated
½ tsp cumin seeds, finely
    ground
1 tsp powdered turmeric
2 red bird's eye chillies, deseeded
    and chopped
2 ripe tomatoes, deseeded and
    chopped
½ tsp sea salt
1 small handful coriander leaves,
    chopped

1. Whisk the eggs in a bowl, then set aside.

2. Put a heavy-based non-stick saucepan over a medium–low heat and add half the butter. When it begins to foam gently, add the onions and gently fry them until soft. Try not to let them colour.

3. Add the ginger, spices and chillies, give it a quick stir to combine, then add the tomatoes.

4. Add the sea salt to the bowl of eggs, give them another quick whisk, then tip them into the pan along with the remaining butter, and cook gently, stirring continuously to prevent the mixture from catching and to help form small, delicate clumps of soft, spiced egg.

5. Keep cooking until you're happy with the consistency, then remove from the heat, stir in the coriander and serve immediately on warmed plates with hot, buttered toast.

# IRISH RAREBIT

*This is a big shout out to my adopted homeland and it's a really tasty way to use up bits and pieces such as cold cuts of ham or gammon and cheese – with a fried egg on top.*

**SERVES 4**

45g (1½oz) unsalted butter, at
    room temperature
45g (1½oz) plain flour
300ml (10fl oz) Irish stout
125ml (4fl oz) double cream
150g (5½oz) mature Cheddar
    cheese, grated
1 tsp English mustard
1 tsp black peppercorns, finely
    ground
Scant ¼ tsp finely ground mace
4 thick slices soda bread or
    sourdough
Light olive oil, for frying
4 eggs
400g (14oz) gammon or ham,
    pulled or chopped
A little cayenne pepper

1. Put a large saucepan over a medium heat. Add the butter, stir lightly with a small whisk, then when the butter has melted, add the flour. Whisk to form a roux and cook for 30 seconds.

2. Measure the stout and cream into a jug. Turn up the heat under the roux, then pour the liquid bit by bit into the pan, whisking all the time to combine well with the roux. Once all the liquid has been added, keep whisking until you see the first bubbles appear, then continue to cook for another 2 minutes.

3. Add the cheese, mustard, black pepper and mace, and stir continuously to combine. Once the cheese has melted, continue to cook gently for 5 minutes, with only the odd bubble or two popping up, stirring occasionally. Set aside.

4. Toast the bread and leave to cool. Heat the olive oil in a large frying pan and fry the eggs; the whites should be just set, the yolks still soft.

5. Meanwhile, preheat the grill to its hottest setting. Arrange the gammon on the toast, place in a grill pan, coat generously with the cheese sauce and put under the grill for 1–2 minutes until the sauce bubbles and only just lightly scorches.

5. Put a slice of the toast on each of four warmed plates and top with a fried egg, then sprinkle with a pinch of cayenne pepper to serve.

# CHEESE IN A BOX

*This is a beautifully simple, moreish dish that is perfect for the cold winter months. I make it from October to April, when the French Vacherin Mont d'Or is available. It's a cow's-milk cheese from the Jura mountains. The Swiss also produce this cheese. Take a peek inside the box; the rind of the cheese should have a wavy surface with a wonderful aroma of freshly rained-on undergrowth. If you can't find Vacherin Mont d'Or you could use Camembert – as long as it comes in a wooden box that you can put in the oven. This goes perfectly with smoked ham and turmeric boiled potatoes, and the pickles help cut through the richness and add crunch.*

**SERVES 4**

500g (1lb 2oz) Vacherin Mont d'Or, in its box, at room temperature

1kg (2lb 4oz) waxy potatoes, such as Charlotte, peeled, halved or quartered

1 pinch sea salt

1 heaped tsp powdered turmeric

1–2 knobs unsalted butter

½ tsp black peppercorns, finely ground

A mix of pickled shallots or onions and cornichons

500g (1lb 2oz) joint lightly smoked cooked ham or gammon

1. Preheat the oven to 200°C (gas mark 6). Put the cheese in its box on a baking tray, remove the lid and gently slash the surface of the cheese twice with a sharp knife, just scoring the rind so that you have two shallow incisions about 5cm (2in) long.

2. Put the lid back on, then put the box into the oven for 15 minutes or until the cheese is nicely runny and melted.

3. Meanwhile, put the potatoes in a large saucepan. Add the salt and turmeric and cover with cold water. Boil the potatoes for 20 minutes or until tender. Drain well, then tip them into a warmed serving dish, dot with the butter, sprinkle on the pepper and take them straight to the table. Swiftly follow the potatoes with the pickles and your box of cheese on a large warmed plate, keeping the lid on so that the cheese stays warm and runny.

4. Carve the ham joint at the table. Spoon some lovely warm turmeric potatoes onto warmed plates. Follow with a spoonful or so of the Vacherin Mont d'Or, with slices of ham and the pickles – glorious!

# Cheese & Onion Flaky Puff Pie

*A delicious, simple pie that's best eaten slightly warm – any leftovers are brilliant eaten at room temperature with Sizzled Tomatoes (see page 182).*

**SERVES 6**

1 tsp black peppercorns
4 cloves
Seeds of 3 green cardamom pods
7 gratings nutmeg
300g (10½oz) Ardrahan or
    Lancashire cheese, grated
100g (3½oz) mature Gruyère or
    Comté cheese, grated
50g (1¾oz) unsalted butter
700g (1lb 9oz) onions, roughly
    sliced
3 garlic cloves, lightly crushed
    and left whole
320–375g (11–13oz) butter puff
    pastry (ready-rolled is fine)
Flour, for dusting
1 medium egg, lightly beaten
1 tbsp whole milk

1. Finely grind the peppercorns, cloves and cardamom seeds using a mortar and pestle, then add the nutmeg and mix well.

2. Preheat the oven to 200°C (gas mark 6). In a small bowl mix the two cheeses together and set aside.

3. Put a heavy-based sauté pan over a medium heat. Add the butter and allow it to melt, then add the onions and garlic and fry gently until both are really soft and translucent, about 20 minutes. Add the spice mix, stir it through, then cook for 30 seconds. Remove from the heat and set aside to cool.

4. On a lightly floured work surface, roll out the pastry very thin, about 2mm thick. Cut the pastry in half and use one half to line a 23cm (9in) pie plate, allowing a little to hang over the edges.

5. Remove the cloves of garlic from the spiced onion, spread a layer of the onion over the pie base, then a layer of mixed cheeses and repeat to fill the pie generously.

6. Mix the egg with the milk and use this egg wash to brush around the edge of the pastry, then gently put on the other piece of pastry for the lid. Gently press to seal, then cut away any excess pastry, and crimp the edges together.

7. Brush more egg wash over the top. Make a small hole in the centre to allow the steam to escape, then put the pie on the middle shelf of the oven and bake for 20 minutes. Reduce the temperature to 180°C (gas mark 4) and bake for another 20 minutes or so until the pastry is golden and the filling oozing. Leave to cool for 4 minutes, then slice into generous wedges and serve with English mustard and a bitter leaf salad, such as chicory, dandelion and mustard leaves.

144

# MAC 'N' CHEESE

*Mum used to roll this one out all the time when we were young – to the point that I didn't eat it for quite a while! I have, however, picked up the 'Mac' mantle once again, and once again have fallen in love with it. Tempered clove adds a fruity note to the cheese, while the mace adds a truly delicious depth of flavour, fragrance and tingly, clean finish.*

**SERVES 4–6**

1 tsp sea salt
320g (11oz) dried macaroni
Splash of light olive oil

FOR THE SAUCE
1 tbsp sunflower oil
9 cloves
40g (1½oz) unsalted butter
50g (1¾oz) plain flour
775ml (1⅓ pints) whole milk
125ml (4fl oz) single cream
250g (9oz) mature Cheddar
    cheese, grated
2 tsp French mustard
2 tsp English mustard
1 tsp black peppercorns, finely
    ground
Scant ¼ tsp finely ground mace

FOR THE TOPPING
100g (3½oz) fresh breadcrumbs
2 tbsp olive oil
40g (1½oz) Parmesan cheese,
    finely grated
½ tsp cayenne pepper
1 thyme sprig, leaves only
1 small handful flat-leaf parsley
    leaves, finely chopped

1. Put 1 litre (1¾ pints) water into a large saucepan and bring to a rolling boil. Add the salt and pasta, bring back up to a rolling boil and cook for 11 minutes (or follow the instructions on the packet). Drain, rinse and coat with a drizzle of light olive oil, then pour into a roasting tin or ovenproof dish about 30 × 25cm (12 × 10in) and about 4.5cm (1¾in) deep. Set aside.

2. To make the sauce, put a large saucepan over a high heat, pour in the oil and, when smoking hot, carefully drop in the cloves – they will splutter and expand in size. Remove the pan from the heat, add the butter, stir lightly with a small whisk, then when the butter has melted, remove the cloves with a spoon and discard them, retaining all the butter and oil.

3. Put the pan back on the heat, turn the heat down to medium, add the flour, and whisk to form a roux, then cook for 30 seconds or so.

4. Measure the milk and cream into a jug, then pour it bit by bit into the pan, whisking all the time to combine well with the roux. Once all the liquid has been added, keep whisking until you see the first bubbles appear, then continue to cook for 2 minutes.

5. Add the cheese, mustards, pepper and mace and stir continuously to combine. Once the cheese has melted, continue to cook gently for 5 minutes, with only the odd bubble or two popping up, stirring occasionally. Pour into the roasting tin, covering the macaroni. Set aside.

6. Preheat the oven to 190°C (gas mark 5). Mix all the topping ingredients in a bowl, then scatter evenly over the macaroni and sauce. Put the roasting tin onto the middle shelf of the oven and cook for 15 minutes or until the crumbs turn golden brown and the sauce bubbles up through the topping.

# GRAINS
# & PULSES

GRAINS AND PULSES PROVIDE THE PERFECT BLANK CANVAS FOR DOTS, SPLASHES AND WHIRLS OF SPICE INTENSITY. Earthy, perfumed or pungent spices provide kicks of flavour as they nestle in soft, subtle grains.

Plainly cooked rice is a natural accompaniment to spicy food in many cultures, and for this I would always choose aged basmati rice: in India the best rice is aged for at least a year before use, which makes a huge difference to the flavour. However, in this chapter I'm featuring rice as a centrepiece, pairing it with floral perfumed saffron or fragrant garam masala. But for my Asafoetida Risotto I've 'gone against the grain' and created a dish to truly challenge the purists. The risotto gains depth from the subtly sulphurous asafoetida, relying on an acidulated butter sauce, walnut and celery leaf to cut through glorious richness.

My passion for lentils and pulses started when I was young. I have fond memories of Mum and Dad organising their dinner parties. The day before Dad would fill large plastic bowls of water to soak chickpeas and various lentils. He'd go to his spice cupboard, pull out the various brightly coloured tins and arrange them on the counter. Next day, the magic would start. Peeling potatoes, pulling cauliflower florets, spilling frozen peas over the tiled floor. Dad would start chopping, frying and hunting for the 'large enough' pots. Mum cleaning up after Dad, smiling, scolding, laughing. Then the aromas, the glorious aromas.

My Tarka Dhal tempers the spices in hot oil to round the flavour and create a down-to-earth flavour sympathetic to the creamy-earthy little moong dahl (split mung beans). I use channa dahl (split chickpeas) for its al dente texture, its earthy-sweet, pea-like taste and to act as the foil to the sweet aged basmati rice and the fragrant spice lift of Garam Masala in my Pistachio and Rose Pilau.

Chickpeas have a delicate bite and sweet earthy flavour. The salad of Chickpea, Nectarine and Feta is a celebration of summer flavours. Intended to burst with 'sunshine', I've made a dressing incorporating my floral, fragrant Garam Masala with orange, mirin and rapeseed. The mix of vibrant flavours gives a different taste to every satisfying bite.

*Previous page: Vibrant, earthy turmeric needs a light touch to showcase its gingery clean warmth.*

# BERBER COUSCOUS

*Tagine and couscous dishes have their roots planted firmly in the indigenous Berber people of North Africa. These proud people uphold culinary traditions observed for thousands of years: honey, ewe's milk, goat's cheese and butter, perfumed spices, barley, game and meats. Bedouins brought dates and different grains to the region; the Moors introduced olives, herbs and complex, flavoured dishes; Jewish sects added salting methods; and the French gave everything general finesse. And now I'm adding my own twist!*

*Couscous is a much-revered product – a labour of love prepared from wheat, millet or barley flours. Traditionally, Berber women took sacks of wheat to be ground into semolina and laboriously formed the now-familiar small balls, rolling the moistened flour between the palms of their hands. As with pasta, there are different types or sizes of couscous for different methods of cooking: 'mhammsa' is 3mm (⅛in), 'keskou' 2mm (1/16in) and ultrafine 'seffa' is a mere 1mm. For this recipe, I'm not suggesting we make our own couscous, but do try to find the fine or ultrafine, pre-cooked types. These will make a lighter dish and a difference you'll really notice.*

*I've included the traditional Moroccan 'tfaia' topping of spicy caramelised onions and sultanas, adding another layer of flavour to this fragant dish.*

## SERVES 4

### FOR THE MEAT OR BARLEY

**2 tsp cumin seeds**
**1 tsp coriander seeds**
**7 cloves**
**4 tsp Kashmiri chilli flakes**
**500g (1lb 2oz) rump beef steak, chopped into bite-sized chunks, or 250g (9oz) barley grains mixed with 600ml (1 pint) water**
**1 large onion (about 350g/12oz), chopped into chunky dice**
**1 tsp sea salt**
**At least 750ml (26fl oz) good-quality dark chicken stock**

1. Finely grind the cumin seeds, coriander and cloves using a mortar and pestle, then add the chilli flakes and mix well.

2. Put the beef chunks in a flameproof casserole over a medium–high heat. Add the onion, spices, salt and enough stock to cover the meat by 3cm (1¼in). (Alternatively put the barley, onion, spices, salt and stock into the casserole.)

3. Bring to a boil, then turn down the heat to a gentle bubble, put the lid half on and allow to cook for 1½–2 hours until the meat is tender. Don't let the pan dry out. (If using barley it should need only 35–40 minutes until the grains are tender.)

[ *Continued* ]

## FOR THE COUSCOUS

500g (1lb 2oz) fine or ultrafine
    couscous
1 pinch sea salt
2 tbsp olive oil
2 tsp unsalted butter, diced

## FOR THE TFAIA

10 saffron threads
75g (2¾oz) sultanas
1 tbsp olive oil
30g (1oz) unsalted butter
3 large onions, thinly sliced
1 tsp sea salt
1 tsp black peppercorns, finely
    ground
1 heaped tsp finely ground
    cinnamon
2 tsp powdered ginger
1–2 gratings nutmeg
2 tbsp runny honey

4. Meanwhile, preheat the oven to 180°C (gas mark 4) and make the couscous. Pour the couscous into a heatproof bowl or ovenproof dish, stir the salt into 500ml (18fl oz) warm water and pour into the couscous. Leave for 10 minutes.

5. Pour the oil over the couscous and, using your hands, gently mix the ingredients together, rather like making soda bread: gently, gently.

6. Scatter the butter over the surface, cover tightly with foil and put the dish into the oven for 10–12 minutes. Take out and keep warm, replacing the foil with a tea towel. Set aside.

7. For the tfaia, soak the saffron in 4 tablespoons warm water for at least 15 minutes. Soak the sultanas in 3 tablespoons warm water for 10 minutes, then drain them. Set aside.

8. Put the oil and butter in a large heavy-based frying pan over a medium heat. Allow the butter to melt, then add the onions and salt, and fry gently for 5 minutes.

9. Turn down the heat slightly, add the spices, adding nutmeg to taste, the saffron threads and their soaking water and the honey, then stir. Cover and cook gently for 15 minutes or until the onions are soft and 'melted'.

10. Remove the lid and add the drained sultanas, stir them through and continue to cook for another 10 minutes, uncovered. Take off the heat and set aside.

11. Spoon all the couscous into a large serving dish, then make a small well in the middle. Strain the meat (or barley) and onions, reserving the juices in a small bowl or jug, and put the meat and onion (or spiced barley and onion) into the well, top with the tfaia and serve immediately, with the meat juices served separately.

# Paella Túnel

*There are many versions of paella, but here I take it back to its roots, add a spice or two and cook a dish that recalls the land workers of the Albufera, the freshwater lagoon on the Valencia coast, the true home of paella. More than 1000 years ago, the Moors first cultivated rice in this Mediterranean Spanish region, and the famous Spanish dish arose from there. There's no 'official' recipe, but rice is the star ingredient, so if you can find them, use one of the three main Valencian varieties: Bahía, Senia or Bomba. The starch content ('white pearl') is what it's all about: the rice shouldn't be fluffy, but must have a bit of bite while soaking up the glorious cooking juices. Túnel is a Mallorcan herb liqueur with hints of anise and juniper – use pastis if you can't find it. Butter beans are part of a traditional paella: you need to soak them overnight before putting this dish together.*

**SERVES 4–6**

150g (5½oz) dried butter beans, lima beans or garrafón beans
12–15 saffron threads
6 chicken thighs, bone-in, trimmed of excess skin, chopped in half across the bone
1 wild rabbit, portioned into small cuts; ask your butcher (optional, but worth it)
3 tsp coarse sea salt
250g (9oz) large flat green beans (ideally flat runner beans; if not, use mangetout)
Several splashes olive oil
4 garlic cloves, lightly crushed
2 large onions, chopped
2 green peppers, quartered, deseeded and diced
2 small thyme sprigs, leaves only

1. Soak the dried butter beans overnight in 500ml (18fl oz) cold water. The next day, drain and set aside. Soak the saffron threads in 4 tablespoons warm water.

2. To make the spice blend, finely grind the peppercorns, cumin and coriander seeds and star anise using a mortar and pestle, then add the paprika, turmeric and chilli flakes. Set aside.

3. Lay out the chicken and rabbit pieces, if using, and sprinkle with the salt, then massage it briefly into the meat. Put the green beans in a saucepan of boiling water and boil for 1 minute to blanch them, then refresh in a bowl of ice-cold water, drain, slice and set aside.

4. Put a 46cm (18in) diameter deep frying pan (better still, a paella pan) over a medium heat, add 2 large splashes of oil, then add the chicken thighs, scraping all the salt into the pan, and fry for 3–4 minutes until lightly browned, turning them over as they cook.

5. Add the garlic, onions, green peppers and thyme and toss or stir it all around. Add the rabbit pieces and another splash of olive oil and continue to fry for another 5 minutes.

[ *Continued* ]

1 fresh red finger chilli, deseeded
    and roughly diced
400g (14oz) tin chopped
    tomatoes, or in summer, use
    the ripest plum tomatoes and
    coarsely grate them
1 rosemary sprig, about 7.5cm
    (3in), leaves only
200g (7oz) paella rice
150g (5½oz) live mussels,
    scrubbed and de-bearded
150g (5½oz) live clams or
    cockles, scrubbed
12 raw large tiger prawns, shell
    on, deveined
Zest of ½ lemon
3 lemons, halved, to garnish

### FOR THE SPICE BLEND
2 tsp black peppercorns
½ tsp cumin seeds
1 tsp coriander seeds
1 star anise
2 tsp sweet Spanish pimentón
    paprika
1 tsp powdered turmeric
2 tsp dried chilli flakes

### FOR THE REDUCTION
4 tbsp white wine vinegar
100ml (3½fl oz) Túnel de
    Mallorca (or a French pastis)

6. When the meat is a nutty-brown colour, add the chilli, stir, then add the tomatoes, green beans and soaked butter beans. Turn down the heat a little and cook for another 8–10 minutes.

7. Next, add the spice blend and stir, then pour in 1 litre (1¾ pints) warm water, add the rosemary and finally add the saffron and its soaking water. Turn up the heat to high, bring to a strong, rolling bubble, then gently pour in the rice. Jiggle and shake the pan to distribute things evenly and cook for 1 minute.

8. Lower the heat to medium, stir gently to combine the ingredients, then leave to bubble gently for 25–35 minutes.

9. Meanwhile, to make the reduction, put the white wine vinegar and the Túnel or pastis in a small non-stick saucepan and stir over a medium–high heat until reduced to the consistency of runny honey. Set aside.

10. Discard any mussels or clams that do not close when the shell is tapped. When the rice is nearly cooked, add the prawns, mussels and clams. Cover and cook gently for 3–5 minutes until the seafood is just cooked and the rice is soft but still with a little bite. Discard any mussels or clams that remain closed.

11. Turn off the heat and sprinkle with the lemon zest. Take the paella to the table, put it on a trivet and cover with a clean tea towel to rest for 3–4 minutes.

12. Remove the tea towel, drizzle the Túnel reduction over the rice, and serve on warmed plates with lemon halves and finger bowls at the ready.

# ASAFOETIDA RISOTTO WITH WALNUTS & CELERY LEAF

*I think risottos are one of the ultimate comfort dishes, and I love to serve this one with a crisp green salad on the side. When you're cooking risotto, remember: only add liquid that's been heated to a gentle bubble, don't flood the rice with stock and always be generous with the amount of stock you start with, because some rice varieties absorb more than you might expect.*

**SERVES 4–6**

### FOR THE ACIDULATED BUTTER
**100g (3½oz) shallots, finely chopped**
**100ml (3½fl oz) white wine vinegar**
**125g (4½oz) unsalted butter, cubed and chilled**

### FOR THE RISOTTO
**1–1.2 litres (1¾–2 pints) hot light chicken stock**
**A generous splash light olive oil**
**30g (1oz) unsalted butter**
**50g (1¾oz) celery leaves chopped into 5mm (¼in) pieces, plus 1 tbsp whole leaves to garnish**
**50g (1¾oz) shallots, finely chopped**
**½ garlic clove, finely chopped**
**250g (9oz) Arborio rice**
**¼ tsp asafoetida resin**
**50g (1¾oz) acidulated butter (see above)**
**75g (2¾oz) Parmesan cheese, freshly grated**
**A splash walnut oil**

1. Make the acidulated butter well in advance, as it needs to freeze. Put the shallots and vinegar in a small saucepan and simmer gently until the vinegar has almost reduced by half, then remove the pan from the heat. Add the cubed butter, whisking as you go to form a smooth sauce – a beurre blanc – then pour into an ice-cube tray. Leave to cool, then store in your freezer. The cubes make handy-sized portions to work with.

2. Now for the risotto. Keep the stock simmering in a pan over a low heat. Put a sauté pan over a medium heat, splash in a little olive oil and add the butter. When the butter just begins to foam, add the celery leaves, shallots and garlic, and fry gently for a couple of minutes. Add the rice and stir to coat it in the buttery oil and vegetables. Stir continuously until you hear the rice 'cracking' – about 3–5 minutes. This means that the rice is releasing its starch.

3. Add the asafoetida and continue cooking for a minute or so. Add a ladle of the hot stock, then carry on stirring and continuously adding just enough stock to keep the mixture moist. The rice will take 15–20 minutes to cook, depending on the variety and age of rice you're using.

4. When the rice has softened slightly but still has a little bite, add the acidulated butter, Parmesan, walnut oil and a little more stock so that it has a slack, but not sloppy, consistency. Stir, remove from the heat and cover the pan three-quarters with its lid for 2–3 minutes to relax the rice and allow it to absorb the extra stock.

5. Time to serve! The risotto should have a 'molten' consistency now, so serve it on warmed plates, flatten it with the back of the spoon, then sprinkle with celery leaves to garnish.

# PISTACHIO & ROSE PILAU

*I came up with this gloriously fragrant version of pilau rice because I wanted something light, perfumed, and interesting to serve as an accompaniment to curry dishes. Actually this works wonderfully well with any saucy dish. I love the layers upon layers of perfume, natural sweetness and vibrant colours.*

**SERVES 4–6**

¼ butternut squash, peeled
   and diced into 2.5cm (1in)
   chunks
A splash rapeseed oil
30g (1oz) unsalted butter
½ onion, finely diced
375g (13oz) best-quality
   aged basmati rice, rinsed
   thoroughly and drained
100g (3½oz) channa dhal (split
   chickpeas)
1.2 litres (2 pints) vegetable
   stock or hot water
1 tsp powdered turmeric
2 tsp Garam Masala blend (see
   page 267), plus a little extra
   to serve
1 heaped tsp sea salt
1 handful bright green pistachio
   nuts, lightly crushed
2 tbsp dried rose petals,
   roughly chopped
1 large handful each coriander
   leaves, flat-leaf parsley and
   chives, finely chopped

1. Preheat the oven to 180°C (gas mark 4). Put the squash in a roasting tin with the oil, and roast it in the oven for 20–25 minutes until just soft and a little coloured. Set aside.

2. Melt the butter, or a splash of oil, in a flameproof casserole over a gentle heat, then add the onion and sweat for 5 minutes or until it is soft.

3. Add the rice and channa dhal, then stir for a minute or two, coating all the grains with the melted butter.

4. Next, pour the stock into the casserole, sprinkle in the turmeric and Garam Masala, and give it a quick but gentle stir.

5. Cover the casserole with a tight-fitting lid or foil and put on a middle shelf in the oven. After 10–15 minutes, check to see if all the liquid has been absorbed. If there's still some liquid remaining, return the covered casserole to the oven and give it a few more minutes until all the liquid has been absorbed but the rice is still moist and glossy.

6. Remove from the oven, take off the lid, or gingerly rip off the foil, add the salt and fluff gently with a fork. Stir through the butternut squash, pistachio nuts and rose petals, sprinkle with the herbs and a little more Garam Masala and serve immediately.

# Vanilla & Long Pepper Porridge with Sugared Banana, Cardamom & Lime

*I eat porridge every morning, rain or shine. Not always with cardamom syrup and bananas, I must confess. Vanilla in porridge is nothing new, but the addition of long pepper here offsets its creaminess, backing it up with heat, and the whole dish is wonderfully fragrant. Recently I've started to use unsweetened almond milk in place of cow's milk: it adds a delicious toasted nutty flavour to my morning porridge.*

**SERVES 4**

### FOR THE PORRIDGE
**1 vanilla pod, split lengthways**
**200g (7oz) jumbo oats**
**600ml (1 pint) whole milk**
**600ml (1 pint) water**
**½ long pepper spike, grated**
**1 tsp vanilla extract**

### FOR THE CARDAMOM–LIME SYRUP
**6 green cardamom pods**
**700g (1lb 9oz) golden caster sugar**
**Zest and juice of 2 limes**

### FOR THE BANANAS
**2 short, sweet, only-just-ripe bananas**
**Icing sugar, sifted**

1. Scrape out the seeds from the vanilla pod. Put the pod and seeds into a large heavy-based saucepan and add all the remaining porridge ingredients. Ideally, the ingredients should come no more than a third of the way up the pan.

2. Put the pan over a medium heat, stir the mixture well and cook until it just begins to bubble. Keep stirring from time to time.

3. When you see the porridge gently bubbling, turn the heat down to very low so that it is only just simmering. Cook for 30–40 minutes, stirring frequently, until the starchy flavour has disappeared and the porridge has taken on an unctuous, whipped-cream texture.

4. While the porridge is cooking, make the syrup: put the cardamom pods on a chopping board and give them a firm, decisive, controlled bash with the bottom of a saucepan. This will slightly open up the pods to expose their fragrant seeds.

5. Put the sugar, 300ml (10fl oz) cold water and the smashed cardamom pods in a saucepan over a medium heat and give everything a gentle stir. Make sure there are no sugar crystals up the side of the pan, as these will burn and cause problems. Don't be tempted to stir, but, from time to time swirl the pan around. Once you're sure all the sugar has dissolved, allow the syrup to bubble for 2 minutes.

6. Remove the pan from the heat, and add the lime zest and juice. Stir well, then set aside.

7. Peel the bananas, then slice them on the diagonal about 3mm (⅛in) thick. Put the banana slices on a dinner plate and dredge with icing sugar.

8. If you have a chef's blowtorch, this is the perfect time to use it. Simply flame the bananas until the sugar just starts to catch and colour to a light caramel. If you don't have a blowtorch, set the grill to its highest setting, put the banana slices on a grill pan, and put the pan close to the flames. Watching carefully, heat the bananas until the sugar just begins to colour.

9. To serve, remove the vanilla pod from the porridge, scrape any porridge from the pod back into the pan and give it a good stir. Spoon generous servings into your favourite breakfast bowls, place 3 or 5 banana slices in a star shape in the centre of each bowl, then spoon a little syrup over the bananas. (Or simply serve the porridge and let everyone help themselves to bananas and syrup.)

# Red Lentil Dhal with Tomato, Coconut & Lime

*This dish is inspired by the Malay cooking style of the south Malabari Indians. Fragrant cinnamon and cloves combine with red lentils, creamy coconut, a zesty kick of fresh lime and chilli. It's a brilliant recipe, one of the originals we've been serving at farmers' markets for years: a vegetarian bowl of absolute comforting delight.*

## SERVES 8

500g (1lb 2oz) red lentils
1 small handful cashew nuts
2 tsp black peppercorns
1 tsp cumin seeds
1 tsp coriander seeds
½ tsp cloves
½ tsp finely ground cinnamon
1 tsp powdered turmeric
60g (2¼oz) unsalted butter or 3 tbsp vegetable oil
250g (9oz) onions, cut into chunky dice
2 red onions, diced
6 garlic cloves, finely chopped
1 red chilli, deseeded and finely chopped
125g (4½oz) fresh ginger, grated or blitzed
2 × 400g (14oz) tins chopped tomatoes
1 tbsp golden caster sugar
2 tsp sea salt
400ml (14fl oz) coconut milk
600ml (1 pint) vegetable stock or water
Juice of 1 lime
Coriander leaves, chopped
1 small handful coconut flakes

1. Soak the lentils in enough water to cover for 10 minutes. Put the cashew nuts in a dry frying pan and toast over a medium heat for 5 minutes, or until lightly golden, tossing the pan frequently. Chop roughly and set aside.

2. Finely grind the peppercorns, cumin and coriander seeds and cloves using a mortar and pestle, then mix in the cinnamon and turmeric. Set aside.

3. Heat the butter in a large flameproof casserole or saucepan over a medium heat. Add the white and red onions, the garlic, chilli and ginger, and cook gently for 5 minutes or until softened.

4. Add the spice mix and cook gently for a couple more minutes.

5. Add the tomatoes, sugar, salt and coconut milk, and simmer for 5–10 minutes, stirring occasionally.

6. Rinse the lentils well and add to the casserole. Simmer, adding the stock bit by bit as it's absorbed. Stir occasionally to prevent it from sticking. Cook over a medium heat for 15–20 minutes until soft.

7. Stir in the lime juice, sprinkle with fresh coriander, coconut shavings and the cashew nuts and serve immediately with fragrant basmati rice or Indian flatbreads.

# TARKA DHAL

*Here's the way my father taught me to make tarka dhal. It's really simple and tastes wonderful. You'll need to have a skimmer to hand, as the turmeric and lentils produce a foam that you need to skim off the surface from time to time as they cook. This is just the impurities and excess starch coming to the surface. Remember to work quickly at the 'tarka' stage so as not to burn the spices.*

**SERVES 6–8**

250g (9oz) moong dhal, red lentils or your favourite type of lentil, rinsed well
About 500ml (18fl oz) vegetable stock or water
1 tsp powdered turmeric
400g (14oz) tin chopped tomatoes
Sea salt
4 tbsp sunflower oil
2 tsp coriander seeds
1 tsp cumin seeds
4 garlic cloves, finely chopped
1 red bird's eye chilli, deseeded and chopped, or 1 tsp chilli flakes (optional, and according to your heat tolerance)
Coriander leaves, finely chopped

1. Put the dhal into a saucepan and add the vegetable stock to cover. Add the turmeric.

2. Bring to the boil, half-cover with a lid, then turn down the heat. Simmer gently until the lentils are just about tender enough to eat; 10–15 minutes if using moong dhal.

3. Add the tomatoes and salt to taste. Stir and leave to simmer gently for another 2–3 minutes. Turn off the heat, cover, and set the saucepan to one side.

4. Now you're ready for the 'tarka' stage. Add the oil to a sauté or high-sided frying pan and put it over a high heat until the oil starts to smoke.

5. Add the coriander and cumin seeds. Take the pan off the heat and swirl the seeds around in the pan, then immediately add the garlic and chilli, if using. Keeping a firm grip on the pan's handle, swirl all the spices around in the oil, taking the pan off and on the heat as you do so to prevent the garlic and spices from burning. You need to keep just enough heat to fry everything.

6. When the spices and garlic are a light brown, nutty colour (this should only take about 1 minute maximum), turn off the heat and pour the hot oil and spices into the lentil saucepan. Immediately replace the lid. Be sure to stand well back! Be prepared for lots of steam and sizzling, hissing sounds as you add the hot oil to the lentils. Gently swirl the lentil pan to combine all the flavours.

7. Leave the pan for a couple of minutes before lifting the lid. Savour the gorgeous spicy aromas as you sprinkle with the fresh coriander. Serve immediately with aged basmati rice and a sliced onion and tomato salad.

# Spicy Chickpeas on Toast

*This is based on one of Dad's recipes. When Mum was in hospital having my younger brother, if we weren't given rice pudding and jam at each meal then he'd conjure up his favourite chickpea chana masala. This is my version of beans on toast: quick, tasty, good for you and happy memories for me!*

## SERVES 4 AS A SNACK OR LIGHT SUPPER

2 tbsp ghee (clarified butter), unsalted butter or a couple of splashes vegetable oil

1 large onion, chopped into 2cm (¾ in) dice

60g (2¼ oz) fresh ginger, grated

5 garlic cloves: 4 finely chopped, 1 halved

3 tsp coriander seeds

1½ tsp cumin seeds

2 tsp black peppercorns

2 tsp powdered turmeric

1 tsp sea salt

400g (14oz) tin chickpeas, drained and rinsed (250g/9oz drained weight)

400g (14oz) tin chopped tomatoes

4 slices sourdough bread

Butter, for spreading

2–3 tsp Garam Masala blend (see page 267) (optional)

Coriander leaves, roughly chopped

2 tsp thick, black Indian tamarind paste

1. Put the ghee into a heavy-based saucepan over a medium heat. Add the onion, ginger and the chopped garlic, and cook gently over a low heat until the onions have softened and the garlic gives off its gorgeous fragrance. Try not to colour the garlic; this will give it and the end dish a bitter flavour.

2. Finely grind the coriander and cumin seeds and peppercorns using a mortar and pestle. Add all the spices to the pan and add the salt, then stir for a couple of minutes to combine all the flavours. It may look a bit dry at this stage, but don't worry: it's all good!

3. Pour the chickpeas and chopped tomatoes into the pan and add 50ml (2fl oz) water, then turn up the heat and gently stir. Heat the mixture until it just starts to bubble, then turn the heat down and simmer gently for 15 minutes.

4. Toast the bread, then rub with the cut edges of the halved garlic clove. Spread generously with butter and put on warmed plates. Spoon on the chickpeas, sprinkle with the Garam Masala, if using, and the fresh coriander. Drizzle each slice with ½ teaspoon tamarind paste and serve immediately.

# CHICKPEA SALAD WITH NECTARINE, FETA & MINT

*The combination of fresh, invigorating garden mint, sweet, juicy nectarines, soft-bite nutty chickpeas and gently salty feta cheese is brought beautifully together with my clean-finishing, vibrant summer dressing – this is one to savour. This surprisingly quick salad goes with any meal, from sausages to steak, from fish to juicy chicken thighs. Its freshness is the key. So grab a glass of your favourite tipple, picnic rugs, friends, family and enjoy a pure taste of summer.*

**SERVES 4–6**

½ red onion, sliced very thinly
Juice of 2 limes
2 ripe nectarines
3 × 400g (14oz) tins chickpeas, drained and rinsed (750g/ 1lb 10oz drained weight)
40g (1½oz) feta cheese, diced into 1cm (½in) cubes
1 handful rocket leaves, torn
1 large handful mint leaves, very thinly sliced

FOR THE DRESSING
5 tbsp rapeseed oil
3 tbsp fresh orange juice
1 tsp orange zest
1 tsp Worcestershire sauce
1 heaped tsp Garam Masala blend (see page 267)
2 tsp mirin (sweet Japanese rice wine)
1 tsp white wine vinegar
½ tsp sea salt
125g (4½oz) soft goat's cheese

1. Put the sliced onion in a bowl and add the lime juice. Set aside for at least 30 minutes.

2. Skin the nectarines by scoring a cross into the base of each fruit and popping it into boiling water for 1 minute; carefully remove it and peel away the skin.

3. Put the nectarines onto a chopping board and cut each into quarters, slicing down around the stone. Then chop into small, even pieces.

4. Mix all the dressing ingredients, except the goat's cheese, together in a small bowl, then stir in the goat's cheese until well combined. Set aside.

5. Lift the onion slices out of the lime juice. Holding them in one hand over the sink, squeeze out the liquid with a firm but gentle grip, and put them in a large mixing bowl. Add the chickpeas and dressing, and mix well so that they are all nicely coated.

6. Add the feta cheese, nectarine pieces, rocket and mint, and gently and carefully fold together just to combine. Chill before serving for an extra-refreshing effect!

# WINTER VEGETABLES

BRASSICAS, TUBERS, SQUASHES, ALLIUMS AND MUSHROOMS ARE THE HEARTY HEAVYWEIGHTS OF THE VEGETABLE WORLD. When cooking and spicing this group it's good to play with warmth and perfume: warmth of ginger, pepper, chillies; perfume of cubeb, cardamom, mace and saffron. Fragrant Garam Masala, a touch of amchoor or asafoetida, or a pinch of chilli give a kick to creamy winter soups and bakes.

I adore cabbage of all types, with their beautiful textured leaves: my favourites, Savoy, Primo and January King, have just the right combination of sweetness and astringency, perfect with pepper, chilli, cumin, coriander, cubeb, turmeric and ginger. My Celebration Lentil Cabbage includes green cardamom and mace to lift and brighten the lentils, while Kashmiri chillies help marry the rich béchamel sauce to astringent cabbage.

I moved to Ireland not terribly passionate about potatoes. However, my wife Olive, like most inhabitants of the Emerald Isle, is a stalwart supporter of floury potatoes: Golden Wonders, Queens, Kerr's Pinks and, at a push, Roosters. For my Vada Pav (potato buns) and Aloo Tikki (potato fritters) I suggest Maris Pipers, but any floury variety is perfect. Potatoes provide a blank canvas for spicing: define buttery mash with nutmeg and white pepper; lift roast spuds with coriander and cumin; when frying, throw in a little chilli and Szechuan pepper; liven up boiled potatoes with green cardamom, vanilla and a grating of long pepper.

Squashes and alliums can share many of the same spice notes: ginger, coriander, fennel, clove, turmeric and white pepper, to bring out natural sweetness, add background heat, and balance sulphurous and bitter notes. At the age of 13, I had a revelation involving the humble onion. It was Saturday or Sunday evening, the TV was on, it may have been Keith Floyd, or Delia. Anyway, they popped a large onion into the oven, bit of olive oil, pinch of salt and simply roasted it off. That was it. I couldn't believe the simplicity. So I tootled off to the kitchen and did the same. About three quarters of an hour later, hey presto, I produced a wonderfully soft, sweet and deliciously pungent supper with crusty bread. And that's the inspiration for my Allium Crumble.

*Previous page: Caramel to the nose, tangy to the tongue, dried mango powder (amchoor) creates a satisfying, subtle, sweet–sour contrast to winter vegetables.*

# JERUSALEM ARTICHOKE SOUP

*I first made a basic version of this recipe many years ago as part of my Ballymaloe Cookery School exam. I chose it for its comfort factor, earthy flavour and the health-giving natural fibre (inulin) content of the artichokes.*

**SERVES 4**

30g (1oz) butter
300g (10½oz) onions, roughly
    chopped
1 tsp sea salt
250g (9oz) floury potatoes, such
    as Maris Piper, peeled and
    roughly chopped
600g (1lb 5oz) Jerusalem
    artichokes, peeled and
    roughly chopped
500ml (18fl oz) chicken stock
300ml (10½fl oz) whole milk,
    plus extra if needed
1 tsp black peppercorns
1 tsp cumin seeds
2 tsp fennel seeds
1 tsp Kashmiri chilli flakes
4 slices sourdough bread, cut
    into 2cm (¾in) dice
4 tbsp light olive oil
4 tbsp soured cream
1 small bunch chives, very thinly
    sliced

1. Put a large saucepan over a medium heat. Add the butter, allow to melt, then add the onions and salt, and fry gently for 5 minutes or until the onions are soft, stirring frequently.

2. Add the potatoes and artichokes, stir well, and cover with a piece of greaseproof paper. Turn down the heat slightly, cover and cook gently for 20 minutes, stirring occasionally.

3. Add the stock and milk, turn up the heat and cook at a gentle bubble for 15–20 minutes until the potatoes and artichokes are completely soft.

4. Remove from the heat and blitz with a stick blender or in a food processor to a smooth consistency. Add a little more milk if needed, then adjust the seasoning and set aside.

5. Meanwhile, preheat the oven to 200°C (gas mark 6) and put a roasting tin into the oven. Finely grind the peppercorns, cumin and fennel seeds using a mortar and pestle, then add the chilli flakes. Put the diced bread in a bowl. Mix the spices with the oil and pour the mixture over the bread.

6. Stir well and tip into the heated roasting tin in an even layer. Put the tin into the oven and roast the bread for about 10 minutes, turning it over from time to time until it's golden all over. Remove from the oven, tip the bread onto kitchen paper to drain, then set aside and allow to cool.

7. Ladle generous amounts of the soup into warmed bowls, drizzle each bowl with 1 tablespoon soured cream, scatter over a handful of the spiced bread, then add the chives and serve immediately.

# CREAM OF YOUNG PUMPKIN SOUP

*The wonderfully fruity, almost smoky flavour and delicate heat of the Kashmiri chilli work so well with the taste of new-season pumpkin. The pumpkin seeds and croûtons add crunch and texture to this unctuous soup – something to bite into is somehow always more satisfying than merely a slurp or two.*

**SERVES 4**

100g (3½oz) unsalted butter
2–3 small pumpkins, or ½ large
    butternut squash, peeled and
    cut into chunks
4 shallots, finely chopped
1 garlic clove, chopped
2 tsp Kashmiri chilli flakes
2 tsp coriander seeds, finely
    ground
1 tsp powdered turmeric
1 litre (1¾ pints) vegetable
    stock
200ml (7fl oz) double cream
1 tsp ground black pepper
30g (1oz) Parmesan cheese,
    grated

## FOR THE CROÛTONS
3 tbsp rapeseed oil
1 handful stale bread, cut into
    small cubes
Sea salt and freshly ground black
    pepper

## TO SERVE
1 small handful dried pumpkin
    seeds
1 small handful chives, finely
    chopped or snipped with
    scissors
1 tsp Kashmiri chilli flakes

1. Put a large heavy-based saucepan over a medium–low heat, add the butter and allow to melt. Add the pumpkin chunks and shallots and cook gently in the butter, without getting any colour, for 6–7 minutes until the edges of the pumpkin are starting to soften.

2. Add the spices and cook for 1 minute. Add the stock and simmer for 5 minutes.

3. Add the cream, black pepper and cheese, then bring just to the boil and remove from the heat.

4. Pour the soup into a food processor or whizz with a stick blender to a smooth consistency. Set aside to keep warm.

5. To make the croûtons, heat the oil and gently fry the bread cubes until they're golden brown, then season with salt and black pepper.

6. Dry-roast the pumpkin seeds in a non-stick pan over a medium heat until just toasted.

7. Pour the soup into warmed bowls, then sprinkle the croûtons, pumpkin seeds, chives and Kashmiri chilli flakes over the top and serve immediately.

# Cauliflower Cheese with Spiced Mornay Sauce

*This is a brilliant accompaniment to steak or lamb roasts, or simply serve by itself as a comfort-food supper.*

**SERVES 4–6**

1 pinch sea salt

1 cauliflower, outer leaves removed and chopped into 2cm (¾in) slices; florets separated into golf-ball-sized chunks

FOR THE MORNAY SAUCE

30g (1oz) unsalted butter

30g (1oz) plain flour

400ml (14fl oz) whole milk

50ml (2fl oz) single cream

75g (2¾oz) mature Cheddar cheese, grated, plus 50g (1¾oz) grated cheese for the topping

50g (1¾oz) mature Emmenthal cheese, grated

30g (1oz) Parmesan cheese, grated

2 tsp French mustard

1 tsp English mustard

1 tsp black peppercorns, finely ground

¼ tsp Szechuan pepper, finely ground

¼ tsp cayenne pepper

Scant ¼ tsp finely ground mace

1. Pour enough cold water into a saucepan, big enough to hold the cauliflower, to come 3cm (1¼in) up the sides of the pan. Add the salt and the cauliflower leaves, then put the florets on top.

2. Bring to the boil over a medium heat, then turn down the heat, cover the pan and simmer for 12–15 minutes until the florets are just tender; when pierced with a knife there will be just a little resistance.

3. Remove from the heat and drain. Put the cooked greens into a roasting tin and put the florets on top. Set aside.

4. Preheat the oven to 200°C (gas mark 6). To make the sauce, put a large saucepan over a medium heat. Add the butter, stir lightly with a small whisk, and when it has melted add the flour and whisk to form a roux. Cook for 30 seconds.

5. Pour the milk and cream into a jug, then pour it bit by bit into the pan, whisking all the time to combine well with the roux. Once all the liquid is added, keep whisking and allow the sauce to cook until you see the first bubbles appear, then continue to cook for 2 minutes.

6. Next add the cheeses, mustards, peppers and mace, stirring continuously to combine. Once the cheese has melted, continue to cook gently for 5 minutes, with only the odd bubble or two popping up, stirring occasionally.

7. Pour all the sauce into the roasting tin, covering the cauliflower, then sprinkle over the extra grated Cheddar. Put on the middle shelf of the oven, and bake for 15–20 minutes or until the cheese melts and the sauce begins to scorch without burning. Serve immediately.

# WINTER LEAVES & SPICED SQUASH

SERVES 4 AS A SNACK OR
LIGHT SUPPER

## FOR THE DRIED FRUIT

1 tbsp each diced dried apricots,
   pitted prunes and figs, and
   sultanas
2 tbsp runny honey
90ml (3fl oz) warm jasmine tea
About 12 saffron threads
1 tsp rose water

## FOR THE SALAD

¼ tsp cubeb peppercorns
¼ tsp finely ground mace
¼ tsp amchoor
2 tsp finely ground cassia
½ tsp powdered ginger
2 tbsp rapeseed oil
500g (1lb 2oz) butternut squash,
   peeled, deseeded and cut into
   small wedges
1 green bird's eye chilli,
   deseeded and finely chopped
1 tsp sea salt
2 small heads radicchio
2 small heads chicory,
   ideally 1 green and 1 red
1 head frisée lettuce
3 handfuls watercress
2 fresh raw chestnuts

## FOR THE DRESSING

1 tbsp Dijon mustard
2 tbsp runny honey
1 tsp red wine vinegar
½ tsp sea salt

*This is a great-tasting salad that looks really splendid if you're able to find different varieties of winter leaves and squashes. That way, you'll not only have an attractive visual selection, but one that excites the palate.*

1. Preheat the oven to 190°C (gas mark 5). Pop all the ingredients for the dried fruit into a saucepan, put over a medium heat, bring up to a bubble and cook for 2 minutes. Remove from the heat, set aside and leave to infuse for 45 minutes, stirring occasionally, until all the fruits soften and plump up, then drain.

2. Mix the spices for the salad together. Put the oil, squash, spice mix, chilli and salt in a bowl, and mix well. Transfer to a large ovenproof frying pan or flameproof casserole and fry for 1 minute over a high heat. Toss the ingredients around in the pan, then pop it into the oven and roast for 15–20 minutes until just soft and charring around the edges. Set aside to cool to room temperature.

3. Put all the dressing ingredients in a screwtop jar and add 2 tablespoons boiling water. Shake well, then set aside.

4. Carefully separate the leaves of the salad vegetables and arrange on a large serving platter.

5. Put the squash pieces on the leaves, scatter over the fruits, pour on the tepid dressing and shave the chestnuts over the top, using a vegetable peeler. Serve immediately.

# Chicory, Watercress, & Grilled Squash Salad

*This simple winter salad makes a beautiful starter or main course. The spiced blood orange dressing incorporates wonderful, fragrant garam masala, which may sound bizarre but tastes excellent and has to be tried. This recipe makes more dressing than is needed for this salad, so you'll have some left over to use with other salads. I love sheep's cheese, but you could use goat's or even a blue cheese at a push.*

## SERVES 4–6

### FOR THE DRESSING
**150ml (5fl oz) rapeseed oil**
**100ml (3½fl oz) blood-orange juice (about 2 juicy oranges), strained**
**Zest of ½ blood orange**
**1 tsp Worcestershire sauce**
**2 tsp Garam Masala blend (see page 267)**
**1 tbsp mirin (sweet Japanese rice wine)**
**1 tbsp white wine vinegar**
**1 tsp sea salt**

### FOR THE SALAD
**50g (1¾oz) skinned hazelnuts**
**1 butternut squash, cut in half lengthways, deseeded and peeled**
**1 head green chicory**
**½ head red chicory, cut lengthways**
**200g (7oz) fresh wild watercress, large stalks removed (you can keep these for a soup stock)**
**100g (3½oz) sheep's cheese, crumbled into small lumps**

1. Put all the dressing ingredients into a clean screwtop jar and shake well. Set aside.

2. Put the hazelnuts for the salad in a dry pan and toast over a medium heat until lightly golden. Roughly chop and set aside.

3. Put the squash flat-side down on a chopping board and, using a sharp knife, carefully cut thin slices the length of the vegetable. You're aiming for them to be no more than 3mm (⅛in) thick.

4. Put a griddle pan over a high heat until drops of water immediately sizzle and evaporate. (You can use a hot grill or heavy-based frying pan if you don't have a griddle pan.) Put a couple of squash slices on the griddle and cook until they char on one side, then flip the slices over and char the other side. Repeat until all the slices are similarly toasted and suitably floppy. Set aside.

5. Chop the base off each chicory head, then carefully peel away whole leaves, one at a time, until you have stripped off all the leaves.

6. Put the toasted squash slices, the watercress and the chicory leaves in a large mixing bowl. Shake the dressing and pour 2 tablespoons of it over the leaves.

7. Using your hands, carefully tumble the leaves around to coat in the dressing, then lift, gently shake off any excess dressing, and transfer them to a large platter or salad bowl. Sprinkle with the cheese, then the chopped hazelnuts and serve.

# CAULIFLOWER CHEESE WITH SPICED MORNAY SAUCE

*This is a brilliant accompaniment to steak or lamb roasts, or simply serve by itself as a comfort-food supper.*

**SERVES 4–6**

1 pinch sea salt

1 cauliflower, outer leaves removed and chopped into 2cm (¾in) slices; florets separated into golf-ball-sized chunks

### FOR THE MORNAY SAUCE

30g (1oz) unsalted butter

30g (1oz) plain flour

400ml (14fl oz) whole milk

50ml (2fl oz) single cream

75g (2¾oz) mature Cheddar cheese, grated, plus 50g (1¾oz) grated cheese for the topping

50g (1¾oz) mature Emmenthal cheese, grated

30g (1oz) Parmesan cheese, grated

2 tsp French mustard

1 tsp English mustard

1 tsp black peppercorns, finely ground

¼ tsp Szechuan pepper, finely ground

¼ tsp cayenne pepper

Scant ¼ tsp finely ground mace

1. Pour enough cold water into a saucepan, big enough to hold the cauliflower, to come 3cm (1¼in) up the sides of the pan. Add the salt and the cauliflower leaves, then put the florets on top.

2. Bring to the boil over a medium heat, then turn down the heat, cover the pan and simmer for 12–15 minutes until the florets are just tender; when pierced with a knife there will be just a little resistance.

3. Remove from the heat and drain. Put the cooked greens into a roasting tin and put the florets on top. Set aside.

4. Preheat the oven to 200°C (gas mark 6). To make the sauce, put a large saucepan over a medium heat. Add the butter, stir lightly with a small whisk, and when it has melted add the flour and whisk to form a roux. Cook for 30 seconds.

5. Pour the milk and cream into a jug, then pour it bit by bit into the pan, whisking all the time to combine well with the roux. Once all the liquid is added, keep whisking and allow the sauce to cook until you see the first bubbles appear, then continue to cook for 2 minutes.

6. Next add the cheeses, mustards, peppers and mace, stirring continuously to combine. Once the cheese has melted, continue to cook gently for 5 minutes, with only the odd bubble or two popping up, stirring occasionally.

7. Pour all the sauce into the roasting tin, covering the cauliflower, then sprinkle over the extra grated Cheddar. Put on the middle shelf of the oven, and bake for 15–20 minutes or until the cheese melts and the sauce begins to scorch without burning. Serve immediately.

# SHIITAKE & SAVOY UPSIDE-DOWN CAKE

*Cabbage is one of my favourite ingredients. I wanted to create a vegetarian terrine; this idea came together over a couple of months of thought – and many a cabbage later! It's based on a very posh-sounding technique, the 'chartreuse', which basically means things wrapped up in cabbage. If the egg mixture leaks out a little, don't worry; it simply fills the cabbage-vein divots – giving the end product a slightly otherworldly, pretty hip appearance.*

### SERVES 4–6

450g (1lb) waxy potatoes, unpeeled

1 large Savoy cabbage, leaves plucked off, hard central veins cut out and discarded

½ tsp cubeb peppercorns

2 tsp white peppercorns

1 tsp cumin seeds

30g (1oz) unsalted butter

2 tbsp olive oil

2 large onions, sliced

1 tsp Kashmiri chilli flakes

4 garlic cloves, finely chopped

175g (6oz) fresh shiitake mushrooms, halved

1 tsp sea salt

300ml (10fl oz) double cream

5 large egg yolks (use the egg whites to make meringues, see page 206)

Sunflower oil, for greasing

Sea salt and freshly ground black pepper

1. In a saucepan, boil the potatoes in enough water to cover for 25 minutes or until soft. Then, holding the hot potatoes in a clean tea towel, peel them, then slice into rounds about 5mm (¼in) thick.

2. Put the cabbage leaves in a pan of boiling salted water and boil for 1 minute to blanch them. Drain and pop into a bowl of ice-cold water. Leave until completely cold. Drain and pat dry with kitchen paper.

3. Finely grind the cubebs, white peppercorns and cumin seeds using a mortar and pestle. Heat the butter and olive oil in a frying pan. Add the onions and cook gently until soft. Add the spices, chilli flakes, garlic, mushrooms and salt, stir and cook for 1 minute. Pour in the cream, turn up the heat and bring to the boil, then simmer rapidly for 5 minutes. Stir and pour the mixture into a heatproof bowl. Set aside to cool completely.

4. Preheat the oven to 180°C (gas mark 4). Stir the egg yolks into the mushroom mixture, one at a time, and season with salt and pepper to taste. Add the potatoes and gently fold to combine everything together.

5. Lightly oil a 1kg (2lb 4oz) loaf tin and line its sides and base with the blanched cabbage leaves so that they overlap each other slightly and fall over the top. Reserve a couple of leaves to cover. Pour in the mushroom mixture and cover with the reserved leaves. Stand the tin in a roasting tin of hot water, cover with a sheet of moistened greaseproof paper and bake for 1 hour. Leave to cool in the tin for 10 minutes, then invert the tin onto a board. Cut the terrine into thick slices and serve immediately.

# CELEBRATION LENTIL CABBAGE

SERVES 4

A little light olive oil

1 large onion, cut into 5mm
(¼in) dice

1 carrot, cut into 5mm (¼in)
dice

¼ head celery, cut into 8mm
(⅜in) slices, leaves reserved
and finely sliced for garnish

3 Jerusalem artichokes, peeled
and cut into 5mm (¼in)
slices

¼ small head celeriac, peeled
and cut into 5mm (¼in) dice

1 garlic clove, roughly chopped

Seeds of 2 green cardamom pods

1 tsp black peppercorns

1 tsp cumin seeds

250g (9oz) Puy lentils, rinsed

¼ tsp finely ground mace

750ml (26fl oz) vegetable stock

50g (1¾oz) unsalted butter,
plus extra for greasing

1 tsp sea salt

2 small, tight Primo cabbages,
halved through the root

2 tsp Kashmiri chilli flakes

30g (1oz) plain flour

350ml (12fl oz) whole milk

100ml (3½fl oz) single cream

2 tsp horseradish cream

50g (1¾oz) hard sheep's cheese
or cow's cheese, finely grated

*This dish can be made really quickly if the lentils are prepared in advance. The combination of nutty spiced lentils, bright cabbage and the warmth of the chilli cream makes a brilliant vegetarian main course.*

1. Put a large saucepan over a medium heat. Add a large slug of oil and the vegetables and garlic, then fry gently for 5 minutes, stirring occasionally. Finely grind the whole spices using a mortar and pestle.

2. Add the lentils and the spice mix and mace to the pan. Stir everything to coat in the oil, then add the vegetable stock and 30g (1oz) of the butter, bring up to a bubble, stir, cover and simmer gently for 40 minutes or until the lentils have lost their bite. Stir in the salt and set aside.

3. Grease a large shallow ovenproof dish, big enough to fit the cabbages snugly inside, and spoon in the warm lentils so that they're about 1.5cm (⅝in) thick over the base.

4. Put the cabbage halves in boiling salted water for 3 minutes to blanch them. Drain well, then lay them, evenly spaced, over the lentils in the dish, alternating top to tail and gently pressing them into the lentils.

5. Preheat the grill to medium. Put a large saucepan over a medium heat, add the remaining butter and stir lightly with a small whisk. When the butter has melted, add the chilli flakes and flour, and whisk to combine. Cook for 30 seconds.

6. Pour the milk and cream into a jug, then pour it bit by bit into the pan, whisking all the time to combine well with the roux. Once all the liquid is in, add the horseradish. Keep whisking and allow the sauce to cook until you see the first bubbles appear, then continue to cook for 2 minutes.

7. Pour this chilli béchamel over the cabbage, sprinkle generously with grated cheese, then pop it under the grill until the whole dish is piping hot and the chilli sauce is a beautiful speckled golden-brown. Remove from the grill, sprinkle with the reserved celery leaves and serve at once.

# GRILLED CHILLI CABBAGE

*This chilli and charred cabbage filled with spicy lamb is my stodge-free take on a chilli dog. It's a great alternative for those days you don't want a carb overload. It can be a little messy to eat, but that's half the point; just have a roll of kitchen paper to hand and you'll be fine!*

## SERVES 4

2 January King cabbages
(Savoys are a great
alternative)
3 tbsp rapeseed oil, plus extra for
basting
575g (1lb 5oz) onions: 500g
(1lb 2oz) thinly sliced, 75g
(2¾oz) finely chopped
3 garlic cloves, finely chopped
1 green finger chilli, deseeded
and finely diced
½ tsp Kashmiri chilli flakes
1 heaped tsp black peppercorns,
finely ground
1 heaped tsp coriander seeds,
finely ground
1 tsp powdered ginger
1 tsp powdered turmeric
1 heaped tsp sea salt
1kg (2lb 4oz) minced lamb
400g (14oz) tin chopped
tomatoes
250g (9oz) crème fraîche
125g (4½oz) Cheddar cheese,
grated

1. Gently snap off six outer leaves from each cabbage, then cut out and discard the central, woody veins. Put the leaves in a large pan of boiling salted water for 30–45 seconds to blanch them, then immediately put them in a bowl of ice-cold water to cool completely.

2. Cut each cabbage in half through their poles, cut out the central stalk and discard, then slice the leaves very thinly into ribbons. Set aside.

3. Put the oil a large saucepan over a medium heat. Add the sliced onions and fry gently until soft, then add the garlic, chilli and chilli flakes, the spices, salt and 2 small handfuls of the thinly sliced cabbage leaves. Fry gently for 1 minute, until wilted.

4. Add the lamb and cook over a medium heat, stirring, until the meat is only just no longer pink.

5. Add the tomatoes and mix well, then bring up to a bubble and simmer over a low heat for 20 minutes or until the meat is tender. Take the pan off the heat, add 200g (7oz) of the crème fraîche and stir well. Put the pan back on the heat, bring back to a gentle simmer and cook for another 1 minute. Remove from the heat and set aside.

6. Preheat the grill to high. Take the large cabbage leaves from the water, drain well and pat them dry with kitchen paper. Rub them with a little oil on both sides. Put them under the grill and grill both sides briefly until just scorched. Repeat until all the leaves are done, then set them aside.

7. In a small bowl, mix the cheese with the remaining crème fraîche and the chopped onions. Take a charred cabbage leaf, spoon on some of the lamb mixture, top with some of the cabbage ribbons, then the cheese mix. Put on the grill pan and repeat until the pan is snugly full. Put under the heat, cook for 1 minute until the cheese melts, then remove from the heat, gingerly roll up each leaf and serve immediately.

# ALOO TIKKI – POTATO FRITTERS WITH SIZZLED TOMATOES

*My dad often used to make us fried potato cakes when he got into the kitchen when Mum was out. They're a staple of any street-food vendor in northern India and a must-have whenever you're walking around the streets of Old Delhi in winter. This is my version – simple, effective and totally delicious. If you have a splash guard, then I'd recommend using it here, because the tomato sauce really spits. A bit messy, I grant you, but essential for the finished dish, so don't be tempted to turn down the heat – but do be careful not to burn it.*

### MAKES 8 PATTIES

500g (1lb 2 oz) floury potatoes, such as Maris Piper, peeled
3–4 tbsp sunflower oil
150g (5½oz) onion, diced
30g (1oz) fresh ginger, finely grated
2 green chillies, deseeded and finely chopped (use less if you don't want it too hot)
3 tsp Garam Masala blend (see page 267)
1 tsp powdered turmeric
2 tsp black mustard seeds
1 tsp sea salt
1 handful mint leaves, torn or chopped
1 small handful coriander leaves, chopped

1. Put the potatoes in a saucepan and cover generously with water. Bring to the boil and boil for 20 minutes or until tender. Drain and lightly mash. Set aside.

2. Heat 1 tablespoon oil in a heavy-based frying pan or sauté pan over a medium heat. Add the onion and fry gently for 3 minutes, then add the ginger and continue cooking until the onion is soft.

3. Add the chillies, the Garam Masala, turmeric, mustard seeds and salt. Stir and cook for 2 minutes more, then turn off the heat, set aside and allow to cool to tepid.

4. Add the herbs and mashed potato and mix thoroughly. Divide the potato mix into eight mounds, then form them into evenly sized balls.

5. Add a little more oil to the frying pan over a medium heat. When hot, add three or four balls. Gently press them down into flat but chunky patties and cook for about 10 minutes until light brown on each side. Repeat until you've cooked all the potato fritters. Serve immediately with Sizzled Tomatoes (see page 182).

[ *Continued* ]

## FOR THE SIZZLED TOMATOES

**3 tbsp olive oil, plus a little extra**
**1 garlic clove, thinly sliced**
**400g (14oz) tin whole plum
    tomatoes, drained**
**1 pinch finely ground black
    pepper**
**Sea salt**

1. Put a large saucepan over a medium–low heat. Add the olive oil and garlic slices and cook for a few minutes to soften without browning.

2. Add the tomatoes, pepper and salt to taste, then turn up the heat and cook fiercely, stirring to make sure it doesn't burn.

3. The tomatoes will release all of their juices. When all the thin liquid has evaporated, add a splash more olive oil, adjust the seasoning and serve hot.

# Vada Pav – Potato Buns

**SERVES 6**

FOR THE RELISHES

2 garlic bulbs, skin on

1 tbsp light olive oil

3 tbsp thick, black Indian
  tamarind paste

Juice of 1 lime

1 tsp sea salt

½ tsp cumin seeds, finely ground

½ tsp black peppercorns, finely
  ground

¼ tsp cayenne pepper

15g (½oz) fresh ginger, grated

A few tbsp Chilli, Coriander &
  Lime Relish (see page 257)

FOR THE BATTER

500g (1lb 2oz) gram (chickpea)
  flour

Juice of 1 lime

1 tsp sea salt

FOR THE POTATO CAKES

500g (1lb 2oz) floury potatoes,
  such as Maris Piper, peeled

1 tbsp light olive oil

150g (5½oz) onion, diced

20g (¾oz) fresh ginger, finely
  grated

1–2 green chillies, deseeded and
  finely chopped

2 tsp black mustard seeds

1 tsp powdered turmeric

1 tsp sea salt

1 large handful coriander leaves,
  torn or chopped

Sunflower oil, for deep-frying

6 soft baps, buns, pav rolls or
  barm cakes, cut almost
  in half, to serve

*We were visiting cousins in Mumbai when they mentioned these potato buns one night. The next morning they delivered about eight to us – fantastic! This is perfect street food; once thought of as a poor man's lunch, today the 'Bombay Burger' is revered. It's traditionally served with three relishes: garlic, chilli and tamarind.*

1. Preheat the oven to 180°C (gas mark 4) and put the garlic in a small roasting tin. Roast for 30 minutes or until golden and softened. Cool, then pop the cloves out of their skins into a small bowl. Mix the roasted garlic with the oil and set aside. In another bowl, mix the tamarind paste, lime juice, salt, spices and ginger and set aside.

2. Next, put the gram flour for the batter in a bowl and whisk in about 300ml (10fl oz) cold water to make a batter that has a consistency a bit thicker than double cream. Set aside.

3. Now for the cakes. Boil the potatoes for 20 minutes or until tender. Drain and roughly mash, then set aside.

4. Heat the oil in heavy-based frying pan or sauté pan over a medium heat. Add the onion and fry gently for 2–3 minutes, then add the ginger and continue cooking until the onion is soft. Add the chillies to taste, the mustard seeds, turmeric and salt. Stir and cook for 2 minutes, then turn off the heat, set aside and allow to cool until tepid.

5. Add the coriander and mashed potato and mix thoroughly. Divide the potato mix into six mounds, then form each mound into a patty.

6. Pour the sunflower oil into an electric deep-fat fryer set to 170°C. (Alternatively, pour the oil into a large saucepan until one-third full and heat it over a medium heat. After about 4–5 minutes, drop a cube of white bread into the hot oil. If it takes 3 seconds to turn golden brown, it's the right heat. If not, adjust the heat accordingly.) Dip each patty into the batter and coat well, drain off any excess batter, then gently lower into the hot oil. Don't crowd the pan; cook in two or three batches as required. Deep-fry until crisp and golden, then transfer to kitchen paper to drain.

7. Put a potato patty into a bun, coat with a little garlic relish, then serve with the tamarind and chilli relishes.

# ALLIUM CRUMBLE

SERVES 4–6

## FOR THE SPICED BUTTER

2 tsp coriander seeds
2 tsp fennel seeds
2 tsp white peppercorns
3 cloves
150g (5½oz) unsalted butter, at
    room temperature
1 heaped tsp powdered ginger
1 tsp black onion (nigella) seeds
½ tsp powdered turmeric
Zest of ½ lemon
1 small handful parsley, leaves
    chopped
1 tbsp brandy

## FOR THE CRUMBLE

150g (5½oz) fresh breadcrumbs
2 tbsp olive oil
40g (1½oz) Parmesan cheese,
    finely grated
½ tsp cayenne pepper
1 small handful chives, finely
    chopped

## FOR THE ONIONS

4 onions, halved through the
    root, each half cut into 4
    slices
4 red onions, halved through
    root, each half cut into 3
    slices
5 banana shallots, halved
    through the root
2 leeks, cut on the diagonal into
    4cm (1½in) pieces
Generous splash rapeseed oil

*Onions, shallots and leeks are all members of the allium family. Here, they get together in a spicy butter under a crumble topping. This is brilliant as a side dish or a light supper.*

1. Preheat the oven to 190°C (gas mark 5). Finely grind the whole spices for the spiced butter using a mortar and pestle. In a small bowl, mix all the spiced butter ingredients together really well. Set aside.

2. In another small bowl, mix all the crumble ingredients. Set aside.

3. Put all the onions, shallots and leeks, cut-side up, in a large roasting tin or ovenproof dish, about 40 × 25 × 4½cm (16 × 10 × 1¾in), and splash a little of the oil over them. Put the tin on the middle shelf of the oven. Roast for 35–40 minutes until just softening and becoming a little charred.

4. Remove the dish from the oven, give it a quick, gentle stir, dot the spiced butter all around it, then put it back in the oven for 5 minutes. Remove once more and scatter the crumble mixture evenly over the surface of the onions.

5. Put the dish back in the oven and cook for a final 5–10 minutes, or until the crumbs are golden brown and the butter begins to bubble up through the topping.

6. Allow to cool slightly and serve with crisp green salad leaves.

# BHARVA BAINGAN

*This classic north Indian stuffed aubergine recipe was described to me in full by both a cousin and an aunt when I was last visiting India. Here's my version – taking equal influence from both sources, you understand! It's a delicious veggie accompaniment to a meal, or is great served simply with flatbread, chilli and cucumber raita.*

## SERVES 4 AS A SIDE DISH

2 onions
4 tsp cumin seeds
3 tsp coriander seeds
2 tsp fennel seeds
¼ tsp asafoetida resin
Sea salt
5 tbsp mustard oil
8–10 baby aubergines, halved along two-thirds of their length, but held together at the stalk
1½ tsp amchoor

1. Grate the onions coarsely into a sieve over a bowl. Discard any juices in the bowl. Finely grind the cumin, coriander and fennel seeds using a mortar and pestle. In a bowl, mix the ground spices with the asafoetida, grated onion and salt to taste. Set aside.

2. Heat the oil in a large frying pan over a medium heat, add the aubergines and fry for 5–8 minutes.

3. Remove the pan from the heat and carefully stuff the aubergines, spooning the spiced onion mix into the cut slits. Let any excess fall into the pan. Lie them on their sides in the pan and return it to the heat. (Some of the stuffing will escape during cooking, but that's all part and parcel of this dish.)

4. Cover and cook for 12–15 minutes, turning the aubergines over halfway through, until the oil separates from the onion mix and the aubergines are beginning to collapse. Remove the lid, sprinkle with the amchoor and a pinch of salt, then turn up the heat and cook to finish off for 2 minutes. Serve immediately.

# SUMMER VEGETABLES

SUMMER VEGETABLES ARE DELICATE CREATURES OF THE LIGHT. NATURE GETS ALL EXCITED AT THIS TIME OF YEAR and brings out an array of dazzling colours and amazing flavours. It's that feeling of abundance and rich colour I'm trying to reflect throughout the recipes in this chapter, mingling subtle fresh flavours with a light touch. Star anise and saffron compete for aromatic dominance, yet combine elegantly and brilliantly; add cumin's earthy sweetness, black pepper's rounded heat, long pepper's off-the-wall perfume, clove's fruitiness for a twist; cayenne for intense red colour and heat.

At the beginning of the season broad beans are at their best, sweet and tender. My Broad Beans and Anchovy Eggs takes a classic mix of flavours as its starting point, but the spices I've used take it in another direction. The long pepper and clove add high-note sunshine sparkle to the grounding effect of turmeric, with a touch of cayenne added as a little 'devilment'.

One of my all-time summer favourite salads has to be the Niçoise. Soft-boiled eggs with yolks oozing, anchovies, green beans, olives and a good coating of lemon dressing. I've rolled the tuna in coriander, Szechuan and black pepper to add zesty zing to the firm flesh, added a lightly spiced saffron aïoli and popped it all into lightly charred olive bread for a slight bitter note and crisp texture.

In my Charentes Cold Plate, the black pepper peach dressing with a splash of vodka, Charentais melon and a touch of saffron all bring heady perfume and suggest the height of summer lunch decadence. Fresh black pepper adds both perfume and an underlying heat to the peach dressing; black olives provide a salty hit, toasted almonds add sweet crunch.

Playing on physical sensations of hot and cold, my Heritage Soup uses green cardamom to accentuate the natural sweetness of courgettes and add a heady pine perfume that works so well with the denser, creamier, warm potato soup. I recommend you serve this with a glass of chilled Albariño, Picpoul de Pinet or the much-maligned Muscadet.

*Previous page: Star anise adds richness, perfume and depth and can broaden out deep notes to provide a firm foundation to many dishes.*

# BROAD BEANS & ANCHOVY EGGS WITH CRISP PANCETTA

*A celebration of summer eating – so simple, yet so delicious. Accented with the flavours of lemon and chervil, it's the perfect summer lunch starter, best enjoyed in the open air.*

**SERVES 4**

9 eggs
12 slices pancetta
150g (5½oz) shelled broad
    beans (about 1.5kg/3lb 5oz
    pods)
50g (1¾oz) tin Spanish Ortiz
    anchovy fillets in olive oil,
    drained and oil reserved
2 tsp best-quality mayonnaise
1 clove, finely ground
½ tsp powdered turmeric
7 gratings long pepper
½ tsp cayenne pepper, plus extra
    for dusting
1 small handful curly parsley
    leaves, finely chopped
12 chervil sprigs, plus chervil
    leaves to garnish
Sea salt

## FOR THE LEMON DRESSING

3 tbsp fruity olive oil
Juice of ½ lemon
1 pinch sea salt

1. Preheat the oven to 190°C (gas mark 5). Put the eggs in a large saucepan of boiling water, bring back to the boil and cook for 6 minutes. Drain and refill the pan with cold water. Drain and refill the pan again, then drain again. Peel off the shells and cut the eggs in half. They should have a soft centre. Lay the pancetta on a baking sheet, cover with another baking sheet and bake for 7–10 minutes until crisp. Set aside.

2. Put the beans in a saucepan of boiling salted water for 1 minute to blanch them, then drain and plunge them into ice-cold water. Peel off the outer skins and discard. Set the beans aside on a plate.

3. Put six of the egg halves and all the yolks in a bowl and crush them with a fork. Add a tiny drizzle of the anchovy oil, the mayonnaise, spices and four anchovy fillets, then work everything together into a rough paste.

4. Add the parsley, mix to combine well, then spoon into a piping bag with a fluted nozzle. Pop into the fridge.

5. Put all the lemon dressing ingredients into a screwtop jar and add 4 teaspoons cold water. Shake well, then set aside.

6. Take the 12 remaining egg halves, season with a little salt, then pipe the anchovy paste generously onto each egg half. Dust with a little cayenne pepper. Set aside.

7. In a small bowl, coat the broad beans with the dressing, then arrange them along the centre of a long platter. Dress with chervil sprigs, then put the egg halves on the beans. Lean the pancetta crisps against the eggs and garnish generously with chervil leaves.

# Niçoise Pan Bagnat

*Pan bagnat is a brilliant sandwich that encapsulates the spirit of the Côte d'Azur. It's all about classic Provençal flavours and textures, layered between olive oil bread. Salade niçoise is one of my favourites; here it is, in a sandwich. Preparation is the key here: searing tuna, soft-boiling eggs, making aïoli and the like. The king of all sandwiches, it takes a little time to construct – so take a deep breath and off we go.*

### MAKES 2–3 SANDWICHES

2 eggs
1 handful extra-fine green beans
2 tsp black peppercorns
½ tsp Szechuan pepper
2 tsp coriander seeds
150g (5½oz) fresh yellowfin
    tuna loin
1 fresh ciabatta loaf
2 tsp pitted and roughly chopped
    green olives
2 very ripe plum tomatoes,
    thinly sliced
1 small romaine or sweetheart
    lettuce, shredded
1 red onion, thinly sliced
1 small handful basil leaves
1 small bunch wild rocket
50g (1¾oz) tin Spanish Ortiz
    anchovy fillets in olive oil,
    drained and oil reserved

1. Put the eggs in a large saucepan of boiling water and boil for 3½ minutes. Drain and refill the pan with cold water. Drain and refill the pan again, then drain again. Peel off the shells and slice each egg into six.

2. Steam the green beans for 5 minutes or until just soft, then cool and cut in half. Coarsely grind the peppercorns and coriander seeds using a mortar and pestle.

3. Put a griddle pan or heavy-based frying pan over a high heat. Tip the coarsely ground spices onto a plate, roll the tuna loin on the plate to coat it well all over, then put on the griddle for 30–45 seconds on each side, to sear the tuna rare. Slice thinly and set aside.

## FOR THE LEMON DRESSING

2 garlic cloves
1 pinch sea salt
Juice of 1 lemon
75ml (2½fl oz) fruity olive oil
1 tbsp anchovy oil from the tin
   (see above)
½ tsp black peppercorns, finely
   ground

## FOR THE SAFFRON AÏOLI

1 floury potato, such as Maris
   Piper, unpeeled
4 saffron threads
1 garlic clove
1 pinch sea salt
1 medium egg yolk
2–3 tbsp fruity olive oil, or more
   if needed
Juice of 1 lemon

4. To make the dressing, chop the garlic with the salt until it forms a paste. In a small bowl, mix all the dressing ingredients with a fork to bring them together. Set aside.

5. To make the aïoli, put the potato in a saucepan and cover generously with water. Boil for 20 minutes or until tender. Peel and cool. Meanwhile, put the saffron in a bowl and add 1 teaspoon warm water.

6. Chop the garlic with the salt until it forms a paste. In a small bowl, combine the potato, saffron and its soaking liquid, egg yolk and garlic, gently working them into a smooth paste, using a fork. Drizzle in the olive oil while whisking with a fork until the aïoli has a lovely velvety texture. Add the lemon juice and salt to taste. Set aside.

7. Preheat the grill to hot or return the griddle pan to a high heat. Cut the bread in half horizontally and put under the grill or on the griddle to lightly toast or char the cut surfaces. Drizzle 2–3 teaspoons lemon dressing over the bottom half of the loaf to moisten it, then spread the chopped green olives on top, followed by the saffron aïoli.

8. Now for the layers: first add the sliced tomatoes, then the lettuce, sliced eggs and beans, and drizzle with a little more lemon dressing. Next, add the sliced seared tuna, then the sliced onion, basil leaves, rocket leaves and finally a single line of anchovies.

9. Cover the sandwich with the top half of the loaf and press down gently. Put an upturned plate on top of the loaf and leave for 10 minutes to rest. Slice the loaf into two or three pieces and serve.

# My Bologna Sarnie

*Modena, the home of Ferrari, is where I got the inspiration for this delicious finger sandwich. It's a superb combination of flavours and textures – crushed peas, mortadella, Bel Paese cheese and anise mayo – and simple to construct. Perfect for afternoon teas or canapés.*

### SERVES 2 HUNGRY PEOPLE

1 tbsp light olive oil
3 star anise, slightly cracked
2 tsp finely chopped shallots
85g (3oz) defrosted frozen, or
     tinned small young peas
2 tsp good-quality mayonnaise
1 tsp finely chopped tarragon
     leaves
8 slices good-quality white
     bread, sliced 8mm (⅜in)
     thick
4 wafer-thin slices mortadella or
     Italian cooked ham
½ tsp black peppercorns, finely
     ground
A little sea salt
4 Bel Paese portions, or any soft
     cheese

1. Put the oil in a small saucepan and fry the star anise over a gentle heat for 5 minutes.

2. Add the shallots and continue to cook for 3 minutes or until they're only just soft. Add 3 tablespoons water; the mixture will thicken and emulsify slightly. Remove the star anise, then add the peas and cook for 2 minutes or until soft.

3. Remove the pan from the heat and dip the bottom into a bowl of iced water. When the peas are completely cold, crush them with a fork, then add the mayonnaise and tarragon, and gently mix them together.

4. Spread a thick layer of the pea mixture over four slices of the bread, then top with the mortadella or ham. Season the remaining four slices with pepper and just a sprinkle of sea salt, then spread on the Bel Paese and sandwich together with the ham-topped slices. Gently press the bread down, then cover and chill for 45 minutes to firm up the mixture.

5. Using a serrated knife, remove the crusts and cut into fingers or triangles, trying not to squeeze out the mixture as you go. Serve with a chilled glass of something you love; they're the perfect apéritif foil.

# CHARENTE COLD PLATE

*Refreshing, summery and full of flavour; this is my 'sunshine-on-a-plate'.*

**SERVES 4**

100g (3½oz) golden caster
   sugar
300g (10½oz) peaches
½ tsp black peppercorns, finely
   ground
1 tbsp vodka
1 small handful blanched
   almonds
75g (2¾oz) Puy lentils
12 saffron threads
Juice of ½ lemon
½ fennel bulb, very thinly sliced,
   feathery fronds reserved
1 large carrot, shaved into
   ribbons with a veg peeler
½ Charentais melon, balled with
   a melon baller
7 pitted black olives, finely
   chopped
1 small handful pine nuts
A generous splash best-quality
   fruity olive oil
1 large handful fresh mint
   leaves, some very finely
   chopped, a few left whole

1. Put 75ml (2½fl oz) water and the sugar in a saucepan, stir and put over a medium heat. Skin the peaches by scoring a cross into the base of each fruit and popping it into boiling water for 1 minute; carefully remove it and peel away the skin. Halve and stone the peaches and chop them roughly, reserving any juices.

2. Once the sugar has dissolved, add the peach pieces, their juices and the black pepper to the pan and allow to bubble gently for 5–8 minutes.

3. Take off the heat, pour in the vodka, then transfer to a food processor or blender and blitz to a smooth paste. Allow to cool, then pop the mixture into the fridge to chill completely.

4. Put the almonds in a small pan and dry-toast them over a medium heat until golden. Leave to cool, then roughly chop. Set aside.

5. Put the lentils in a small saucepan, cover well with cold water and put over a high heat. Bring to the boil, then turn down the heat and simmer gently for 15 minutes or until cooked but still with a little bite. Drain, rinse under cold water, then set aside to cool completely.

6. Put the saffron in a small bowl, add 2 tablespoons hot water and set aside to steep for at least 15 minutes, then add the lemon juice and stir.

7. To assemble the plate, arrange the fennel, the fennel fronds and carrots on a large serving platter, then add the melon balls and drizzle generously with the peach purée. Scatter over the olives, pine nuts and lentils, then spoon the saffron and its soaking water over the salad. Finish off with a splash or two of the olive oil, sprinkle with the mint and serve immediately.

# HERITAGE SOUP

SERVES 4–6

*Two soups in one bowl. The earthy, creamy potato soup is served hot, the delicate courgette and cardamom soup is chilled, making a lovely contrast of hot and cold, creamy and dense, and light and fragrant.*

### FOR THE POTATO SOUP

**5 new-season waxy heritage potatoes, such as Home Guard or Charlotte, peeled and cut into chunks**
**150g (5½oz) unsalted butter**
**1 onion, cut into chunks**
**1 leek, white only, cut into chunks**
**600ml (1 pint) whole milk**
**100ml (3½fl oz) double cream**
**1 tsp sea salt**
**A little freshly ground white pepper**

1. Put the potatoes in a large saucepan over a medium–low heat and add the butter. Cover and cook them gently for 30 minutes, stirring frequently.

2. Add the onion and leek, then cover and cook gently for another 15 minutes. Add the milk and 300ml (10fl oz) water, bring to a gentle simmer and allow to bubble gently, uncovered, for 25 minutes. Add the cream, then pour the mixture into a food processor or blender and blitz until smooth and creamy. Season with salt and pepper to taste. Set aside.

### FOR THE COURGETTE & CARDAMOM SOUP

**150g (5½oz) unsalted butter, chilled**
**4 small, firm courgettes, thinly sliced**
**3 shallots, finely chopped**
**Seeds of 6–8 green cardamom pods, finely ground**
**3 handfuls spinach, thick fibrous stalks removed**
**200ml (7fl oz) buttermilk**

1. Put a shallow pan over a medium–low heat and add 100g (3½oz) of the butter. Add the courgettes, shallots and most of the ground cardamom and cook gently for 10 minutes or until the vegetables are really soft. Try not to colour the veg at all. Add the spinach and allow it to wilt, then remove the pan from the heat and leave to cool completely. Chill for at least 10 minutes.

2. Put everything into a food processor or blender and blitz, then add the buttermilk, the remaining cold butter and the remaining ground cardamom. Blitz again until it's really smooth and glossy.

3. Cover and put it into the fridge until ready to serve.

### TO SERVE

**Seeds of 2 green cardamom pods, finely ground**
**8–12 chervil sprigs**

1. Heat the potato soup until hot, but not boiling. Check the seasoning and adjust it if necessary. Meanwhile, whisk the courgette soup or quickly whizz it with a stick blender to froth it – like a cappuccino. Check the seasoning. Ladle the potato soup into warmed bowls, then pour on the chilled courgette soup. Garnish with a light dusting of green cardamom and a couple of sprigs of fresh chervil – beautiful, simple and delicious! Serve with warm soda bread.

# JUST RAW SALAD

*A superb, fresh and strikingly beautiful salad to serve as a starter, main or when you want to treat yourself or friends to a light snack bursting with vibrant flavours. Just be careful if you're using a mandolin and avoid nipping your fingertips.*

**SERVES 2**

2 heritage golden and candy-
    striped beetroot, peeled
3 carrots
7–8 radishes
1 fennel bulb, trimmed
1 star anise, finely ground
75ml (2½fl oz) extra virgin
    olive oil
2 tbsp lemon juice
1 small dried red bird's eye chilli,
    crumbled
½ tsp coarsely ground black
    pepper
Sea salt
1 fresh pomegranate, halved
50–100g (1¾–3½oz) mature
    crumbly goat's cheese
Generous bunch of flat-leaf
    parsley, finely chopped
1 small handful pea shoots,
    stalks removed

1. Using a mandolin or a sharp knife, taking great care, very thinly slice the beetroot, carrots, radishes and fennel, then put them all in a bowl.

2. Add the star anise, olive oil and lemon juice, then sprinkle in the chilli, black pepper and salt to taste. Leave the salad to rest for 5 minutes, then toss everything together. Transfer to a serving platter.

3. Hold a pomegranate half in one hand just above a small bowl, cut-side down. With your other hand, firmly and repeatedly strike the pomegranate with a wooden spoon to release the seeds and juice into the bowl.

4. Remove any white pith from the seeds, then scatter them over the salad, followed by the gorgeous red juices.

5. Now, just crumble the goat's cheese over the top, sprinkle the parsley over that and top with the pea shoots. Serve immediately.

# BAKED AUBERGINES WITH CRUMBLY GOAT'S CHEESE

*Simple earthy flavours make this a great snack or addition to a picnic basket or a summer salad table.*

**SERVES 4**

2 tsp cumin seeds

4 aubergines

2 tbsp extra virgin olive oil, plus extra for drizzling

1 red finger chilli, deseeded and finely diced

Juice of 1 lemon

Olive oil, for grilling

1 tsp sea salt

1 small handful flat-leaf parsley, finely chopped

175g (6oz) crumbly local goat's cheese, or Valençay St Maure

1. Put the cumin seeds in a small pan and lightly dry-toast over a medium heat to release their aroma. Lightly crush them in a mortar and pestle, and set aside.

2. Cut the aubergines in half lengthways and gently score the exposed flesh to create a criss-cross pattern on each half.

3. In a small bowl, mix the olive oil with the chilli and lemon juice, then set aside.

4. Preheat the oven to 200°C (gas mark 6). Put a griddle pan over a high heat until it's very hot. Rub a little olive oil on the exposed flesh of the aubergine halves, then put them, cut-side down, in the griddle pan and cook for 3 minutes. Turn them over and cook their skins for another 1 minute.

5. Take the aubergines from the pan and put them into a large roasting tin or baking tray, flesh-side up. Put the roasting tin on a high shelf in the oven and cook the aubergines for 15 minutes. Take them out, drizzle them with half the chilli-lemon juice mixture, then pop them back in the oven and cook until they have collapsed and are soft.

6. Put the aubergines on a warmed serving platter and drizzle with olive oil. Sprinkle evenly with the salt, the toasted cumin seeds and parsley, then crumble the cheese on top. Serve immediately.

# WINTER FRUIT

WINTER FRUITS, COMFORT AND SPICE. Fruit and nuts foraged from hedgerows or fresh from farmers' markets, and their exotic imported cousins oranges, pomegranates and passion fruits. Match their sweet notes with creamy floral vanilla or heady cinnamon, or lift the fruit with the sweet floral astringency of rose or saffron, the menthol perfume of green cardamom or aromatic star anise.

Plums and Miso Candied Pistachios is a fireside feast. Sticky umami pistachios, soft plum flesh, rich mascarpone warmed with black pepper and scented with rose and vanilla. As food tends to be a little heavier at this time of year, this sweet treat stands out as a dish of indulgence with very little guilt factor. In absolute contrast, I created the Chestnut Meringue, combining sweet, light meringue with a dense chestnut mousse, made brighter with green cardamom and rose, warmed and rounded out with cinnamon, and served with pears poached in a sugar syrup 'spiced' with whiskey.

For winter fruit colours I think of rusty reds, deep oranges, mellow yellows and nutty browns. Main spice notes are perfumed and fruity, earthy, rich and floral. These characteristics work to enrich the depth of flavour and bring out both the sultry character and the unique richness winter fruits offer.

I based my Polenta Tea Cake on my friend Stefano's recipe; I love the simplicity of the method. For my version of this classic combination of north Italian ingredients, I add fruity notes of clementine and dried cherries, and plenty of perfumed oomph with the spicing: clove to back up the fruit, fennel for a comforting anise twist, black pepper for depth and green cardamom for a high-end 'ping'. I pair the cake with a passion fruit mascarpone cream, to focus attention on all the fruity flavours.

*Previous page: The floral astringency of rose balances and contrasts with its sweet, heady perfume. Wonderful with windfall apples and brambles, or use to lift the richness of cream and mascarpone to serve with fruity puds.*

# Celeriac & Beets with Blood Orange & Walnut

*This side dish works well with game or beef. It's zingy, textured and earthy, with a healthy sprinkling of spice for good measure. You can prepare the vegetables and the dressing ahead; when you're ready to serve, pop the vegetables back in the oven to heat up and follow step 4.*

**SERVES 4**

3 beetroot (a mix of heritage
    varieties is great), peeled,
    halved though the poles, then
    each half cut into wedges
½ celeriac (about 250g/9oz), cut
    into 2.5cm (1in) dice
Generous splash rapeseed oil
2 tsp sea salt
2 blood oranges

FOR THE DRESSING
75g (2¾oz) walnuts
2 tbsp runny honey
30g (1oz) fresh ginger, peeled
    and very finely grated
1 tbsp white wine vinegar
Juice of ½ lemon
1 tbsp silver tequila
1 star anise, finely ground
1 tsp black peppercorns, finely
    ground
2 tsp black cumin seeds
½ tsp carom seeds
7 gratings long pepper
½ tsp sea salt
1 large handful curly parsley,
    leaves finely chopped

1. Preheat the oven to 180°C (gas mark 4). Put the beetroot, celeriac, oil and salt in a roasting tin and mix to coat all the ingredients. Roast for 35–40 minutes until the vegetables are just becoming soft without being too squidgy.

2. Meanwhile, using a sharp knife, slice of the tops and bottoms of the oranges, then cut off the peel and pith. Cut 1 orange into 2cm (¾in) discs, and for the second orange cut between the membrane into individual segments. Remove all the pips but reserve the juice.

3. For the dressing, put the walnuts in a small pan and dry-toast over a medium heat until lightly browned. Chop roughly. Put the honey, ginger, vinegar, lemon juice, tequila, and ground and whole spices in a small saucepan. Put over a medium heat, bring up to a bubble and simmer gently for 1 minute, stirring. Remove from the heat, add the salt and reserved orange juice, stir, then add the parsley and stir briefly to combine.

4. Remove the vegetables from the oven and immediately, but carefully, stir in the orange discs. Drizzle over the dressing, sprinkle on the walnuts, and dot the orange segments over the top.

# PLUMS & MISO CANDIED PISTACHIOS WITH ROSE VODKA SAUCE

*This is a delicious combination of taste and texture and the most wonderful of light, fruity desserts. The miso pistachio nuts are something I came up with after a trip to meet my friend Ben at the Nordic Food Lab in Copenhagen. They add crunch, with a subtle umami twist. Try to find plums that are really ripe, juicy and ready for eating. Using different varieties of plums makes presentation that much more intriguing.*

**SERVES 4**

**250g (9oz) pistachio nuts**
**Sunflower oil, for greasing**
**1 tbsp miso paste (sweet white is good, but any good-quality miso is fine)**
**4 tbsp runny honey**
**12 plums, such as Victoria, greengage, Opal, Reeve or even yellow**
**At least 24 juicy wild blackberries**
**1 vanilla pod, split lengthways**
**12 tbsp mascarpone cheese**
**2 tsp rose water**
**1 tsp black peppercorns, finely ground**
**1 tbsp vodka**
**6 tbsp light muscovado sugar**

1. Preheat the oven to 150°C (gas mark 2). Put the pistachio nuts onto an oiled baking tray and cook on the middle shelf of the oven for 10 minutes. Meanwhile, in a small bowl, mix the miso paste with 1 tablespoon water, stir, then add the honey and stir again to combine well.

2. Take the warm nuts from the oven and tip them into the miso bowl, stir well, then tip the mixture back onto the baking tray. Return it to the oven and cook for 5–10 minutes until the nuts start to colour slightly. Take them out, pour them onto a plate and set aside to cool.

3. Preheat the grill to high. Cut each plum in half, removing and discarding the stones. Put the plums, hollow-side up, on a shallow baking tray, then put a blackberry or two into each plum half.

4. Scrape out the seeds from the vanilla pod. In a bowl, mix together the mascarpone, rose water, pepper, vodka and vanilla seeds. Carefully spoon the creamy mixture over the plums, sprinkle with the sugar, and put the tray onto the top rack of your grill. Grill for 15–20 minutes until the plums just begin to collapse.

5. Spoon the plums and as much of the gorgeously gooey mascarpone mix as you like onto a large, warmed serving platter, top generously with the miso pistachio nuts and let everyone dig in!

# CHESTNUT MERINGUE

*With its saffron-poached pears, whisky syrup and whipped cream, this is a wonderfully indulgent winter treat. I love meringues, and this method is simple to get right. The mousse, fruit and syrup make it something really special.*

**SERVES 4**

## FOR THE PEARS

**700g (1lb 9oz) demerara sugar**
**12 saffron threads**
**2 strips of lemon zest, pared**
    **with a veg peeler**
**6 Comice pears, peeled, cored**
    **and each cut into 4 slices**
**50ml (2fl oz) whisky**

## FOR THE MERINGUE

**6 large egg whites**
**350g (12oz) golden caster sugar**

1. To cook the pears, put the sugar and 300ml (10fl oz) water into a heavy-based saucepan. Stir once, then put over a medium heat until the sugar has dissolved, swirling the pan from time to time, but do not stir. Add the saffron and lemon zest, and gently swirl the pan a little more.

2. Add the pears and cover with a piece of greaseproof paper. Turn the heat down to a gentle constant bubble, and cook for 15–20 minutes until the fruit softens and becomes translucent – just so that there's no resistance when you poke them with the point of a sharp knife.

3. Remove the pears with a slotted spoon and put them on a wire rack over a plate to collect the juices. Turn up the heat under the pan, reduce the syrup by half and then pour in the whisky. Swirl the pan to combine, and set aside.

4. To make the meringue, preheat the oven to 160°C (gas mark 3). Line a baking tray with a sheet of baking parchment. Put the egg whites and sugar into a clean, grease-free bowl and whisk to form smooth, stiff, glossy peaks – about 12–15 minutes with an electric hand whisk.

5. Put a small dot of meringue mixture under the four corners of the parchment to stick it to the tray. Take a large metal spoon and dollop the meringue onto the baking parchment to form a large doughnut-type shape about 20cm (8in) in diameter. Be a little creative with your meringue by shaping the edges of the ring into turret-like peaks.

6. Pop it in the oven and bake for 10 minutes, then turn the oven down to 140°C (gas mark 1) and continue to bake for another 50 minutes, then remove from the oven and set aside to cool completely.

## FOR THE MOUSSE

**400g (14oz) cooked and peeled chestnuts**

**175ml (6fl oz) whole milk, plus extra if needed**

**1 tiny pinch sea salt**

**2 large egg yolks**

**175g (6oz) light muscovado sugar**

**60g (2¼oz) crème fraîche**

**100ml (3½fl oz) double cream, plus extra whipped cream to serve**

**1 tsp dried rose petals, finely chopped**

**Seeds of 3 green cardamom pods, finely ground**

**1 tsp finely ground cinnamon**

7. For the mousse, put the chestnuts, milk and salt into a saucepan. Put the saucepan over a medium heat, partially cover, and bring to a gentle simmer. Bubble gently for 10 minutes or until the chestnuts are soft.

8. Put the chestnuts and hot milk into a blender or food processor and blitz to a smooth purée. You may need to add a little more milk so that you end up with a very thick, but only just pliable, paste. Transfer to a bowl and put a sheet of clingfilm on the paste's surface. Set aside to cool.

9. Meanwhile, put the egg yolks into a mixing bowl and, using an electric hand whisk, whip until they become pale and fluffy. Set aside.

10. Put the muscovado sugar and 125ml (4fl oz) water into a saucepan and stir thoroughly just once. Put the pan over a medium heat and bubble gently to make a clear syrup. After 5 minutes, take a metal spoon, dip it into the sugar solution, then raise the spoon to about the same level as the rim of the pan, tilt the spoon and allow the syrup to fall from the spoon back into the pan. Repeat until you see a gloopy drop fall from the spoon. It should no longer run freely but be more like molten jam: this is the soft ball stage.

11. Remove the pan from the heat. Using your electric whisk, immediately pour the hot sugar syrup into the egg yolks, whisking constantly. Keep whisking for 5 minutes or until the mixture has cooled. Set aside.

12. Make sure the chestnut paste is at room temperature, then add it to the yolk mixture and mix in. Add the crème fraîche and mix again. Whip the cream to soft peaks, then fold the cream and spices into the chestnut mixture and mix thoroughly but gently to combine. Put the meringue on a large serving platter and spoon the mousse into the centre, arrange the pear segments on the mousse, drizzle over the whisky sauce and serve with a little whipped cream.

# POLENTA TEA CAKE

*Although this is simple to make, it does take a little patience to cook and cool but it produces a totally satisfying, deep-crust crunch with a moreish moist centre and delicious polenta bite. I've used the spices here to brighten up the richness and add some oomph to the subtle, zesty clementine flavour.*

## MAKES ABOUT 20 SLICES

2 tsp fennel seeds
5 cloves
Seeds of 5 green cardamom pods
1 tsp coriander seeds
1 tsp black peppercorns
100g (3½oz) dried cherries, halved
225g (8oz) polenta
200g (7oz) demerara sugar
1 pinch sea salt
175g (6oz) plain flour
1 tsp baking powder
1 tsp bicarbonate of soda
50g (1¾oz) walnuts, roughly chopped
3 clementines
250g (9oz) ricotta cheese
100g (3½oz) unsalted butter, melted, plus extra for greasing
1 medium egg white

### TO SERVE

200g (7oz) mascarpone cheese
Pulp and seeds of 2 passion fruits
1 tsp icing sugar, sifted

1. Preheat the oven to 170°C (gas mark 3). Lightly butter a 900g (2lb) loaf tin, line it with greaseproof paper and butter it again.

2. Finely grind the spices in a mortar and pestle. Add the cherries to the spices and mix to coat them thoroughly.

3. Put the polenta, sugar and salt in a large bowl and mix together, then sift in the flour, baking powder and bicarbonate of soda. Add the walnuts, spices and cherries, and mix well to combine. Grate the zest of the clementines into the same bowl and mix well.

4. Put the ricotta in a separate bowl, give it a quick whisk, then add 250ml (9fl oz) water and the melted butter. Squeeze in the juice of two of the clementines. Whisk again.

5. Pour the wet ingredients into the dry ingredients, stirring with a wooden spoon or rubber spatula. Mix the batter well, stirring, and scraping the base and sides of the bowl until you have an unctuous mixture.

6. In a clean, grease-free bowl, whisk the egg white to stiff peaks. Carefully fold it into the batter, then pour the batter into your lined loaf tin. Put the loaf on a middle shelf of the oven and bake for 1 hour 20 minutes or until a skewer inserted into the centre comes out clean.

7. Remove the tin from the oven and put it on a wire rack. Leave the loaf to cool for 30 minutes, then turn it out of the tin to cool completely. Carefully tear away the greaseproof paper. Store in a cake tin for up to one week, or freeze for up to two months.

8. To serve, mix the mascarpone, passion-fruit pulp and seeds, and icing sugar together in a bowl. Slice the cake and serve with a dollop of the passion-fruit mascarpone or a thick layer of butter.

# BLACKBERRY, APPLE & COMICE PEAR COMPÔTE

*This is a very simple dessert. It's fruity, light and packed full of generous flavours with virtually no guilt factor attached. As such, it makes the perfect New Year's Day pudding for when you might still be reeling from your enjoyment of Christmas meals and party excesses.*

**SERVES 4–6**

700g (1lb 9oz) demerara sugar
1 star anise, lightly crushed
2 green cardamom pods, crushed
3 cloves
4 black peppercorns, crushed
½ tsp Szechuan pepper
½ tsp dried rose petals, finely
    chopped
2 strips of lemon zest, pared
    with a veg peeler
2 eating apples, peeled, cored
    and each cut into 16 thin
    slices
4 pears, such as Comice, peeled,
    cored and each cut into 8
    slices
150g (5½oz) blackberries, fresh
    or defrosted frozen
Clotted cream (optional),
    to serve

1. Put the sugar and 300ml (10fl oz) water in a heavy-based pan, stir to combine, then put over a medium heat until the sugar has dissolved, swirling the pan from time to time but not stirring.

2. Add the spices and strips of lemon zest, and gently swirl the pan a little more.

3. Add the apples and pears and cover with a piece of greaseproof paper. Turn the heat down to a gentle constant bubble, and cook for 10–15 minutes until the fruit softens and becomes translucent – just so that there's no resistance when you poke them with the point of a sharp knife.

4. Remove the fruit slices from the pan using a slotted spoon and put them on a plate to rest. Turn the heat up under the pan and reduce the syrup by half.

5. Next, carefully pour the syrup through a fine sieve, discard the spices and zest, then return the syrup to the pan and heat gently. When warm to the touch, pop in the blackberries, then return the cooked pears and apples to the syrup and warm through for no more than 30 seconds. Turn off the heat and transfer to a serving bowl.

6. Serve immediately with a couple of generous dollops of clotted cream or my Slaked Passion-fruit Ice (see opposite) and tuck in.

# SLAKED PASSION-FRUIT ICE

*This is called slaked ice, rather than sorbet, because I'm using milk rather than water. It's a really refreshing dessert. I came up with this idea when I wanted something a little lighter than ice cream. It's a kind of guilt-free version, with a little lactic hit and a beautiful floral punch.*

**SERVES 10–12**

750ml (26fl oz) whole milk
10 saffron threads
4 large eggs, separated
400g (14oz) golden caster sugar
100ml (3½fl oz) strained lemon
    juice (from 2 lemons)
Pulp of 10 passion fruits,
    rubbed through a sieve to
    remove the seeds

1. Put 75ml (2½fl oz) of the milk and the saffron in a small saucepan. Put over a medium heat until you see a gentle shimmer, then take off the heat and leave to infuse and cool completely.

2. In a small bowl, lightly whisk the remaining milk with the cooled saffron milk, then add the egg yolks and whisk well. Add the sugar, lemon juice and passion-fruit pulp. Mix well, then set the bowl aside.

3. In a clean, grease-free bowl, whisk the egg whites to stiff peaks, then add them to the bowl of fruit pulp and fold through to combine the mixture thoroughly.

4. Pop the bowl into the freezer for 2 hours. Remove from the freezer, transfer the mixture to a food processor or blender, blitz, then pour and scrape the semi-frozen mixture back into the bowl, smoothing it down with the back of a metal spoon.

5. Put the mixture back into the freezer for another 1 hour or so. Serve generous scoops with my Blackberry, Apple & Comice Pear Compôte (see opposite).

SUMMER FRUIT

THIS CHAPTER IS CRAMMED WITH ALL MY SUMMER FRUIT FAVOURITES:
figs, raspberries, blackcurrants, peaches, cherries and apricots. As these fruits ripen on the bush or tree they produce wonderful natural sugars, and their own distinctive perfumes. Beguiled by their beauty, we're rewarded with every sweet, sour, satisfying bite.

It's the combination of natural sugars and perfumes that make summer fruits so interesting to me – so many mixed and varied flavours. So the group of spices that I work with edge toward the more challenging, working in subtle opposition to the natural fruity notes; spices help my palate understand the complex beauty of these delicate fruits. After all, many spices are also fruits: the complex, almost citrus notes of allspice or equally complex long pepper (a flower spike packed with minuscule 'fruit'), the twisted heat of cubeb, the sweet anise perfume of fennel or richer notes of star anise. Summer fruit, fresh from the garden (or shop shelf!), can work so well with soft green aromatic leaves of fresh herbs, lifting fruity flavours to another level. Combine the pungency of peppers, twists of anise perfume from fennel, add a touch of basil freshness and you have the inspiration for my Apricot Crunches.

A recent wonderful olfactory experience in Pollença, Spain, is part of the inspiration for my Black Figs with Goat's Cheese and Rocket salad. The sun was beaming down, I was running around shooting water pistols at my niece and nephew, and I stopped to take a much-needed rest under a fig tree in the garden. As the sun poured onto the thick, leafy canopy, the fruit gave up the most delicious, deep, heady perfume, similar to vanilla, but with a fruity, tobacco twist. The kind of fragrance you can almost taste. Then a wasp, probably also enjoying a similar experience, stung me and so moved me on!

I adore the light texture of a clafoutis and my version, incorporating raspberries and light spicing, is a refreshing twist on the French classic. Star anise reflects and reinforces the deep fruity richness of raspberries. Nutmeg and green cardamom add diamond-bright sparkle and both work well with the orange aromas of Grand Marnier. Fresh black pepper is a personal indulgence, but I think it brings further depth and clarity, cutting through rich, buttery flavours.

*Previous page: Long pepper brings perfumed notes of allspice, pepper, nutmeg and cloves to all it touches, adding definition and clarity to the myriad of flavours in summer fruits.*

# APRICOT CRUNCHES

*Great as a snack at elevenses, high tea or simply as a dessert, these crunches are simple to construct – and far too easy to devour. Serve them with homemade lemonade or a cup of fragrant Earl Grey tea.*

**SERVES 4**

100g (3½oz) golden caster
    sugar
12 fresh apricots, halved and
    stones removed
1 tsp black peppercorns, coarsely
    ground
5–6 gratings long pepper
1 tbsp vodka
1 French baguette, sliced
    in half lengthways
1 tsp allspice berries
2 tsp fennel seeds
½ tsp cubeb pepper
400g (14oz) mascarpone cheese
3 tbsp whole milk
1 handful fresh basil leaves, torn

1. Put 75ml (2½fl oz) water and the sugar into a saucepan, stir and put over a medium heat. Once the sugar has dissolved, add the apricot halves, black pepper and long pepper and bubble gently for about 5–8 minutes, or until the apricots are soft without breaking up too much.

2. Take off the heat, add the vodka, pour into a small bowl and set aside to cool completely. Cover with clingfilm and put in the fridge.

3. Preheat the oven to 200°C (gas mark 6). Put the baguette halves on a baking tray and put in the oven for 12–15 minutes until lightly toasted. Remove and allow to cool completely.

4. Coarsely grind the spices using a mortar and pestle. Mix the mascarpone, milk and spice mix in a small bowl. Put in the fridge.

5. When it's time to serve, spread the baguette halves generously with spiced mascarpone, then add the apricots and basil. Slice each half into 10–12 diagonal pieces with a serrated knife and serve.

# BLACK FIGS WITH GOAT'S CHEESE & ROCKET

*I absolutely love figs, fresh or dried, and so this dish is all about the figs. I first had a salad similar to this at a birthday barbecue back in the mid-nineties and totally loved it. I knew I'd be doing something with it one day so, with a few tweaks, here it is for you to enjoy. When buying figs, make sure they feel heavy, have a little 'squidge' to them and don't smell at all sour. Only buy those that are fully ripe and with flesh that has a honeyed, ripe sweetness.*

**SERVES 4**

8 ripe black figs, halved
3 tbsp runny honey
4 tsp French pastis (optional)
2 tsp fennel seeds, coarsely
    ground
1 tsp black peppercorns, coarsely
    ground
50g (1¾oz) sunflower seeds
100ml (3½fl oz) balsamic
    vinegar
200g (7oz) peppery wild rocket
    leaves
100g (3½oz) goat's cheese,
    crumbled
Zest of ½ orange

1. Preheat the oven to 180°C (gas mark 4). Put the figs, cut-side up, on a roasting tin and drizzle them as evenly as possible with 2 tablespoons of the honey and the pastis, if using. Sprinkle with the ground fennel seeds and black pepper.

2. Put on a middle shelf in the oven for 10–12 minutes until they start to collapse slightly. Put the sunflower seeds in a small saucepan and dry-toast over a medium heat until lightly golden. Set aside.

3. Pour the balsamic vinegar into a small saucepan and put over a medium heat. Bring up to a steady, rolling simmer and allow to reduce by half, then set aside and leave to cool.

4. When the figs are soft, take them out of the oven and delicately cut each half in half again. Set aside.

5. Scatter a large serving platter with the rocket leaves, then dot with the figs and goat's cheese, then grate over the orange zest. Drizzle over the remaining honey and the reduced balsamic vinegar, and top with the sunflower seeds before serving.

# CHERRY BRIOCHE PUD

*Indulgent only just comes somewhere near to describing this pudding's beauty. This is bread pudding with a delightful tweak of fresh cherry, fennel, pistachio cream – nothing too fancy, just a flavour combination that really works.*

**SERVES 4**

2 tbsp Grand Marnier, Cointreau or kirsch (or a mix)

150g (5½oz) fresh cherries, pitted and lightly crushed so that they still hold most of their shape

50g (1¾oz) dried or sour cherries

1 tbsp golden caster sugar

1 tsp black peppercorns, finely ground

300ml (10fl oz) whole milk

300ml (10fl oz) double cream

1 vanilla pod, split lengthways

6 medium egg yolks (use the whites to make meringue, see page 206)

125g (4½oz) demerara sugar

1 small pinch sea salt

100g (3½oz) unsalted butter, at room temperature

4 tsp fennel seeds, finely ground

12 slices brioche, about 1cm (½in) thick

4 tbsp orange marmalade (with peel)

75g (2¾oz) green pistachio nuts, roughly chopped

1. Pour your chosen alcohol into a small saucepan, put over a gentle heat and warm for 1 minute – don't allow it to bubble. Add both types of cherries, the caster sugar and pepper, swirl the pan around, then set it aside to cool for 2 hours.

2. Pour the milk and cream into another saucepan over a medium heat. Scrape out the seeds from the vanilla pod. Add the seeds and pod to the milky mixture. Heat gently until it just starts to simmer.

3. Meanwhile, put the egg yolks in a large heatproof bowl with the demerara sugar and salt, and whisk well.

4. Pour the hot milk mixture into the bowl, giving it all a vigorous whisk. Remove the vanilla pod from this custard mixture and set aside.

5. In a small bowl, mix the butter with the ground fennel seeds, then spread a little on the brioche slices, reserving a couple of teaspoons. Spread the buttered slices with the marmalade, then cut into triangles.

6. Lightly butter a large pie dish, at least 2 litres (3½ pints) capacity, with the reserved spiced butter, then layer it neatly with the brioche triangles, scattering the cherries and their liquor on top.

7. Pour the warm custard over the slices and finish with a scattering of pistachio nuts, then carefully put the dish into the fridge to rest for 30 minutes.

8. Preheat the oven to 180°C (gas mark 4). Put the dish on the middle shelf of the oven and bake for 25–35 minutes until the pudding puffs up and the brioche is a glorious nut-brown colour. Serve warm with chilled pouring cream.

# BLACKCURRANT SUMMER PUDDING

*This is my favourite summer dessert. It's tangy, soft-textured and has just the right amount of sweetness, with the spices adding depth and clarity to the finish. We chose this as our wedding dessert. Using sponge makes a real difference; it's best to make your own, but you could use bought Madeira cake, cut into batons, at a push.*

**SERVES 8–10**

### FOR THE SPONGE

**1 vanilla pod, split lengthways**
**125g (4½oz) unsalted butter**
**175g (6oz) golden caster sugar**
**175g (6oz) plain flour**
**1 tsp baking powder**
**3 large eggs, at room
    temperature**
**5 tsp whole milk**

### FOR THE PUDDING

**½ star anise**
**1 tsp black peppercorns**
**4 cloves**
**½ long pepper, smashed**
**2 green cardamom pods**
**600g (1lb 5oz) demerara sugar**
**20g (¾oz) fresh ginger, roughly
    chopped**
**900g (2lb) fresh or defrosted
    frozen blackcurrants**
**5 tsp crème de cassis**

1. Preheat the oven to 180°C (gas mark 4). Grease and flour two 18cm (7in) cake tins. Scrape out the seeds from the vanilla pod. In a large mixing bowl, cream the butter and sugar together, then add the vanilla seeds and mix well. Sift the flour and baking powder into a second bowl. Whisking all the time, add an egg to the butter mixture, then add a spoonful of flour and whisk lightly. Repeat until all the flour and eggs are combined, then add the milk and mix to incorporate. Divide the batter evenly between the two tins, leaving a slight indent in the centre of each. Put on the middle shelf of the oven and bake for 20 minutes or until a skewer pushed into the centre comes out clean. Cool on a wire rack. Remove the cakes from the tins and slice each into 2cm (¾in) thick lengths, then cover with a tea towel and set aside.

2. Lightly crush the spices using a mortar and pestle. Put the sugar, ginger, 750ml (26fl oz) water and the spices in a large saucepan, then stir and put over a medium heat. Cook until the sugar has dissolved, then allow it to bubble for 3 minutes. Leave to cool, then strain through a fine sieve into a jug. Discard the spices. Set the syrup aside. Put the blackcurrants in a large saucepan over a medium heat. As soon as the berries begin to burst, add the spiced sugar syrup, stir well, and bring to a gentle bubble. Add the cassis, stir and take off the heat.

3. Line the base and sides of a 1.8 litre (3 pint) pudding basin, or two 900ml (1½ pint) basins, with the cake slices, cutting the lengths to fit. Reserve some cake to form a lid. Drizzle the sponge with the warm syrup, then fill the lined basin with the blackcurrants to about 3cm (1¼in) from the top. Add more syrup to cover the fruit, then cover with one even layer of cake slices. Drizzle with syrup.

4. Put a small plate on top and weight it down with something heavy. Allow to cool. Put it in the fridge for 24 hours before carefully turning out onto a serving plate. Serve with chilled pouring cream.

# Raspberry Clafoutis

*Here's a beautiful light yet rich version of this popular dessert. My recipe tends to be a little more full-on than the traditional, but the spices help to lessen the richness and anyway, desserts are supposed to be indulgent! You can serve the clafoutis with chilled pouring cream, but I like it with my lightly scented Tejpatta Ice Cream (see page 234).*

**SERVES 6**

### FOR THE FRUIT

½ tsp black peppercorns
½ star anise
Seeds of 2 green cardamom pods
2 cloves
75g (2¾oz) golden caster sugar
4 gratings nutmeg
500g (1lb 2oz) raspberries
2 tbsp Grand Marnier or
    Cointreau

### FOR THE BATTER

75g (2¾oz) plain flour
20g (¾oz) ground almonds
40g (1½oz) golden caster sugar
1 pinch sea salt
3 large eggs, plus 1 yolk, lightly
    beaten
200ml (7fl oz) whole milk
75ml (2½fl oz) double cream
30g (1oz) unsalted butter,
    melted, plus extra for
    greasing

1. Preheat the oven to 200°C (gas mark 6). Lightly grease a 1-litre (1¾ pint) or 23cm (9in) pie dish. Finely grind the spices using a mortar and pestle.

2. Mix the sugar and all the spices together, then take 1 teaspoon of the mix and set it aside for later. Tip some of the remaining spiced sugar into the buttered pie dish and roll it around to coat the base and sides as evenly as possible. Set aside.

3. Pour the raspberries, the remaining spiced sugar and the liqueur into a small bowl, toss around gently to combine, then cover and set aside for 30–40 minutes.

4. Meanwhile, make the batter. Put the flour and almonds in a large mixing bowl, add the sugar and salt, then the eggs and yolk, and whisk lightly. Add the milk, cream and melted butter, then whisk lightly to a smooth batter.

5. Tip in the raspberries and their macerating liquor, give them a quick but gentle stir, then pour everything into the pie dish and bake in the centre of the oven for 25–30 minutes until the mix is just set with a little comforting wobble.

6. Remove from the oven, sprinkle with the reserved spiced sugar, then pop under a hot grill to caramelise if you'd like a little extra texture. Allow to cool slightly before serving warm with Tejpatta Ice Cream.

# APPLE SORBET & PEACH GAZPACHO

*This recipe is refreshing and chock-full of summery flavours. Use the ripest peaches and melon you can find, as this will make a surprising difference. It's best to make the sorbet the day before you want to serve the gazpacho.*

## SERVES 4

### FOR THE APPLE SORBET
**175g (6oz) golden caster sugar**
**5 crunchy green cooking apples**
**Juice of 2 lemons**
**125ml (4fl oz) best-quality cloudy apple juice**
**2 tsp Calvados (optional)**

### FOR THE GARNISH
**2 tbsp golden caster sugar**
**2 cloves, finely ground**
**4 small sprigs redcurrants or whitecurrants**
**1 medium egg white, lightly whipped and foamy**

### FOR THE GAZPACHO
**1 small handful blanched almonds**
**6 ripe white peaches, stoned, halved and chilled**
**150ml (5fl oz) Prosecco, chilled**
**2 tsp icing sugar**
**3 cloves, finely ground**
**1 ripe Charentais melon, halved and deseeded**
**5 pitted green olives, dried with kitchen paper, finely chopped**

1. To make the sorbet, put the sugar and 125ml (4fl oz) water into a small saucepan over a medium heat and simmer for 1 minute, then remove from the heat and leave to cool. Cut the apples into quarters, core them, leaving the skin on, then put them in a food processor or blender with the lemon juice and briefly blitz. Add the cooled sugar syrup, the apple juice and Calvados, if using, and blitz to a smooth purée.

2. Line a deep baking tray with baking parchment, pour in the purée and put it in the freezer for at least 3 hours or until semi-frozen. Remove from the freezer and put the mixture back into the food processor, then blitz again. Pour and scrape the mix back into the lined tray, smoothing it down with the back of a metal spoon. Put back into the freezer for at least 1 hour, then shape into golf-ball-sized balls and return to the freezer.

3. To make the garnish, mix the sugar and cloves. Dip a sprig of redcurrants into the whipped egg white, then into the spiced sugar, and gently lay it on a wire rack. Repeat with the other sprigs, then leave to dry.

4. Put four soup bowls into the fridge. Put the almonds for the gazpacho in a small pan over a medium heat and dry-toast until golden. Roughly chop them and set aside.

5. Put the peach halves, Prosecco, icing sugar and clove powder into your food processor or blender and blitz to a smooth paste. Pass the paste through a sieve into a jug or bowl, pushing the pulp through with the back of a ladle. Put in the fridge.

6. Cut out little balls from the melon using a melon baller; you should get about 20. Set aside.

7. Take the bowls from the fridge, rub them dry with a tea towel, then put a ball of apple sorbet in the middle of each. Pour in the peach and Prosecco mixture (it may need a quick whizz first), add five melon balls, a sprinkle of nuts and then the olives. Put the candied redcurrants on the side and serve immediately.

# BLACKBERRY-PEPPER FROZEN YOGURT & LEMON SHORTBREAD

*This is based on my recipe for kulfi (see page 244), an Indian style of ice cream. It's a really easy way to make a creamy, textured frozen dessert. And the great news is that this frozen yogurt contains 50–60% less fat than commercial ice creams and up to 80% less fat than homemade ones.*

### SERVES 6

100g (3½oz) golden caster
    sugar
500g (1lb 2oz) fresh or
    defrosted frozen blackberries
1 tsp black pepper, finely ground
1 tbsp vodka (optional)
400g (14oz) tin condensed milk
300g (10½oz) full-fat natural
    yogurt
2 large egg whites

1. Put the sugar and 5 tablespoons water into a saucepan, stir and put over a medium heat. Once the sugar has dissolved, add the blackberries and black pepper, and allow to bubble gently for 5–8 minutes until the blackberries are just softened.

2. Take off the heat, add the vodka, if using, then pour all the ingredients into a food processor and blitz to a smooth purée. (Alternatively, use a balloon whisk to beat the fruits and vodka together thoroughly.) Pass the purée through a sieve into a bowl, pushing the pulp through with the back of a ladle. Discard the seeds. Leave the purée to cool completely, but don't chill.

3. Put the blackberry purée, condensed milk and yogurt into a large mixing bowl. Whisk the ingredients together thoroughly, using a stick blender if you like.

4. In a clean, grease-free bowl, whisk the egg whites until stiff. Carefully fold the egg whites through the creamy, fruity mixture until all the ingredients are mixed well and you have a thick, sticky mousse.

5. Pour the mousse into a plastic container, pop it into your freezer and allow it to set for at least 6 hours or overnight.

## FOR THE SHORTBREAD

1 vanilla pod, split lengthways
60g (2¼oz) golden caster sugar
125g (4½oz) salted butter, at
    room temperature, cubed
175g (6oz) plain flour
Zest of ¼ lemon
Icing sugar, for dusting

1. Preheat the oven to 180°C (gas mark 4). Line a baking tray with baking parchment. Scrape out the seeds from the vanilla pod. Put the vanilla seeds and the remaining ingredients, except the icing sugar, into a big mixing bowl and use your fingertips to rub the butter through the dry ingredients until the mixture looks like coarse breadcrumbs. Bring all the ingredients together into a ball.

2. Sift the icing sugar over a work surface and also use to dust the rolling pin. Roll out the dough to 5mm (¼in) thick. Cut out shapes using a cookie cutter, and space apart on the tray. Bake for 10–15 minutes or until they're a pale beige colour. Use a palette knife to gently lift the shortbread onto a wire rack to cool. Serve with the Blackberry-Pepper Frozen Yogurt.

# PEACH CARDINAL

*This simple, summery dessert is light yet indulgent enough to satisfy. Poached peaches, Angostura, raspberry sauce, vanilla ice cream, almonds – and a touch of spice. Foodie heaven!*

### SERVES 4

250g (9oz) demerara sugar
1 vanilla pod, split lengthways
1 tsp black peppercorns
30g (1oz) fresh ginger, peeled
½ red finger chilli
1 tbsp rose water
4 large, ripe peaches, peeled if
    you like (see page 193)
A few splashes Angostura bitters
100ml (3½fl oz) double cream,
    lightly whipped
2 tbsp toasted flaked almonds
4 scoops best-quality vanilla ice
    cream

## FOR THE RASPBERRY SAUCE

200g (7oz) fresh raspberries
100g (3½oz) icing sugar
Juice of ½ fresh lime

1. Put the demerara sugar and 750ml (26fl oz) water into a saucepan, stir well and put over a medium heat. Once the sugar has dissolved, allow to bubble gently for 1 minute. Add the spices, fresh ginger, chilli and rose water, and continue to bubble gently for another 3 minutes.

2. Turn up the heat, add the whole peaches and bring back to a gentle bubble, then turn the heat down and gently poach for 10 minutes.

3. Remove the peaches, set aside and leave to cool, then put in the fridge to chill. Strain the syrup into sterilised bottles (see page 255) and reserve for another time you'd like to poach fruit.

4. To make the sauce, put the raspberries, icing sugar and lime juice into a food processor or blender and blitz to a smooth purée. Push through a fine sieve into a small bowl or jug, pushing the pulp through with the back of a ladle. Discard the seeds.

5. To serve, put a peach into each serving bowl. Splash with a couple of drops of Angostura, lightly coat with a spoonful or two of raspberry sauce and top with a little whipped cream and some flaked almonds. Add a neat ball of ice cream to the side and serve immediately.

# BLUEBERRY & LYCHEE SORBET

*I love the colour and texture of this sorbet; I prefer sorbets not to be too jagged and icy. The flecks of blueberry skin simply add to its appeal. I've used nutmeg to add a fragrant, bitter note as well as black pepper for background heat and to cut through sweetness. The clove backs up the fruity notes while the vanilla provides a complementary perfume.*

**SERVES 4–6**

125g (4½oz) golden caster sugar
1 clove, smashed
400g (14oz) blueberries
200g (7oz) tin pitted lychees, drained (125g/4½oz drained weight)
1 tbsp lemon juice
1 tbsp vodka
1 small pinch sea salt
4 gratings of nutmeg
¾ tsp black peppercorns, finely ground
1 tsp vanilla extract
Fresh mint leaves, torn, to decorate

1. Line a deep baking tray with baking parchment. Put the sugar, 4 tablespoons water and the clove in a saucepan over a medium heat. Swirl the pan around gently as the water starts to bubble; this helps to dissolve the sugar.

2. Once the sugar has completely dissolved, pour the mixture through a sieve into a small bowl, then set aside and allow to cool.

3. Put all the remaining ingredients – except the mint leaves – into a food processor or blender, add the cooled sugar syrup and blitz to a smooth purée. Pour the purée into the lined tray and put it in the freezer for at least 3 hours or until semi-frozen.

4. Remove from the freezer, pop it back into your food processor, blitz again, then pour and scrape the semi-frozen fruit mix back into the lined tray. Smooth it down with the back of a metal spoon, then put it back into the freezer for another 1 hour.

5. Serve generous scoops of the sorbet with torn leaves of fresh mint and Thyme & Pepper Lozenge Biscuits (see page 229) for a refreshing treat.

# THYME & PEPPER LOZENGE BISCUITS

*Simple biscuits – the perfect crunchy partner to any fruit sorbet.*

**MAKES ABOUT 10**

40g (1½oz) plain flour
40g (1½oz) icing sugar
2 medium egg whites, lightly whipped with a fork
1–2 gratings orange zest
40g (1½oz) salted butter, melted and cooled
1 tsp black peppercorns, coarsely ground
½ tsp thyme leaves

1. Preheat the oven to 150°C (gas mark 2). Lay a sheet of baking parchment or a silicone sheet on a baking sheet.

2. Sift the flour and sugar into a bowl, then steadily pour the egg whites into the flour, stirring all the time with a fork.

3. Add the orange zest to the melted butter, then pour this into the egg mixture and stir thoroughly to a smooth paste. Take a large tablespoon of the mixture and dollop it onto your lined baking sheet, then spread the mixture with the back of a spoon into a lozenge shape, about 3 x 12cm (1¼ × 4½in). Don't worry too much about dimensions; let the mix take its own shape.

4. Repeat until you have used all the mixture, then bake in the oven for 4–6 minutes until the biscuits turn a very light brown colour.

5. Immediately scatter the pepper and thyme across the biscuits' surface. Leave them on the baking sheet to cool completely, then carefully remove them using a palette knife.

6. There, done! Serve alongside the Blueberry & Lychee Sorbet (see page 226) for a little wow and crunch factor.

# SWEET THINGS

My father is Indian and my mother from Yorkshire. I never stood a chance of not being a pudding-head, a sweet tooth, a dessert junkie. It's in my genes! As children, though we were only allowed to buy sweets once a week, there was the odd road trip. Mum and Dad would pack us all into the maroon Peugeot and we'd head down to London to visit relatives. We'd always make time to go to Drummond Street for a splurge on Indian sweets. And when Dad came back from his visits home to India he'd bring a brightly coloured, sticky box or two full of sweet treats.

This chapter offers a really intriguing number of possibilities when it comes to spice. Gorgeous, sweetly warming ginger, intoxicating nutmeg, the freshest of cloves to reinforce and heighten fruity intensity for a homely comfort-food factor. When balancing sugars, I look for intense, clean spices, sweetly aromatic with vibrant perfume. Fresh Mixed Spice (see page 266) is just such a blend: the ultimate mixed spice for Christmas cake and mincemeat.

Spice can be used to tone down sweetness in a dish. In Gingerbread Mess, I use cubeb and dried rose petals to offset the cake's deep sugary notes, green cardamom and powdered ginger to heighten flavour and highlight warmth, star anise for depth and Szechuan pepper to twist and back up the citrus notes of the fresh ginger.

I've included a couple of traditional Indian sweets, Halwa and Kulfi, and I must say, I am rather pleased with the Knickerbocker Glory presentation of the kulfi. The Greek yogurt adds a little lactic bite, the black cardamom a subtle smoky balance to the honey brittle and the touch of salt brings a little 'weight' to its mid notes.

My biggest projects were the Chocolate Pot, the Triple Chocolate Meringue Cream Pie and my Christmas Cake. With the chocolate pot, I wanted to create more than just a pure chocolate hit and so added subtle salt butterscotch, then the merest hint of clove, black pepper, nutmeg and whiskey to add different layers of defining depth. Nutmeg is traditionally used to bring out cacao notes in the spice world, and I have employed the same technique here. And for a real show-stopping dessert, do try the triple chocolate pie. With its Garam Masala biscuit base, intense orange-chocolate filling and the sticky rose-meringue topping, it really is something special. The Christmas Cake looks a little daunting, but that's the nature of the beast – with the vanilla, black pepper, Mixed Spice and Angostura bitters, juicy macerated fruits and deep, sweet notes of dark muscovado sugar, I don't use any white icing; that would just take it over the top.

*Previous page: Cubeb, or Javanese pepper, is a spice I often use in place of allspice, for its assertive flavour and 'twisted' perfume.*

# TRINITY COLLEGE VANILLA CREAM

*My twist on crème brûlée: the shiny caramel topping is made separately, and flavoured with green cardamom and freeze-dried raspberries. I make this in a large, shallow bowl around 4cm (1¼ inches) deep with a 1.2 litre (2 pint) capacity, to really show off the caramel shards.*

## SERVES 6–8

2 vanilla pods, split lengthways

750ml (about 1¼ pints) double cream

8 large egg yolks (use the egg whites to make meringues, see page 206)

75g (2¾oz) golden caster sugar

75ml (2½fl oz) semi-skimmed milk

1. Scrape out the seeds from the vanilla pods. Put the cream in a saucepan over a low heat and add the vanilla pods and seeds. Heat until a few bubbles appear, then take off the heat.

2. In a bowl, beat together the egg yolks and the sugar, then stir in the milk.

3. Pour a small amount of the hot cream onto the yolk mixture, whisk, then tip the yolk mixture back into the pan and cook over a very gentle heat until the mixture thickens, stirring almost constantly.

4. When the mixture coats the back of a wooden spoon, remove the vanilla pods and pour the mixture into a blender to blitz, or use a stick blender. Pour into a wide, shallow heatproof bowl and leave to cool.

5. Cover with clingfilm and chill in the fridge for up to 48 hours.

## FOR THE CROQUANT CARAMEL

Sunflower oil, for greasing

35g (1¼oz) almonds

250g (9oz) golden caster sugar

1 tbsp runny honey

40g (1½oz) skinned pistachio nuts, roughly chopped

Seeds of 6 green cardamom pods, finely ground

2 tbsp freeze-dried raspberries, roughly broken

1. Oil a baking tray. Put the almonds in small saucepan over a medium heat and dry-toast them until golden. Chop them roughly and set aside. Make a caramel by putting the sugar and honey into a saucepan over a medium–high heat; once the sugar has dissolved, swirl the pan to keep the heat moving through the sugar, but do not stir. If sugar starts to catch on the sides of the pan, brush it down using a moistened pastry brush.

2. Once the sugar has browned to a dark golden caramel, quickly pour it onto your prepared baking tray to form a 2mm (⅟₁₆in) thick layer. Immediately scatter over the nuts, then sprinkle on the ground cardamom and raspberry pieces and leave to cool.

3. To serve, gently smash the croquant with a rolling pin to achieve dramatic shards. Take the vanilla cream from the fridge, remove the clingfilm and scatter the sugar shards over the surface.

# Tejpatta Ice Cream

*This subtle, gently flavoured ice cream goes perfectly well as an accompaniment to fruit puddings, pies and desserts – an alternative to the ubiquitous vanilla ice cream, if you like.*

**MAKES ABOUT 20 SCOOPS**

500ml (18fl oz) double cream
7 large Indian bay leaves (tejpatta), crushed in your hand
4 medium egg yolks (use the egg whites to make meringues, see page 206)
125g (4½oz) golden caster sugar
1 medium egg white

1. Pour 75ml (2½fl oz) of the cream into a saucepan. Add the crushed bay leaves and put over a medium heat. Bring to a gentle simmer, turn down the heat, and allow to bubble for 2 minutes, then turn off the heat and set aside to infuse and cool.

2. Put the egg yolks in a large mixing bowl. Whisk with an electric whisk on high until they're pale, light and fluffy and have doubled in volume – about 6–8 minutes. Set aside.

3. Put the sugar in a saucepan, add 2 tablespoons water, stir, then put the pan over a medium heat. When the sugar starts bubbling and melting, cook for 1 minute more, then take a metal spoon, dip it into the molten sugar solution to catch some syrup and lift it up; when you see a gloopy drop fall from the spoon like runny honey, leaving a thin, wispy thread behind, it's ready. (This is known as the soft ball stage.)

4. Remove the pan from the heat and pour the hot sugar syrup into the whisked egg yolks, whisking constantly until the mixture is room-temperature cool – about 5 minutes.

5. Tip the remaining cream into a large bowl, then pour the infused cream through a sieve into the same bowl and whisk lightly to form soft peaks. Pour the cooled egg–sugar mixture into the whipped cream and thoroughly combine the two, folding gently with a metal spoon or large rubber spatula.

6. Put the egg white in a clean, grease-free bowl and whisk to stiff peaks. Add 1 tablespoon of the whisked egg white to the cream mixture and stir in gently. Add the rest of the egg white and gently fold through the mixture.

7. Pour into a plastic dish or lightly oiled jelly mould and put it in the freezer. It will take at least 6 hours to set completely. To serve, scoop it into balls, or turn out of the mould, if using, and slice.

# Trifle

*This trifle doesn't use jelly but it does use Madeira sponge, poached berries, vanilla custard, grilled almonds and whipped cream. I generally make this from storecupboard and fridge bits; it's so easy! You can, of course, make all the different parts, use leftovers or simply buy your favourites – jam, cake, custard, and so on – and assemble the dish in a jiffy. Don't forget to use your favourite trifle bowl. My mother-in-law has her 'special' trifle bowl she has used since my wife, Olive, was a young girl. Brilliant!*

## SERVES 6

Madeira cake or Savoiardi
　　biscuits (lady fingers)
Raspberry or blackcurrant jam,
　　for spreading
A large slug of sherry
A large slug of Grand Marnier
　　or Cointreau (optional)
450g (1lb) fresh or defrosted
　　frozen blackberries
150g (5½oz) golden caster
　　sugar
1 tsp black peppercorns, finely
　　ground
2 cloves, finely ground
2 vanilla pods
600ml (1 pint) double cream
600ml (1 pint) vanilla custard
　　(see below) or bought

### FOR THE VANILLA CUSTARD

4 large eggs, separated
85g (3oz) golden caster sugar
150ml (5fl oz) whole milk
150ml (5fl oz) double cream
1 vanilla pod

### TO DECORATE

1 handful toasted flaked
　　almonds
1 small handful fresh cherries

1. First, make the custard. In a large heatproof bowl, whisk the egg yolks with the sugar until mousse-like. Pour the milk and cream into a saucepan over a medium heat. Scrape out the seeds from the vanilla pod, and put the seeds and the pod into the milk mixture. Bring to a gentle simmer and allow to bubble for 2–3 minutes. While whisking the eggs, slowly pour the milk through a sieve into the bowl. Set aside to cool.

2. Cut the Madeira cake into finger shapes, spread with jam and sandwich together in pairs. Wedge them into the base of your trifle bowl. Drizzle the cake with the alcohol until well moistened. Set aside.

3. Put the berries, 100g (3½oz) of the sugar, pepper and cloves in a saucepan. Cut a vanilla pod in half and scrape out the seeds. Add to the pan and put over a medium heat. Bring to a gentle bubble, then turn off the heat and leave to infuse for 15 minutes. Strain the berries through a sieve over a heatproof bowl, then set aside. Put the strained juice and vanilla pod back into the pan and reduce over a medium–high heat for 2–3 minutes until the liquor thickens slightly. Remove the pan from the heat, take out the vanilla pod, then pour the juice back into its bowl and leave to cool.

4. Whip the cream to soft peaks. Cut the remaining vanilla pod in half and scrape out the seeds. Add to the whipped cream. Add the remaining sugar and gently fold the ingredients together until just combined.

5. Scatter the poached berries over the cake fingers and cover with the cooled custard, followed by the whipped cream. Sprinkle over the almonds and dot the creamy surface with fresh cherries. Serve the reserved vanilla berry juices in a little jug, together with, perhaps, some pouring cream and, for real indulgence, a glass of Madeira.

# GINGER & LIME DRIZZLE PUDDING

*This is the ultimate sponge pudding. Light sponge, sweet, citrus sauce and creamy coconut custard. I know it may look a little daunting, but you'll be chuffed with the results.*

**SERVES 6–8**

4 medium eggs, separated
Zest and juice of 2 limes
3cm (1¼in) fresh ginger, finely grated
175g (6oz) light muscovado sugar
2 tbsp white rum
1 tsp white peppercorns
1 tsp fennel seeds
215g (7½oz) self-raising flour
½ tsp sea salt
1 tsp powdered ginger
1 vanilla pod, split lengthways
215g (7½oz) unsalted butter, plus extra for greasing
50g (1¾oz) stem ginger, drained and finely diced

### FOR THE DRIZZLE SAUCE
30g (1oz) unsalted butter
100g (3½oz) light muscovado sugar
200g (7oz) golden syrup
¼ tsp sea salt
2 tsp powdered ginger
Zest and juice of 2 limes

### FOR THE COCONUT CUSTARD
400ml (14fl oz) coconut milk
225ml (8fl oz) single cream
4 medium egg yolks (use the egg whites to make meringues, see page 206)
30g (1oz) golden caster sugar
1 tsp cornflour

1. Butter inside the bowl and lid of a 1.2 litre (2 pint) pudding basin. Put the yolks, lime zest, fresh ginger and sugar in a large mixing bowl and whisk with an electric hand whisk for 2–3 minutes. Set aside. Warm the lime juice and rum in a small saucepan over a medium heat until hot to the touch, but not scalding. Slowly pour the hot lime and rum into the bowl, whisking constantly, until the mixture is really fluffy, about three times its original volume, and has cooled completely.

2. Finely grind the peppercorns and fennel seeds. Sift the flour, salt, pepper, fennel and powdered ginger into the bowl and gently fold through to just combine. Set aside. Scrape out the seeds from the vanilla pod. Melt the butter in a small pan, then stir in the vanilla seeds and stem ginger. Slowly trickle some of the butter mixture into the bowl, and fold gently to combine, then repeat with the remaining butter. Set aside.

3. In a clean, grease-free bowl, whisk the egg whites to stiff peaks. Mix a third of the egg whites through the batter, then gently fold in the remainder. Pour into the pudding basin and cover with the lid. Put the basin in a large saucepan and pour in boiling water to come up one-third of the side of the basin. Cover the pan and simmer gently for 2 hours. Rest for 5 minutes before lifting out.

4. Meanwhile, make the sauce. In a saucepan, gently heat the butter, sugar, syrup, salt and ginger until the sugar has dissolved, then allow to bubble gently for 1 minute. Remove from the heat, add the lime zest and juice. Set aside and keep warm.

5. To make the custard, heat the coconut milk and cream in a large saucepan over a medium heat until the first bubble or two appear. In a small heatproof bowl, whisk together the yolks, sugar and cornflour. Whisk in a third of the hot coconut milk, then pour it back into the pan. Stir with a wooden spoon over a low heat until the custard thickens and lightly coats the back of the spoon. Turn the pudding out onto a warmed serving platter, pour the sauce over and serve with the coconut custard.

# GINGERBREAD MESS

*This is a really amazing pudding, rich, indulgent and wonderful as a treat or celebratory dessert. The cherries, spice and textures will dazzle your palate and delight your friends!*

**SERVES 4–6**

Spice blend: 1 tbsp dried
    rose petals, 1 tsp white
    peppercorns, ½ star anise,
    ¼ tsp cubebs, seeds of 2
    green cardamom pods, ½
    tsp Szechuan pepper, 5 tsp
    powdered ginger
½ cooking apple, such as
    Bramley, peeled, cored,
    chopped
55g (2oz) butter, plus extra for
    greasing
65g (2¼oz) golden syrup
65g (2¼oz) black treacle
40g (1½oz) dark muscovado
    sugar
10g (¼oz) fresh ginger, finely
    grated
Zest of ¼ orange
½ tsp bicarbonate of soda
4 tbsp whole milk
1 medium egg, beaten
100g (3½oz) self-raising flour
30g (1oz) stem ginger, drained
    and finely chopped

FOR THE MERINGUE

3 large egg whites
175g (6oz) golden caster sugar

FOR THE MESS

500ml (18fl oz) double cream,
    lightly whipped and chilled
3 tbsp pitted brandy cherries,
    drained

1. Preheat the oven to 170°C (gas mark 3). Butter a small ovenproof dish or a 450g (1lb) loaf tin, and line it with baking parchment. Finely grind the rose petals and whole spices for the spice blend, then add the powdered ginger. Put the apple and 1 tablespoon water into a small pan over a medium–low heat and cook until puréed. Cool.

2. Put a heavy-based saucepan over a fairly low heat and add the butter, syrup, treacle, sugar, fresh ginger and orange zest. Add 1 heaped teaspoon of your spice blend and stir to combine. Cook gently until everything's dissolved and mixed together. Mix the bicarbonate of soda in a small bowl with 1 tablespoon warm water. Take the pan off the heat, add the milk, egg and dissolved bicarbonate of soda. Stir to only just combine.

3. Sift the flour into a large mixing bowl, then gently pour in the contents of the pan, beating until it's completely combined. Fold in the apple purée and stem ginger. Pour the mix into your prepared dish and bake for 25–35 minutes until a skewer inserted into the centre comes out clean. Put the dish on a wire rack and set aside to cool completely, then cover the dish with clingfilm and pop it into the fridge.

4. To make the meringue, preheat the oven to 140°C (gas mark 1). In a clean, grease-free bowl, whisk the egg whites to soft peaks, then continue whisking while adding 1 tablespoon of the sugar at a time until all the sugar is incorporated and the egg whites form glossy stiff peaks.

5. Line a baking tray with baking parchment. Put tablespoonfuls of the meringue onto the tray, evenly spaced. Bake in the centre of the oven for 1 hour, then turn off the oven, leaving the meringue inside until the oven is completely cooled. Break up the meringues into small nuggets.

6. Add the meringue to the whipped cream and gently fold through. Break off small nuggets of the chilled ginger sponge and add to the bowl. Add the cherries and give the mix one final, gentle stir before pouring the mixture into your favourite serving bowl to serve immediately.

# CARROT HALWA

*The texture of this beautiful sweetmeat could be described as a curiously decadent combination of marshmallow, soft fudge and squidgy brownie rolled into one. Divine for Diwali, the Hindu Festival of Lights, which is celebrated in October, it's a real treat. I love to eat halwa whenever I can! It reminds me of Dad's return home from trips away, opening up garishly coloured cardboard boxes and diving into the sticky, sweet delights wrapped within. This version is really easy to make and goes well with chai tea or coffee, family and friends.*

## MAKES ABOUT 6 THICK, CHUNKY PIECES

**400g (14oz) tin condensed milk**
**Seeds of 2 green cardamom pods, finely ground**
**2 tsp rose water**
**2 tbsp ghee (or a combination of unsalted butter and a little sunflower oil)**
**1kg (2lb 4oz) carrots, coarsely grated**
**8 pistachio nuts, finely chopped**

1. Line a 450g (1lb) loaf tin with baking parchment. Combine the condensed milk, cardamom and rose water in a bowl, then set aside.

2. Put a wide heavy-based saucepan over a medium heat. Add the ghee and allow it to melt, then add the grated carrots. Immediately turn the heat down to low and carefully stir the mixture, allowing the carrot to bubble gently for 20 minutes or until the raw aroma disappears, the colour darkens and the volume has reduced by about two-thirds. Add the condensed milk mixture, scraping the bowl with a rubber spatula to get every last bit.

3. Turn up the heat up slightly, but continue to stir the sticky mixture gently and constantly to combine all the flavours and prevent it from catching. After about 10 minutes, the mixture will have thickened, come away from the sides of the pan and formed a gloopy mass. It'll look a little like soft-set scrambled egg when it's ready.

4. Sprinkle in the pistachio nuts. Mix them through, then carefully spoon the hot mixture into the prepared loaf tin, using a wetted spatula to spread the mixture level.

5. Allow it to cool slightly, then cut the mixture into chunky diamonds or squares and pop the tin into the fridge to allow it to set completely. Serve the halwa chilled.

Tip

*Why not try a handful of chopped almonds and the seeds of 1 vanilla pod instead of the pistachio nuts and green cardamom? Experiment and enjoy your cooking.*

# CHOCOLATE POT AEVAL

*This is a beautiful recipe. It took a bit of time to get right, but I'm chuffed with it. I wanted to add a touch of perfume, a bit of butterscotch and a hint of 'uisce beatha' (that's whiskey in Gaelic), backed up with the warmth of pepper, to a smooth, rich chocolate pot. And here it is – you have to try it. Aeval is a reference to a Celtic fairy queen with similar associations to those of chocolate (look her up…). She hails from Munster, my adopted home, so this seemed the perfect way to honour her!*

**SERVES 4–6**

**450ml (16fl oz) double cream**
**100ml (3½fl oz) whole milk**
**20 black peppercorns**
**3 cloves, finely ground**
**5 gratings nutmeg**
**100g (3½oz) dark chocolate (70% cocoa solids), roughly chopped to gravel-sized chips**
**150g (5½oz) milk chocolate (43% cocoa solids), roughly chopped to gravel-sized chips**
**30g (1oz) salted butter**
**50g (1¾oz) light muscovado sugar**
**70g (2½oz) golden syrup**
**1 small pinch sea salt**
**4 large egg yolks (use the egg whites to make meringues, see page 206)**
**2 tsp Irish whiskey**
**2 tsp vanilla extract**

1. Preheat the oven to 140°C (gas mark 1). Pour the cream and milk into a saucepan. Add the spices and cook over a low heat until bubbles just appear around the edges of the pan. Remove the pan from the heat and leave to infuse for 4–5 minutes.

2. Add the dark and milk chocolate and leave to stand for 1 minute, then use a balloon whisk to gently combine until it's all smooth. Set aside.

3. Put the butter, sugar, syrup and salt in a small saucepan and heat gently over a low heat to just dissolve them together. Stir well, then allow to bubble for 30 seconds before turning off the heat.

4. Tip this butterscotch mixture into the creamy warm chocolate and whisk gently but thoroughly to combine.

5. Put the egg yolks, whiskey and vanilla in a small mixing bowl and whisk together. Add the chocolate-cream mixture and whisk gently to combine.

6. Pour the mixture through a sieve into a jug, then into individual serving dishes, ramekins or espresso cups. Discard the spices.

7. Put the ramekins into a baking dish or roasting tin and pour in warm water to come two-thirds of the way up sides of the dishes. Bake in the oven for 35–40 minutes until set. Leave to cool slightly, then serve with a little crème fraîche or soured cream.

# TRIPLE CHOCOLATE MERINGUE CREAM PIE

*Spiced biscuit base, oozingly rich chocolatey middle and delightfully soft-crunch pistachio meringue. Be sure to leave it to cool completely in the tin or the pie will collapse and you'll end up covering your table in a lake of molten chocolate; I speak from experience!*

**SERVES 12**

### FOR THE BISCUIT BASE
150g (5½oz) salted butter
100g (3½oz) golden caster sugar
70g (2½oz) plain flour
175g (6oz) porridge oats
1 pinch baking powder
2 tsp Garam Masala blend (see page 267)

### FOR THE FILLING
200g (7oz) milk chocolate (43% cocoa solids), broken
300g (10½oz) dark chocolate (70% cocoa solids), broken
200g (7oz) unsalted butter
100ml (3½fl oz) double cream
Finely grated zest of ½ orange
1 tsp black peppercorns, finely ground
4 gratings nutmeg
1 small pinch sea salt
150g (5½oz) plain flour
50g (1¾oz) cocoa powder
6 medium eggs
225g (8oz) light muscovado sugar
1 tbsp black treacle

1. Preheat the oven to 220°C (gas mark 7). Put the butter and sugar into a food processor and cream together at high speed for a few minutes until pale.

2. In a separate bowl, mix together the flour, oats, baking powder and Garam Masala.

3. Turn the food processor to a slow speed and add the dry ingredients, a handful at a time, to avoid clouds of flour engulfing you and your kitchen.

4. As soon as the mixture has come together, turn off the food processor. Turn the base of a 23cm (9in) springform cake tin upside down and place it back in the tin. Close the spring, then spread the biscuit mix over the base of the tin, keeping the edges nice and thin. Bake for 25–30 minutes, until lightly golden.

5. Leave to cool, then pop the tin into the freezer while you make the filling

6. Preheat the oven to 150°C (gas mark 2). Blitz the milk and plain chocolate in a food processor.

7. Put the butter and cream in a large saucepan over a medium heat and allow the butter to melt, stirring frequently. Remove from the heat, add the chocolate, then leave to stand for 1 minute. Gently stir to combine.

8. Add the orange zest, pepper, nutmeg and salt, then stir gently to combine. Set aside to cool.

9. Sift in the flour and cocoa powder, and stir gently and briefly.

10. In a large bowl, lightly beat the eggs to only just combine the yolks and whites. Add the sugar and treacle and stir gently to just combine, then add the chocolate mix and lightly stir to just combine.

## FOR THE MERINGUE

**4 medium egg whites**

**½ tsp cream of tartar or white wine vinegar**

**8 tbsp golden caster sugar, plus 1 tbsp**

**1 vanilla pod, split lengthways**

**100g (3½oz) green pistachio nuts, roughly chopped**

**1 tsp dried rose petals, finely chopped**

11. Pour the mixture onto your chilled biscuit base, then bake for 40 minutes, until just set, with a little wobble. Remove, then turn the oven up to 180°C (gas mark 4).

12. To make the meringue, put the egg whites into a clean, grease-free bowl and whisk until they form soft peaks. Add the cream of tartar, then continue whisking while adding 1 tablespoon of the sugar at a time until all the sugar is incorporated and the egg whites form glossy stiff peaks.

13. Scrape out the seeds from the vanilla pod and add them to the meringue with the pistachio nuts, then fold them through using a spatula. In a separate bowl, mix the remaining sugar with the rose petals and set aside.

14. Top the warm pie generously with the meringue, then sprinkle with the rose sugar and pop it in the oven for 25 minutes until the meringue has just started to take on a little colour.

15. Remove from the oven and leave to cool completely in the tin for at least 10 hours. Run a palette knife around the inside of the tin and release the spring, then serve.

# MANGO & CARDAMOM KULFI

*Kulfi is an Indian style of ice cream and something dear to my heart – I'm such a pudding-head! Dad bought me my first kulfi cone from a street vendor in Connaught Circus, Delhi, back in the late seventies and I was hooked.*

**SERVES 4**

## FOR THE KULFI

**400ml (14fl oz) best-quality
mango purée or 400g (14oz)
fresh mangoes and
2 tsp golden caster sugar
Seeds of 1 black cardamom pod,
finely ground
400g (14oz) tin condensed milk
250ml (9fl oz) double cream
1 large egg white
½ level tsp fine sea salt**

1. First, make the kulfi. If using fresh mangoes, stone the fruit and blitz it in a food processor or blender with the sugar. Put the mango purée in a large mixing bowl and add the cardamom and condensed milk. Using an electric hand whisk, whisk for 3–4 minutes until you see ribbons in the mixture. Add the cream and continue to whisk until you can see the blender making ribbons again.

2. In a clean, grease-free bowl, whisk the egg white to stiff peaks. Fold the egg white and salt gently through the creamy mango mixture, using a spatula, until all ingredients are combined and you have a thick, sticky mousse. Pour the mixture into a bowl, cover with a tea towel and pop it into your freezer. Allow it to set for at least 6 hours or preferably overnight.

## FOR THE HONEY BRITTLE

**Sunflower oil, for greasing
100g (3½oz) flaked almonds
2 tbsp dried mango, cut into
long, thin slivers
150g (5½oz) golden caster
sugar, plus extra for dredging
1 tsp runny honey
Seeds of 4 green cardamom pods**

## TO SERVE

**1 fresh mango, diced
250ml (9fl oz) mango coulis
or purée
250ml (9fl oz) Greek yogurt**

1. Generously oil a large square of baking parchment or foil. Toast the flaked almonds in a dry non-stick pan over a medium heat until golden. Set aside. Dredge the mango slivers in sugar, then tip them into a sieve and gently shake off the excess sugar.

2. Put a saucepan over a medium–low heat, add the sugar and allow it to melt, without stirring, to make a light, golden caramel. Very carefully, add the honey. It will spit, so be careful not to let the molten sugar hit you.

3. Continue to cook until the mixture thickens slightly, then take it off the heat. Work quickly now, before the caramel gets too viscous. Add the toasted almonds and mango slivers and quickly mix them together. Carefully but quickly, pour the sugary mixture onto the parchment in a thin layer – the madder the shape, the better! Sprinkle over the cardamom seeds and allow to cool completely, then crack into shards and set aside.

4. To serve, put a little of the fresh mango dice into four sundae dishes or tall glasses, then add a spoonful of coulis, a dollop of yogurt, and the kulfi. Repeat and finish with brittle shards towering out of the top.

# COFFEE EGG FROTH

*Stefano is a friend from Umbria, whom I met when I first moved to London, when we were working in a restaurant together. He made this for me after a particularly hard week and the odd night out or two. He promised it would pick me up. It worked its magic and I got through the shift. I often have this coffee with its added spice – though less for its 'medicinal' qualities, and more for the simple enjoyment these days.*

## SERVES 4

4 medium egg yolks
4 tsp golden caster sugar
Seeds of 2 green cardamom
    pods, finely ground
4 double shots hot espresso or
    strong coffee

1. In a small bowl, beat the yolks and sugar really well together, either with a balloon whisk or an electric hand whisk, until they're light, voluminous and mousse-like – at least 5 minutes with an electric whisk.

2. Add the ground cardamom and mix well.

3. Pour even amounts into four espresso cups, top up with hot strong coffee, stir well and serve immediately. Simple but 'rock-on' effective!

Variation

*If you serve this coffee in the afternoon, add 2 tablespoons grappa to the mousse mixture while whisking, then add the cardamom and coffee, as above. Superb!*

# FAT-FREE MINCEMEAT

*This recipe uses no butter or suet; it just relies on the freshest of flavours. You'll really notice the difference. It will keep for up to twelve months, so don't just reserve it for Christmas mince pies: try spreading it thick on toasted brioche, or use it as a topping for winter-warming porridge, or to fill baked apples.*

**MAKES 6 X 350G (12OZ) JARS**

50g (1¾oz) almonds
100g (3½oz) muscovado sugar
200g (7oz) eating apples, such
    as Braeburn, cored, peeled
    and chopped
600ml (1 pint) sweet cider,
    preferably local
1 vanilla pod, split lengthways
175g (6oz) raisins
125g (4½oz) currants
225g (8oz) sultanas
85g (3oz) mixed peel
125g (4½oz) dried figs, roughly
    chopped
125g (4½oz) dried apricots,
    roughly chopped
125g (4½oz) prunes, pitted and
    roughly chopped
400g (14oz) cooking apples,
    such as Bramley, peeled,
    cored and grated
1 tsp Mixed Spice blend
    (page 266)
½ tsp finely ground black
    pepper
Finely grated zest of 1 orange
Finely grated zest of 1 lemon
2 tbsp Calvados

1. Put the almonds in a small pan and dry-toast them over a medium heat until golden. Roughly chop and set aside.

2. Put the sugar and 1 tablespoon water in a large heavy-based saucepan. Stir to combine, then heat until the sugar dissolves and starts to bubble. Slide the chopped apples into the hot sugar, being careful not to splash yourself. Stir with a metal spoon until the apple pieces are evenly coated, then allow to cook until they've softened slightly. This will only take a couple of minutes.

3. Again, being very careful not to cause too much splashing, pour the cider into the pan, stirring all the time you're pouring. It'll sizzle and spit, so mind the steam.

4. Scrape out the seeds from the vanilla pod. Slide all the dried fruit into the pan, followed by the grated cooking apple, Mixed Spice, vanilla pod and seeds, and the black pepper.

5. Simmer, partially covered, for 15 minutes or until the fruit has turned slightly pulpy and most of the liquid has evaporated.

6. Remove from the heat and take out the vanilla pod. Allow the mixture to cool slightly, then stir in the lemon and orange zests, almonds and Calvados.

7. Spoon into sterilised jars (see page 255) and seal. Store for up to 12 months unopened. Once open, keep in the fridge and use within six months.

# CHRISTMAS CAKE

*This festive recipe is based on Mum's Christmas cake and a Caribbean fruit cake made by a friend. Don't be put off by the amount of alcohol or the length of time the fruit is steeped in it; it's really easy to make and you'll have all the bottles ready for next year; do use the best-quality ingredients. Rather than icing the cake, I prefer to toast the almond paste, which gives a natural look. I might decorate the serving plate with holly and baubles. Anyway, this is really fun to make, but remember to give yourself enough time and try not to rush things. You need to start the first step at least one week before you want to bake the cake; once baked, it will keep for at least three months in an airtight container. Good luck and enjoy!*

## MAKES 1 CAKE, OR ABOUT 24 SERVINGS

### TO STEEP

**50ml (2fl oz) cloudy, natural apple juice**

**4 tsp espresso or strong black coffee**

**A dash Angostura bitters**

**50g (1¾oz) blanched almonds**

**2 vanilla pods, split lengthways**

**250g (9oz) raisins**

**250g (9oz) sultanas**

**250g (9oz) currants**

**125g (4½oz) sour cherries**

**115g (4oz) natural glacé cherries, halved**

**125g (4½oz) candied orange and lemon, finely chopped**

**2 tsp Mixed Spice blend (see page 266)**

**½ tsp black peppercorns, finely ground**

**1 pinch sea salt**

**50g (1¾oz) black treacle**

**50ml (2fl oz) brandy**

**50ml (2fl oz) Grand Marnier**

**2 tbsp kirsch**

**2 tbsp Madeira**

1. One week before you're going to bake the cake, measure out the apple juice, coffee and bitters into a large saucepan. Put the almonds in a small pan and dry-toast them over a medium heat until golden. Roughly chop, then add to the pan. Scrape out the seeds from the vanilla pods. Add the pods and seeds to the pan. Add the remaining steeping ingredients, but NOT any of the alcohol, ticking off each item on the list as you add it.

2. Stir everything to combine, then put the pan over a low heat and cover. Stirring frequently, allow to cook very gently for 10 minutes.

3. Remove from the heat, give everything another quick stir, then set the pan aside and allow the fruit to cool slightly for 1–2 minutes. Pour in the brandy, Grand Marnier, kirsch and Madeira, and stir once more.

4. Pour the mixture into a large sterilised jar (see page 255) with a lid, or an airtight plastic container. Put the jar in the fridge and leave for seven days, shaking or stirring it from time to time.

5. When you're ready to bake the cake, grease a 20cm (8in) square cake tin, or 23cm (9in) round tin, and line it with a doubled sheet of baking parchment, cut so that it comes 2cm (⅘in) above the top of the tin. Then, measure and cut some brown paper (parcel paper is perfect) so that it wraps nicely around the outside of the tin. This should be much taller than the baking parchment, about 8cm (3¼in) above the top of the tin. Tie in place with kitchen string, and you're ready to start baking.

[ *Continued* ]

## FOR THE CAKE

300g (10½oz) unsalted butter, softened, plus extra for greasing

250g (9oz) dark muscovado sugar

5 large eggs, at room temperature

250g (9oz) self-raising flour

115g (4oz) cooking apples, such as Bramley, peeled, cored and grated

Finely grated zest of ½ orange

Finely grated zest of ½ lemon

2–3 tbsp Grand Marnier

1. Preheat the oven to 140°C (gas mark 1). Put the butter and sugar in a large mixing bowl and cream them together using a hand mixer until they're really well combined, fluffy and pale.

2. Add 1 egg to the bowl and beat it into the mixture, then sift in 1 tablespoon of the flour and mix that in.

3. Now simply add the eggs one at a time, beating each one in really well before adding the next. Sift in the remaining flour, and gently fold it through the mixture using a metal spoon.

4. Put the steeped fruit in a large bowl and remove the vanilla pods. Add the grated apples, and orange and lemon zests. Stir well. Pour the fruit into the cake mixture, scraping out every last syrupy scrap, and carefully fold together until everything is evenly mixed. Be sure to use a gentle touch and don't overwork it.

5. Spoon the mixture into your prepared tin and smooth the surface with the back of the spoon or with a palette knife. Make a slight hollow in the centre of the cake, then wet one of your hands and gently, briefly, lightly pat the cake's surface all over. This will help to maintain a smooth surface while it's cooking. Cover the cake with a doubled sheet of baking parchment, laying it gently on the surface.

6. Put the cake tin on the centre shelf of the oven and bake for 3½ hours without opening the door. Remove the baking parchment from the surface and continue to bake for a further 30 minutes or until the centre feels springy when you touch it lightly.

7. Remove the cake from the oven and put the tin onto a cooling rack. Allow it to cool for 1 hour.

8. Prick the top of the cake all over with a cocktail stick, and 'feed' it with Grand Marnier, carefully spooning the alcohol into the tiny holes. Leave the cake to cool in the tin overnight.

9. Next morning, remove the cake from the tin, leaving the baking parchment around it. Wrap it fully in more baking parchment, then in foil, and store in an airtight tin or a plastic cake box until you need it. The cake will keep nicely for three or four months or so, all wrapped up.

## ALMOND PASTE

**450g (1lb) golden caster sugar**
**450g (1lb) ground almonds, plus**
    **extra if needed**
**2 small eggs**
**2 tbsp Grand Marnier**
**2–3 drops bitter almond extract**
**1 vanilla pod, split lengthways**
**Icing sugar, for dusting**
**1 medium egg white**
**1 tiny pinch fine sea salt**
**2 medium egg yolks**

1. Mix the sugar and almonds together in a bowl. In another bowl, beat the eggs, Grand Marnier and almond extract, and scrape in the seeds from the vanilla pod. Pour this mix into the almond mixture and stir to a stiff paste. The paste should be really stiff, like marzipan, so add an extra sprinkling of ground almonds if necessary.

2. Lay a sheet of greaseproof paper on a work surface and dust it with icing sugar. Roll out half the paste on the greaseproof paper, rubbing your rolling pin with icing sugar as you go, to about 1cm (½in) thick.

3. Lightly mix the egg white with the salt and use to brush the top of your cake, then turn the cake over and put it on the rolled paste, sticky-side down. Gently press the cake down onto the paste. Cut around the cake, leaving a thin border of paste around the edge. Reserve the leftover paste for cutting into shapes later. Set aside.

4. Lift and turn the cake back over and remove the greaseproof paper if it's still sticking to the paste. Use a little of the leftover paste to patch any gaps between the cake and paste, and to ensure the surface is level.

5. Put a piece of string around the outside of the cake to measure its circumference (mark the length with a pen). On another sheet of greaseproof paper, roll out the remaining paste into a strip the same length as your measured string and 1cm (½in) thick. Cut it into two equal lengths.

6. Brush the sides of the cake and one side of the two strips of paste with the egg white. Carefully put the two strips around the sides of the cake, sticky-side to sticky-side. Roll a straight-sided glass against the cake side to smooth it. Tidy up the cake's appearance with your hands, moulding it gently until you're happy with it.

7. Preheat the oven to 220°C (gas mark 7). Mix the egg yolks with 1 tablespoon water. Roll out the remaining almond paste to 5mm (¼in) thick and cut out some festive shapes with a cookie cutter. Brush the cake all over with the egg yolk mix, arrange your cut-out shapes on the cake, then brush them with a little more egg. Carefully lift the cake onto a baking sheet.

8. Pop the cake into the oven for 15 minutes or until the paste turns a light nutty-brown colour. Take it out of the oven and put it onto your cake board. Allow to cool, then decorate the plate with a little holly and maybe a few baubles. That's it. One beautiful, totally yummy Christmas cake!

# RELISHES, CHUTNEYS, JAMS & JELLIES

THIS CHAPTER IS MADE UP OF SOME FAVOURITE RECIPES I'VE MADE OVER THE LAST LITTLE WHILE. If you're wondering which to try first, then I'd recommend the Strawberry, Tequila and Pepper Jam, the Clementine, Date and Chilli Chutney and the Chilli, Coriander and Lime Relish. That way you'll have something for toast, something for lunch and something for when you want a fiery kick for your taste buds!

When making jam or chutney, the trick lies in gauging the setting point. This will come with practice, although I know there's nothing more frustrating than someone telling you, 'it just takes practice'. You could watch videos of jam-making online, ask your friendly local WI member or an experienced family member, or just get stuck in and have a go. It really is quite simple and even your first experiments will yield good, if not necessarily perfect, results.

For my Strawberry, Tequila and Pepper Jam, I wanted a hit of perfume to match the fragrant fruit, plus a touch of bite and heat to enliven the sugary sweetness. It is often said that black pepper enhances the flavour of strawberries. While I agree to a point, I don't think black pepper is the way to go. I always prefer long pepper with fruit. I find the sweet acidity of the fruit makes a great match with the subtle perfume and increased heat of long pepper. The additional pepperiness of tequila brings the two flavours together and orange adds a zesty top note.

I use fresh chilli in my Clementine, Date and Chilli Chutney to cut across the richness of dates and treacly muscovado sugar and the perfumed 'ping' of green cardamom to pick up the orange notes. My wonderfully simple Chilli, Coriander and Lime Relish is all about fresh zing and citrus bite, with an uncompromising hit of fragrant heat. Cumin and mint are an excellent pairing: the cumin works to both 'ground' the relish and add twisted citrus flavours to the fresh mint. This relish is brilliant with meat and fish of all types and is particularly good with my Vada Pav potato buns (see page 183).

*Previous page: Lush pliable vanilla pods, tiny purses full of precious heady aromas. I use vanilla for its creamy sweetness: mellowing the sharpness of rhubarb, emphasising the sweetness of strawberries.*

# Rhubarb Four-Spice Relish

*This is great with rich meats, goose and the like. Freeze some rhubarb from the summer's sweet abundance and bring it out in the depths of winter to make this richly rewarding, simple relish.*

**MAKES 900G (2LB)**

400g (14oz) light muscovado
   sugar
½ star anise
3 cloves
1 small piece blade mace
1 vanilla pod, split lengthways
400g (14oz) rhubarb, cut into
   3cm (1¼in) batons
1 tsp Quatre Épices blend (see
   page 266)
4–5 gratings nutmeg
1 long pepper spike, grated
1 tsp rose water

1. Put the sugar in a heavy-based saucepan with 2 tablespoons water. Give it a quick stir to dampen, then put over a medium heat and allow to dissolve gently.

2. Finely grind the star anise, cloves and mace using a mortar and pestle. Scrape out the seeds from the vanilla pod. When the sugar has dissolved, add the rhubarb, all the spices, vanilla seeds and rose water, then stir and cook for 2 minutes. Remove from the heat.

3. Pour into sterilised jars (see below), seal and leave to cool. Store in the fridge for three weeks unopened. Once open, keep in the fridge and use within one week.

## Sterilising Jars

It's important to make sure the jars you use for storing your jams, chutneys, relishes and preserves are properly sterilised first. There are a couple of ways to do this. Firstly, if you're recycling jars, remove the labels, wash the jars and lids in soapy water and rinse clean. Preheat the oven to 180°C (gas mark 4), put the jars on a baking tray and put them in the oven for about 10 minutes. Boil the lids for 5 minutes and leave to dry. Alternatively, put the jars, right-side up, on a rack in the bottom of a large saucepan, fill the pan with hot (not boiling) water and then boil the jars for 10 minutes; remove them and drain. Boil the lids in water, too – about 5 minutes should be fine. Then remove and allow to dry upside-down on a drying rack. You can fill the jars while they're warm; in fact, it's actually best to do this, as putting hot food into cold jars can cause them to crack – a process known as 'thermal shock'.

# CHILLI, CORIANDER & LIME RELISH

*This zingy, hot, salty and sour relish is a perfect accompaniment to any grilled, fried or curried meat or vegetable dish. Keep a jar in your fridge to liven up any meal.*

**MAKES 500G (1LB 2OZ)**

30g (1oz) green bird's eye
 chillies
40g (1½oz) coriander, leaves
 and thin stalks
15g (½oz) mint leaves
15g (½oz) cumin seeds, finely
 ground
20 garlic cloves
Juice of 1½ lemons
Juice of 6 limes
1 tsp sea salt
1 tsp golden sugar

1. Put everything into a food processor or blender and blitz to a paste, or pulp all the ingredients using a mortar and pestle.

2. Store in a sterilised jar (see page 255) for up ten days. Keep in the fridge both before and after opening.

# CLEMENTINE, DATE & CHILLI CHUTNEY

*I came up with this chutney recipe to go with rich winter meats, especially fowl and game. The combination of orange and cardamom and the soft texture and depth of flavour from dates and muscovado sugar make this one of my favourite chutneys.*

**MAKES 350G (12OZ) – AND A LITTLE LEFT OVER FOR THE COOK!**

3–4 clementines
150ml (5fl oz) best-quality cider vinegar
115g (4oz) dark muscovado sugar
250g (9oz) plump, squidgy dates, pitted and roughly chopped
15g (½oz) fresh ginger, peeled and finely grated
1 red finger chilli, deseeded and very finely chopped
Seeds of 1 large green cardamom pod, finely ground

1. Over a small plate, gently rub 3 clementines across a small grater to remove their zest, then chop them in half widthways and squeeze out their juice into a measuring jug. You may need the fourth clementine to get the right amount of juice: you need 150ml (5fl oz).

2. Put the vinegar, clementine juice and sugar in a saucepan, put over a medium heat, then stir and allow to bubble gently until the sugar has dissolved.

3. Add the dates, ginger and chilli. Stir and lightly squash the dates to combine. Cook for 3–4 minutes until the dates have softened down and the mixture feels a bit oozy and not too stiff, like cold runny honey.

4. Remove from the heat, leave to cool for 2 minutes, then add the clementine zest and cardamom. Stir well.

5. Pour into a sterilised jam jar (see page 255) or serve straight away. Store for six months unopened. Once open, keep in the fridge and use within three months.

# FAT CHILLI PICKLE

*This is a really simple pickle to prepare, but should be left in the cupboard for a least a month before you use it, to allow the flavours to marry and the chillies to soften naturally. It makes a wonderfully fruity, salty hot pickle, brilliant with red meats and vegetable dishes alike. In India we'd use Achar (pickling) or Moti (fat) chillies and call it Moti Mirch ka Achar, but I've been using jalapeños for convenience and calling it chilli pickle.*

**MAKES 350G (12OZ)**

10–12 large chillies, a mix of
    green and red, halved and
    deseeded
1 tbsp black mustard seeds
3 tsp fennel seeds, coarsely
    ground
½ tsp amchoor
1 tbsp sea salt
4 tsp English mustard powder
150ml (5fl oz) grapeseed oil

1. In a bowl, mix the chilli halves with the mustard seeds, fennel seeds, amchoor and salt.

2. In another bowl, whisk the mustard powder with the oil.

3. Pack the chillies snugly into a sterilised jam jar (see page 255) and top with a layer of the mustard oil. Store in a dry, dark cupboard for a month or so, turning the jar over once or twice a day – whenever you remember.

4. Store for up to 12 months unopened. Once open, keep in the fridge and use within six months.

# STRAWBERRY, TEQUILA & PEPPER JAM

*A brilliant jam, this – perfect for a twisted take on the afternoon tea's jam and scones.*

**MAKES ABOUT
700G (1LB 90Z)**

**1 vanilla pod, split lengthways**
**400g (14oz) fresh or defrosted
    frozen strawberries**
**50ml (2fl oz) lemon juice**
**300g (10½oz) golden
    granulated sugar**
**Zest of ¼ orange**
**Butter, for greasing**
**20ml (¾fl oz) silver tequila**
**A little grating of long pepper**

1. Scrape out the seeds from the vanilla pod. Put 350g (12oz) of the strawberries in a large stainless-steel bowl, followed by the lemon juice, vanilla pod and seeds, sugar and orange zest. Stir to combine and leave overnight.

2. Next day, crush the strawberries with a potato masher, leaving a good few lumps. Put a saucer or small plate into your freezer. Cut the remaining strawberries into quarters. Set aside.

3. Very lightly grease a large saucepan with butter, then pour the vanilla-strawberry mix into the pan and put it over a high heat. Bring to the boil, then turn down the heat and, stirring frequently, cook until the sugar dissolves.

4. Turn up the heat and boil for 10 minutes, then remove the vanilla pod (scraping it clean) and test the set of the jam by popping a small bit onto the cold saucer and pushing it with your finger. If it wrinkles, and the channel made with your finger remains fairly well parted, it's ready. If not, put the pan back on the heat for a few moments, then try again.

5. Skim any scum from the surface, then add the quartered strawberries, the tequila and long pepper, and stir through.

6. Decant into sterilised jam jars (see page 255) and enjoy whenever you'd like! Store for up to six months unopened. Once open, keep in the fridge and use within three months.

# CHILLI JAM

*A wonderfully simple recipe that produces a tart-sweet, hot jam that's great with all sorts of savoury dishes. I make it all the time and keep jars of it on hand for whenever it's needed. The key to the perfect result is to ensure no seeds go into the jam.*

## MAKES ABOUT 1KG (2LB 4OZ)

200g (7oz) red peppers, deseeded
   and roughly chopped
100g (3½oz) red finger chillies,
   deseeded and roughly
   chopped
30g (1oz) red bird's eye chillies,
   deseeded and roughly
   chopped
50g (1¾oz) dried Kashmiri
   chillies, deseeded and finely
   chopped
550ml (18fl oz) cider vinegar
1kg (2lb 4oz) jam sugar
Juice of 2 limes

1. First, sterilise three jam jars (see page 255). Set aside. Put the red pepper pieces into a food processor or blender and blitz to a smooth paste. Add all the chillies and pulse to form a textured paste. (Alternatively, chop the peppers and chillies finely, then pulp them using a mortar and pestle.)

2. Put the vinegar and sugar in a large saucepan over a medium-high heat. Swirl the pan, but don't stir, and allow the sugar to dissolve completely, then pour and scrape the pepper and chilli mixture into it.

3. Turn up the heat, bring to a rolling boil, and cook for 12 minutes, bubbling all the time, then remove from the heat.

4. Pour the lime juice through a fine sieve into the chilli mixture and set aside to cool in the pan for 30 minutes. Pour or ladle into the sterilised jam jars. Serve when cooled completely, or store for up to six months unopened. Once open, keep in the fridge and use within three months.

# Mum's Crab Apple Jelly

*I first remember discovering crab-apple jelly upon moving to Ireland, and I came across a recipe when I moved into the 'sweet' section of the Ballymaloe House kitchens. 'Mrs. A', known to everyone else as Myrtle Allen, showed me how to make it; she was brilliant to take the time with me. Then Mum piped up that she used to make it when my brothers and I were children. So, here's my version: perfect for scones, warm brioche, cake fillings or dolloped on ice cream.*

**MAKES ABOUT 1.3KG (3LB)**

**1.2kg (2lb 12oz) crab apples,** or slightly unripe cooking apples, such as Bramley
**½ star anise**
**½ nutmeg**
**1 tsp coriander seeds**
**½ tsp white peppercorns**
**2 blackberries** (they give the jelly a wonderful, warm pink colour)
**Golden granulated sugar, as needed, see method**

1. Cut the apples roughly into quarters, put them into a large saucepan, cover with water, then add the whole spices and blackberries and put over a high heat. Let them bubble away for 20–30 minutes until the apples have collapsed completely.

2. Remove the pan from the heat, give the pulp a quick stir, then pour and scrape into a jelly bag suspended above a large bowl. (Alternatively, use a large square of muslin cloth. Gather up the corners of the cloth and securely suspend it above the bowl.) Leave to drip for 8 hours, or overnight. Don't be tempted to squeeze the bag or you'll end up with a cloudy jelly.

3. Pour the juice into a measuring jug, note the total volume of liquid, then decant it into a preserving pan or heavy-based saucepan. Discard the pulp and spices.

4. Preheat the oven to 140°C (gas mark 1). Put a saucer or small plate into the freezer. For every 600ml (1 pint) of juice measure out 450g (1lb) of sugar. Put the sugar in an ovenproof bowl and put it into the oven to warm through.

5. Put the preserving pan over a medium-high heat, pour in the warm sugar and stir to dissolve, then turn up the heat. Do not stir any more, but simply allow the jelly to bubble for 10 minutes. Test the set of the jelly by dropping a teaspoonful onto the cold saucer and pushing it with your finger. If it wrinkles, it's ready. If not, put the pan back on the heat for a few moments, then try again.

6. Take off the heat and pour through a funnel into sterilised jars (see page 255). Store for up to three months unopened. Once open, keep in the fridge and use within one month.

# BASICS

# SPICE BLENDS

It's difficult to be prescriptive with spicing; it's largely a question of trusting your senses, opening your mind and getting stuck in. That said, the recipes in this book will provide a good starting point to your own journey. The following recipes are for basic spice blends you'll need for some of the recipes in this book. Use whole spices and seeds, freshly ground. Make up only small amounts of these blends at a time, as they'll be past their best in three months. Keep the blends in an airtight jar in a dark, cool storecupboard. Each recipe yields 40–50g (1½–1¾ oz) of blend.

• Ras el hanout is a North African spice blend; the name means 'top of the shop', implying that these are the spice merchant's best spices, and each merchant makes their own blend. My company's version includes dried lavender, rose and orange. But it is always a complex mix of at least 20–30 spices and this is one spice blend I recommend you buy ready-made.

## MIXED SPICE

2 tsp allspice berries
1 tsp coriander seeds
1 tsp black peppercorns
1 tsp cloves
1½ tsp freshly ground cassia
½ tsp freshly ground mace
1 tsp freshly grated nutmeg
1 heaped tsp powdered ginger

Grind all the ingredients using a mortar and pestle, or blitz them in a spice or coffee grinder.

## QUATRE ÉPICES

4 tsp white peppercorns
1½ tsp cloves
1 tsp allspice berries
1½ tsp freshly ground cassia
½ tsp freshly ground mace
¼ tsp freshly grated nutmeg

Grind all the ingredients using a mortar and pestle, or blitz them in a spice or coffee grinder.

## TAGINE

1 heaped tsp sweet paprika
1 tsp powdered ginger
1 tsp powdered turmeric
1 tsp black peppercorns
1 tsp allspice berries
1 tsp coriander seeds
1 tsp freshly ground cassia
½ tsp green cardamom pods
¼ tsp freshly ground mace
4–5 gratings nutmeg

Grind all the ingredients using a mortar and pestle, or blitz them in a spice or coffee grinder.

## PANCH PHORON

2 tsp black mustard seeds
2 tsp black onion (nigella) seeds
2 tsp cumin seeds
2 tsp fennel seeds
2 tsp freshly ground fenugreek seeds

Mix the ingredients together in a small bowl.

# Garam Masala

**2 tsp black peppercorns**
**1½ tsp cumin seeds**
**1 tsp coriander seeds**
**1 tsp fennel seeds**
**1 tsp freshly ground cassia**
**1 star anise**
**1 tsp green cardamom pods**
**½ tsp cloves**
**¼ tsp freshly ground mace**
**12 gratings nutmeg**
**1 black cardamom pod**
**1 tsp dried rose petals**

Grind all the ingredients using a mortar and pestle, or blitz them in a spice or coffee grinder.

# Mouclade

Used for the French mussel dish, mouclade (see page 126), this also serves as an all-purpose curry powder.

**2 heaped tsp powdered turmeric**
**2 tsp coriander seeds**
**1½ tsp cumin seeds**
**1 tsp black peppercorns**
**1 tsp green cardamom pods**
**½ tsp golden caster sugar**
**1 tsp cloves**
**1 tsp freshly ground cassia**
**¼ tsp freshly ground mace**

Grind all the ingredients using a mortar and pestle, or blitz them in a spice or coffee grinder.

## Kitchen tips

• Always read a recipe through before you start to cook. Do you have all the ingredients? Do you need to marinate something overnight? However, once you've made it a few times why not adapt it to your own taste: a little more ginger here, a little less garlic there…

• Preparation is crucial: grind your spices, weigh and chop ingredients so that everything's to hand as you work through the recipe.

• I've created my spice blends to get the balance exactly right, and my recipes often call for ¼, ½ or 1 teaspoon of a spice. Larger mixtures measure ingredients in tablespoons. These are not just rough, 'by eye' spoonfuls but accurate measurements:
1 teaspoon (tsp) = 5ml
1 tablespoon (tbsp) = 15ml
You will ideally need a set of standard measuring spoons – they're inexpensive and metal ones will last a lifetime.

• An electric spice grinder (or coffee mill) is the quickest way to grind spices; a mortar and pestle takes slightly longer, but you can improvise by putting spices in a heavy-duty plastic bag and bashing them with a heavy pan or rolling pin.

• A food processor or blender is a kitchen essential for many home cooks, but there's usually a way to manage without: individual recipes explain how.

• For grating nutmeg and long pepper, lemon and orange zest, I recommend a Microplane grater: the holes are cut by etching rather than stamping through the metal, which means they don't clog.

**A**

aïoli: Algier aïoli 82
    saffron aïoli 127, 191
    spiced aïoli 115
Algier aïoli 82
allspice 13
almond paste 251
aloo tikki (potato fritters) 180
amchoor 13
anardana 13
apples: apple sorbet 223
  blackberry, apple & comice pear
    compote 210
  Mum's crab apple jelly 263
apricot crunches 215
asafoetida 13
    asafoetida risotto 155
Asian sticky beef ribs 55–6
aubergines: baked aubergines with
    crumbly goat's cheese 199
    bharva baingan 185
    seven-pepper tuna 110–11
Ayurveda 22

**B**

bacon 26
  bacon chops with glazed pepper
    pineapple 34–6
  egg & bacon pie 133
  full Irish breakfast 136–7
  poached mutton shoulder 73
bananas, sugared 158–9
beans: duck, pork & beans 96–7
  slow-roast pork neck chops 31
beef 44
  Asian sticky beef ribs 55–6
  beef, carrots & ale 49–51
  beef-on-beef 'dog' 46–8
  Berber couscous 149–50
  chilli beef hash 45
  roast rump with a Tamil crust
    52–3
beetroot: celeriac & beets with
    blood orange & walnut 203
  just raw salad 196

  spiced wood pigeon, artichoke,
    beetroot & chicory salad 94–5
Bengal fry-up 117
Bengali grilled seafood 123–4
Berber couscous 149–50
bharva baingan 185
biryani ka kesar, lamb 62
biscuits: lemon shortbread 225
  thyme & pepper lozenge biscuits
    229
black pudding: black pudding
    salad 33
  full Irish breakfast 136–7
blackberries: blackberry, apple &
    comice pear compote 210
  blackberry-pepper frozen yogurt
    224
  trifle 235
blackcurrant summer pudding 219
blends 10–11
blueberry & lychee sorbet 226
bread: apricot crunches 215
  croûtons 33, 170
  my Bologna sarnie 192
  Niçoise pan bagnat 190–1
breakfast, full Irish 136–7
brioche pud, cherry 218
broad beans & anchovy eggs 189
butternut squash *see* squash
buying spices 8

**C**

cabbage: celebration lentil cabbage
    178
  grilled chilli cabbage 179
  shiitake & Savoy upside-down
    cake 177
Cajun popcorn shrimp 125
cakes: Christmas cake 248–51
  polenta tea cake 209
caramel, croquant 233
caraway seeds 13
cardamom, black 13
cardamom, green 13–14
carom 14
carrots: beef, carrots & ale 49–51
  carrot halwa 239
  coconut mashed roots 51
cashew butter 86
cassia 14

cauliflower cheese 174
cayenne pepper 14
celeriac & beets with blood orange
    & walnut 203
ceviche & corn 105
Charente cold plate 193
cheese 132
  baked aubergines with crumbly
    goat's cheese 199
  black figs with goat's cheese &
    rocket 216
  cauliflower cheese 174
  cheese & onion flaky puff pie 144
  cheese in a box 142
  Irish rarebit 141
  lunchbox frittata 139
  mac 'n' cheese 145
  polenta tea cake 209
cherries: cherry brioche pud 218
  gingerbread mess 238
chestnut meringue 206–7
chicken 78
  chicken Marrakesh 80–2
  Hyderabadi chicken 86
  paella Túnel 153–4
  poached chicken with
    lemongrass & herbs 83
  sofa chicken 84
chickpeas 148
  chickpea chips 110–11
  chickpea salad with nectarine,
    feta & mint 164
  spicy chickpeas on toast 163
chicory, watercress & grilled
    squash salad 173
chillies 14, 21–2
  chilli beef hash 45
  chilli, coriander & lime relish 257
  chilli jam 262
  clementine, date & chilli chutney
    258
  eggs akoori 140
  fat chilli pickle 259
  grilled chilli cabbage 179
  smoked chilli sauce 48
  tomato chilli relish 112
chocolate: chocolate pot Aeval 240
  triple chocolate meringue cream
    pie 242–3
choucroute: pig plate 40–1

chowder, parsnip & salt cod 101
Christmas cake 248–51
chutney: clementine, date & chilli 258
cinnamon 14
clafoutis, raspberry 221
clementine, date & chilli chutney 258
cloves 15
cobbler, crisp haddock 102–3
coconut milk: coconut custard 237
    coconut mashed roots 51
cod: parsnip & salt cod chowder 101
coffee egg froth 246
coriander 15
    chilli, coriander & lime relish 257
coriander seeds 15
    coriander & pomegranate dressing 124
courgettes: heritage soup 195
couscous: Berber couscous 149–50
    tabbouleh 115
crab 120
    crab cakes 121
    seafood gumbo 128–9
crab apple jelly 263
crammed beach fish 115–16
cream: Trinity College vanilla cream 233
croûtons 33, 170
crumble, allium 184
cucumber: pickle 121
cumin 15
cumin, black 15
custard, coconut 237

D
dates: clementine, date & chilli chutney 258
dhal: red lentil dhal 161
    tarka dhal 162
'dirty' dumplings 128–9
dried fruit: Christmas cake 248–51
    fat-free mincemeat 247
duck, pork & beans 96–7
dumplings, 'dirty' 128–9

E
eat-me-with-a-spoon masala 72
eggs 132

broad beans & anchovy eggs 189
egg & bacon pie 133
egg curry 135
eggs akoori 140
full Irish breakfast 136–7
lunchbox frittata 139

F
fennel: fennel salad 105
    orange, fennel & red onion salad 107
    salmon, potato & fennel fishcakes 106–7
fennel seeds 15
fenugreek 15–16
    fenugreek potatoes 36
figs: black figs with goat's cheese & rocket 216
fish 100
    see also mackerel, salmon etc
fishcakes: salmon, potato & fennel 106–7
flavours 20–2
frittata, lunchbox 139
fritters: aloo tikki (potato fritters) 180
    potato fritters 94–5
fruit 202, 214
    see also apples, raspberries etc

G
gammon: pig plate 40–1
garam masala 267
garlic: Algier aïoli 82
gazpacho, peach 223
gherkins: Wally-Wally pickle 61
ginger 16
    ginger & lime drizzle pudding 237
    gingerbread mess 238
grapefruit: ting & ting sauce 79
guinea fowl, roast 92–3
gumbo, seafood 128–9

H
haddock cobbler 102–3
halwa, carrot 239
ham: cheese in a box 142
    my Bologna sarnie 192
    warm lentil & ham hock salad 28–30

haricot beans: duck, pork & beans 96–7
    slow-roast pork neck chops 31
heritage soup 195
hogget 60
    hogget & squash bake 74
honey brittle 244
Hyderabadi chicken 86

I
ice cream: blackberry-pepper frozen yogurt 224
    mango & cardamom kulfi 244
    tejpatta ice cream 234
Indian bay leaf 16
Irish rarebit 141
Irish stew skewers 67

J
jams: chilli jam 262
    strawberry, tequila & pepper jam 260
jelly, Mum's crab apple 263
Jerusalem artichoke soup 169
juniper 16
just raw salad 196

K
Kashmiri chillies 16
kulfi, mango & cardamom 244

L
lamb 60
    eat-me-with-a-spoon masala 72
    grilled chilli cabbage 179
    lamb biryani ka kesar 62
    lamb 'park railings' 61
    meatballs with ras el relish 68
    Olive's Irish stew skewers 67
    Persian lamb tagine 65–6
    spiced lamb cutlets 71
leeks: allium crumble 184
lemon shortbread 225
lemongrass & tamarind mackerel skewers 112
lentils 148
    celebration lentil cabbage 178
    Charente cold plate 193
    red lentil dhal 161
    tarka dhal 162

warm lentil & ham hock salad
  28–30
limes: ginger & lime drizzle
  pudding 237
lunchbox frittata 139
lychees: blueberry & lychee sorbet
  226

M

mac 'n' cheese 145
mace 16–17
mackerel: crammed beach fish
  115–16
  lemongrass & tamarind mackerel
    skewers 112
mango & cardamom kulfi 244
masala, eat-me-with-a-spoon 72
mayonnaise 30
  Algier aïoli 82
  hot pepper mayo 125
  saffron aïoli 127, 191
  Wally-Wally pickle 61
meatballs with ras el relish 68
melon: Charente cold plate 193
meringue: chestnut meringue 206–7
  gingerbread mess 238
  triple chocolate meringue cream
    pie 242–3
mincemeat, fat-free 247
mixed spice 266
mouclade 126, 267
mushrooms: Bengal fry-up 117
  full Irish breakfast 136–7
  shiitake & Savoy upside-down
    cake 177
mussels 120
  Bengali grilled seafood 123–4
  mouclade 126
  paella Túnel 153–4
mustard 17
mutton 60
  poached mutton shoulder 73
my Bologna sarnie 192

N

nectarines: chickpea salad with
  nectarine, feta & mint 164
Niçoise pan bagnat 190–1
nigella seeds 17
nutmeg 17

O

oats: vanilla & long pepper
  porridge 158–9
okra: Bengali grilled seafood with
  okra 123–4
  seafood gumbo 128–9
Olive's Irish stew skewers 67
onions: allium crumble 184
  cheese & onion flaky puff pie
    144
  eat-me-with-a-spoon masala 72
oranges: orange, fennel & red
  onion salad 107
  rhubarb & orange salad 65–6

P

paella Túnel 153–4
pan bagnat, Niçoise 190–1
panch phoron 266
paprika 17
parsnip & salt cod chowder 101
passion-fruit: slaked passion-fruit
  ice 211
peaches: Charente cold plate 193
  peach cardinal 225
  peach gazpacho 223
pears: blackberry, apple & comice
  pear compote 210
  chestnut meringue 206–7
pepper, cubeb 18
pepper, long 18
pepper, Szechuan 18
pepper, white 18
peppercorns 17–18
peppers, chilli jam 262
Persian lamb tagine 65–6
Persian quail 91
pheasant 78
  pot-roasted pheasant 87–8
pickles: cucumber pickle 121
  fat chilli pickle 259
pies: cheese & onion flaky puff
  pie 144
  egg & bacon pie 133
  my Mum's sausage & potato
    pie 37
  triple chocolate meringue cream
    pie 242–3
pig plate 40–1
pigeon 78

spiced wood pigeon, artichoke,
  beetroot & chicory salad 94–5
pilau, pistachio & rose 156
pineapple: bacon chops with
  glazed pepper pineapple 34–6
pistachio nuts: pistachio & rose
  pilau 156
  plums & miso candied pistachios
    204
plums & miso candied pistachios
  204
polenta tea cake 209
pork 26
  duck, pork & beans 96–7
  pig plate 40–1
  potted pepper pork 38
  roast pork shoulder vindaloo 27
  slow-roast pork neck chops 31
porridge, vanilla & long pepper
  158–9
potatoes: aloo tikki (potato fritters)
  180
  cheese in a box 142
  chilli beef hash 45
  coconut mashed roots 51
  fenugreek potatoes 36
  heritage soup 195
  lunchbox frittata 139
  my Mum's sausage & potato
    pie 37
  potato fritters 94–5
  salmon, potato & fennel
    fishcakes 106–7
  shiitake & Savoy upside-down
    cake 177
  vada pav (potato buns) 183
potted pepper pork 38
poussins 78
  spatchcocked jerk poussin 79
prawns: Bengali grilled seafood
  123–4
  Cajun popcorn shrimp 125
  seafood gumbo 128–9
pumpkin: cream of young
  pumpkin soup 170

Q

quail, Persian 91
quatre épices 266

## R

rabbit: paella Túnel 153–4
raita 135
rarebit, Irish 141
ras el relish 68
raspberries: peach cardinal 225
  raspberry clafoutis 221
relishes: chilli, coriander & lime
  relish 257
  ras el relish 68
  rhubarb four-spice relish 255
  tomato chilli relish 112
rhubarb: rhubarb & orange salad
  65–6
  rhubarb four-spice relish 255
rice 148
  asafoetida risotto 155
  lamb biryani ka kesar 62
  paella Túnel 153–4
  pistachio & rose pilau 156
risotto, asafoetida 155
rose petals 18

## S

saffron 18–19
  saffron aïoli 127, 191
salads: black figs with goat's cheese
  & rocket 216
  black pudding salad 33
  chicory, watercress & grilled
  squash salad 173
  fennel salad 105
  just raw salad 196
  old-school squid salad 127
  orange, fennel & red onion salad
  107
  rhubarb & orange salad 65–6
  spiced wood pigeon, artichoke,
  beetroot & chicory salad 94–5
  tabbouleh 115
  warm lentil & ham hock salad
  28–30
  winter leaves & spiced squash
  172
salmon: roast herbed salmon
  108
  salmon, potato & fennel
  fishcakes 106–7
salt cod: parsnip & salt cod
  chowder 101

sandwiches: my Bologna sarnie
  192
  Niçoise pan bagnat 190–1
sardines: crammed beach fish
  115–16
sausages: my Mum's sausage &
  potato pie 37
  pig plate 40–1
sea bass: ceviche & corn 105
seafood gumbo 128–9
seven-pepper tuna 110–11
shellfish 120
shiitake & Savoy upside-down
  cake 177
shortbread, lemon 225
skewers: lemongrass & tamarind
  mackerel skewers 112
  Olive's Irish stew skewers 67
slaked passion-fruit ice 211
smoked haddock: Bengal fry-up
  117
sofa chicken 84
sorbets: apple sorbet 223
  blueberry & lychee sorbet 226
soups: cream of young pumpkin
  soup 170
  heritage soup 195
  Jerusalem artichoke soup 169
  parsnip & salt cod chowder 101
spatchcocked jerk poussin 79
spice blends 266–7
squash: chicory, watercress &
  grilled squash salad 173
  hogget & squash bake 74
  Persian quail 91
  winter leaves & spiced squash
  172
squid 120
  Bengali grilled seafood 123–4
  old-school squid salad 127
star anise 19
sterilising jars 255
strawberry, tequila & pepper jam
  260
summer pudding, blackcurrant
  219
swede: coconut mashed roots 51
sweetcorn: ceviche & corn 105

## T

tabbouleh 115
tagine, Persian lamb 65–6
tagine spice blend 266
tamarind 19
tarka dhal 162
tastes 20–2
tejpatta ice cream 234
thyme & pepper lozenge biscuits
  229
ting & ting sauce 79
toasting spices 10
tomatoes: eat-me-with-a-spoon
  masala 72
  hogget & squash bake 74
  ras el relish 68
  sizzled tomatoes 180–2
  tomato chilli relish 112
trifle 235
Trinity College vanilla cream 233
tuna: Niçoise pan bagnat 190–1
  seven-pepper tuna 110–11
turmeric 19
turnips: poached mutton shoulder
  73

## V

vada pav (potato buns) 183
vanilla 19
  vanilla & long pepper porridge
  158–9
vegetables 168, 188
  see also aubergines; celeriac etc
venison 44
  venison tartare 57
vinaigrette 82, 116
vindaloo, roast pork shoulder 27

## W

Wally-Wally pickle 61
winter leaves & spiced squash 172
wood pigeon see pigeon

## Y

yogurt: blackberry-pepper frozen
  yogurt 224
  eat-me-with-a-spoon masala 72
  raita 135

## Special thanks to:

My beautiful wife, Olive, putting up with my madness, her loving support and patience.

Dearest Mum and Dad, Sunil, Melissa, Flora, Felix, Anil and Sugar, Shai, Simon, Ruby and Ella. My wonderful Irish family, John and Rose Motherway, Martha, Brian, Stephen, Mary and Susan.

My other Irish family, team Green Saffron. Woop!

Max Renzland – dear friend and mentor. Tough times, good times, best of times, all times. Mis en place, chef!

Adam Penney and Mark Broadbent for their encouragement of my food adventures for the last 25 years!

Best man, Adrian Dey. Great man, Aaron G. Top man, Marc Amand.

Ivan Whelan – help, support. Friend always and beyond.

Ben Reade, taste genius, 'Escoffier of the Food Lab', good friend, aye!

Myrtle (Mrs A), Darina and Rory O'C. Rachel's support from day 1 of my Irish journey and continued brilliant friendship.

Jennifer Maher, Noel Kinsella & Liam O'Tuama.

Niall and Joanna McKenna, brilliant people, wonderful support.

Zoe P, The Spice Scribe, wonder scribe, support and brilliance abound

Ross Lewis, Richard Corrigan, Paul Flynn, Vivek Singh, Eric Chavot, Sunil Ghai, Bruno Loubet, Cyrus Todiwala, Torsten Vildgaards, Madhur Jaffrey, Kevin Thornton, Derry Clarke et al for their collective culinary genius and inspiration.

Fiona Lindsay and all at the excellent Limelight, and Cathy Frazer for setting me in motion

Becca Spry for taking a chance on me.

Yuki, Kim, Cynthia, Aya, Valerie – brilliant creatives.

Polly, Claire, Charlotte, Fiona, Krissy, Kom and all at Pavilion; the undeniably wonderful Maggie 'word terrier' Ramsay.

Susan Forrest and all at the excellent Hope Foundation.

## Shout-outs to:

Kathy Littler, Emma Reynolds, Siobhan O'Gorman, David Hare, Tom Doorley, Marie Claire Digby, Gillian Nelis, Allan Jenkins, John Spiteri, Chrissie Walker, Millie Taylor, Asma Khan, Caroline Hennessy, Gerard Baker, Neil Gordon, Robin R, Michael O'C Cork BIC, Aileen Cussen, Jenny Meila, Enda and all at EI, Bord Bia, team Eurotoques, Joe Burke, South Cork LEO, SECAD, Cork Chamber of Commerce, Port of Cork Authority, Maree Gallagher, Asheesh Dewan. Arjan Post, Jan Pap, Jan K and Robert H, Arina; team Holland! Jim Brisby, Daniel, Caroline, Adam & Katie – go Hull! The wonderful Martin Heap. Mairin, Peadar, Mícheál running things in West Cork. Ann, Colin, Graeme, Chris and Jon up Ossett way. Thomas Jackson, Alison McIlroy, Maria Stokes, Glenn Troy. Jim O'Connor – 'we're getting there'. Lucy Kennedy, Martin King, Maura Derrane, Sheana Keane, Bláthnaid Ní Chofaigh and all that have me helped so far. Lot of people, lot of love.

And to all the wonderful local customers and fellow market traders who came out to support, and continue to come out in all weathers to our farmers' market stalls, Mahon Point, Limerick, Midleton, Wilton and retail outlets. The journey continues: bigger, stronger, harder, faster. Thank you kindly. Onward!

www.greensaffron.com

First published in the United Kingdom in 2014 by
Pavilion Books Company Limited
1 Gower Street
London WC1E 6HD

Copyright © Pavilion Books 2014
Text copyright: © Arun Kapil 2014

ISBN: 9781909108479

10 9 8 7 6 5 4 3 2 1

A CIP catalogue record for this book is available from the British Library

Senior commissioning editor: Becca Spry
Designers: Georgina Hewitt and Claire Marshall
Photographer: Yuki Sugiura
Food styling: Valerie Berry and Aya Nishimura
Props styling: Cynthia Inions

Reproduction by Dot Gradations Ltd, UK
Printed by 1010 Printing International Ltd, China

This book can be ordered direct from the publisher at
www.pavilionbooks.com

Front cover image: StockFood/Maja Smend
Author photograph: Joleen Cronin